...ing pleasure
...ing you.

Ken
25 April 2008

Out of Order!

Out of Order!

Anthony Winkler
and
White West Indian Writing

Kim Robinson-Walcott

University of the West Indies Press
Jamaica • Barbados • Trinidad and Tobago

University of the West Indies Press
1A Aqueduct Flats   Mona
Kingston 7   Jamaica
www.uwipress.com

10 09 08 07 06   5 4 3 2 1

Chapter 4 was originally published in *Small Axe*, no. 14 (September 2003): 93–110.
We are grateful to Indiana University Press for permission to reproduce this article.
Earlier versions of chapters 6 and 7 appeared in *Sargasso* 10 (2000): 25–37 and the
Journal of West Indian Literature 9, no. 2 (April 2001): 51–101.

CATALOGUING IN PUBLICATION DATA

Robinson-Walcott, Kim.
Out of order: Anthony Winkler and white West Indian writing /
Kim Robinson-Walcott.
p. cm.
Includes bibliographical references.
ISBN: 976-640-172-1

1. Winkler, Anthony, 1942– – Criticism and interpretation.
2. West Indian literature – History and criticism. 3. West Indian literature – White
authors – History and criticism. I. Title.

PR9265.9.W58Z63 2006   813.54

Cover illustration: Allan Zion, untitled (1999).
Book and cover design by Robert Harris.
Set in Adobe Garamond 11/14 x 27

Printed in the United States of America.

For Bert, in his memory

For Betty, in her honour

For Tony, with respect

For Miles and Sydne, with love

Contents

Acknowledgements / *ix*

Introduction / *1*

Part 1   White West Indian Writers and Winkler

Chapter 1   Winkler and West Indian Whiteness / *9*

Chapter 2   Winkler and White West Indian Writing / *21*

Chapter 3   Transcending the Planter Legacy / *46*

Chapter 4   Claiming an Identity We Thought They Despised / *65*

Part 2   Reading Anthony Winkler

Chapter 5   Writing the Black Protagonist / *85*

Chapter 6   Carnival Meets Dancehall / *111*

Chapter 7   Searching for the Centre / *130*

Notes / *169*

Selected Bibliography / *192*

Index / *201*

Acknowledgements

WITHOUT THE ENCOURAGEMENT, full cooperation, respectful distancing and ultimately the friendship of Anthony Winkler, this book would not have been possible. I also deeply appreciate the support and friendship of his wife, Cathy.

This book is a revised version of my PhD dissertation, "Locating Anthony Winkler" (University of the West Indies, Mona, 2001). Professor Mervyn Morris was my mentor long before he became my thesis supervisor. I thank him for his gentle but firm guidance, his perfectionism, and his generosity of spirit.

The start of this journey was facilitated by Kingston Publishers (now LMH Publishing), where as editor I was introduced to Winkler and his works. I thank Mike Henry and his son Andrew for giving me the freedom to explore these works and to develop a close working relationship with Winkler. The journey was made easier by the financial support of the University of the West Indies which awarded me the Western Union Sir Frank Worrell Scholarship for Excellence. The assistance of Eppie Edwards of the National Library of Jamaica and the staff of the UWI Main Library, West Indies and Special Collections, was invaluable. The journey would not have been completed without the support and encouragement of loved ones. Harclyde Walcott applied his incisive eye to early drafts. Dr Hilary Robotham Westmeier, and her husband Dr Wolfram Westmeier, in their unreserved support of this project, demonstrated the true meaning of friendship. The ambition, dedication and purposefulness of Dr Petrine Archer Straw have long been a source of inspiration. I also thank Dr Norval Edwards, Dr Glyne Griffith, Leeta and Shivaun Hearne, Dr Evelyn O'Callaghan, Professor Kenneth Ramchand, Dr Elaine Savory Fido and Dr Guha Shankar, for their helpful suggestions; Lenworth Burke, Dr Victor Chang, Mary Gray and Dr Leah Rosenberg for their constant encouragement; and Dr Carolyn Cooper, who prodded me unrelentingly when the energy was waning towards the end of the dissertation-writing process. In converting the dissertation to a book, I was greatly helped by the suggestions, gentle nagging and unwavering support of Professor Neville Duncan, and the patience and reassurance of Linda Speth of the University of the West Indies Press.

In particular I thank my parents, Herbert Robinson (who lived to see the award of my PhD but not, sadly, the publication of this book) and Dr Hazel Robinson (whose example I followed in the pursuit of my PhD), both of whose sacrifices to enable the completion of this project can never be repaid; and my children, Miles and Sydne Walcott, for their forbearance and tolerance.

Introduction

"Your Honor! . . . The gentleman is out of order!"
— Anthony C. Winkler, *The Lunatic*

THE JAMAICAN WRITER Anthony C. Winkler has gained recognition as a
popular writer of comic fiction in the twenty-plus years since his first novel,
The Painted Canoe,[1] was published in 1983. That first novel, which was quietly but respectably received, was followed by *The Lunatic*[2] in 1987 – and
with that latter publication Winkler established himself as a bestselling novelist in Jamaica.

The overwhelming popularity of *The Lunatic* was due not only to its
wacky, off-the-wall humour but also, perhaps more so, to its outrageous
bawdiness – a bawdiness which, while delighting many, offended conservative Jamaican sensibilities. A typical Jamaican expression of condemnation in
response to such offensiveness is to label it "out of order", meaning not
merely "unacceptable or wrong" as in British informal usage[3] but, more
vehemently, "rude, disrespectful or offensive" – and, in fact, it is an expression frequently used by characters in Winkler's novels to express their righteous disapproval. It was the view of many readers (and of those who refused

to read the novel based on what they had heard) that *The Lunatic,* with its outrageous situations, its explicit sexual references and its liberal use of Jamaican bad words, was most definitely out of order.

That view extended to Winkler's other early novels, though to a lesser extent. *The Painted Canoe,* which had preceded *The Lunatic,* and *The Great Yacht Race,*[4] which succeeded it (in 1992), both demonstrated outrageous tendencies, although they were comparatively tame. Then came *The Duppy* in 1997,[5] and its religious irreverence brought a new dimension to the categorization of Winkler's work as "out of order".

The expression "out of order" is in fact applicable to Winkler's writing in multiple ways. The standard English meaning of the expression is "not working properly or at all".[6] Readers of his autobiographical work *Going Home to Teach*[7] will be familiar with Winkler's social commentary, which describes Jamaica as a country whose societal structure and institutions are in many respects, largely thanks to its colonial history, out of order. This is a theme portrayed in his novels, especially *The Lunatic* which, I suggest, establishes Jamaica as a madhouse. And in *The Duppy,* Winkler may extend this view to established Judaeo-Christian teachings. So in his out-of-order style, Winkler condemns established Jamaican and Western social and religious institutions and traditions as being out of order.

Winkler's work may be out of order in other, more fundamental, ways. Winkler is white – and it was a surprise to this author that that very fact proved to be surprising to many newcomers to his work, who frequently expressed the view that his novels read as though they had been written by a black Jamaican. What are the qualities in Winkler's writing that produced this mistaken impression?

By exploring the fiction of other white West Indian writers in an attempt to identify any common characteristics and, second and more importantly, by examining a selection of Winkler's works, this study attempts to answer that question, suggesting that Winkler's work may be significantly different – out of synch, out of order – from that of many other white West Indian writers.

There is one important way, however, in which Winkler's work is not out of order. This book suggests that Winkler's books work delightfully well, transcending the boundaries between popular and serious fiction.

Anthony Winkler was born in Kingston, Jamaica in 1942, the second of eight children to Louis Winkler Jr., and his wife Myrtle, *née* Ziadie. Louis was the grandson of Louis and Ida (*née* Milke) Winkler who had emigrated to Jamaica from Hungary in the early 1880s. Myrtle's family had arrived in Jamaica from Lebanon at the turn of the twentieth century, and soon established themselves as dry goods traders. Anthony (Tony) Winkler and his siblings spent their childhood in Kingston, where their father worked as a salesman, before moving in 1950 to Montego Bay, where Louis took up a managerial post. The Winklers stayed in Montego Bay until Louis Winkler lost his job in 1957, at which time the family returned to Kingston. Louis died a year after, and the family found itself in abruptly reduced circumstances. Tony helped his elder brother to support the family until Tony moved to the United States in 1962. He returned home in 1975 with his future wife, intending to stay permanently and assuming a teaching post at a teacher-training college in St Ann. One year later he and his wife returned to the United States, where they have remained since. Winkler and his family have resided in Atlanta since 1978, where he has made a very successful living as a co-author of secondary- and tertiary-level English language textbooks.

While in Jamaica in that period 1975–76, Winkler started the first draft of a novel that would become *The Painted Canoe*. Completed in 1979 and submitted unsuccessfully to various US publishers, it was eventually submitted to the Jamaican publishing house Kingston Publishers, which released it along with two other novels in a newly launched fiction series in 1983. *The Painted Canoe* tells the story of Zachariah, an impoverished Jamaican fisherman whose will to live defies all odds, including getting lost at sea and being afflicted with cancer. That novel gained a quiet but respectable critical reception.

The Lunatic followed in 1987. Aloysius is a homeless madman who lives in the hills of St Ann. A chance encounter with a German tourist, Inga, leads to a series of adventures which expose Aloysius to elements more hazardous than those to which he was previously accustomed when he was living in the wild with only the bushes and trees for company. Inga embroils Aloysius not only in outrageous but also in illegal activities, and it is his implicit goodness which saves him from the consequences of the latter. *The Lunatic,* Winkler's funniest novel and his most raunchy, propelled him to instant fame in Jamaica and brought him critical attention in the United States, where it had been copublished.[8] A Jamaican-made film based on the novel, released in 1991, was enthusiastically received and cemented Winkler's popularity as a writer of comic fiction.

Winkler's third novel, *The Great Yacht Race,* was published in 1992. That novel is set in Montego Bay in the 1950s and, focusing on that city's annual yacht race, deals with a number of characters, mostly from the society's upper echelons, whose lives are entwined. This novel, Winkler's longest, was also his first – a first draft had been written before he went to Jamaica in 1975 and was put aside while he worked on *The Painted Canoe* and then *The Lunatic. The Great Yacht Race* is semi-autobiographical, drawing on Winkler's memories of his life in Montego Bay during the 1950s, and is remarkable in that it is the only one of his works which foregrounds white and brown, and middle- to upper-class, protagonists.

The Great Yacht Race was followed in 1995 by *Going Home to Teach,* an account of Winkler's year in Jamaica spent teaching at a teacher-training college. *Going Home* is much more than that, though: Winkler uses that framework to expound a detailed social commentary on the country of his birth, as well as to provide us with a significant body of autobiographical material. The publication of *Going Home* brought a new dimension of seriousness to Winkler's work and earned him new respect. (It also produced, in response to its discussion of Winkler's experiences as a marginalized white Jamaican, a flurry of enthusiastic endorsements from a number of white Jamaican newspaper columnists shortly after its publication – none of whom, interestingly, mentioned the many negative observations of white Jamaicans contained in the book.)

The Duppy followed in 1997. In that novel, the black Jamaican country shopkeeper Baps dies suddenly and finds himself in a most out-of-order heaven, where Jamaican slackness abounds. Baps is at first (self-)righteously indignant, but eventually comes to appreciate the unaffectedness of Jamaican heaven as opposed to the restrictiveness of the more orthodox American heaven, and ultimately, the goodness and love of God. Despite its positive message, the novel was viewed with distaste by many conservative Jamaican readers, who found the subversion of established Judaeo-Christian teachings in the constructions of heaven and the depiction of God (who manifests as a peenywally) to be distasteful. Nevertheless, or perhaps as a result, the novel was commercially successful – nearly as successful as *The Lunatic*.

A number of trends had by now become evident in Winkler's work. First, all his books were, to varying extents and in various ways, outrageous. Second, they were all located in Jamaica and about Jamaicans. While his books showed a development in style from the conventional form of *The Painted Canoe* to the postmodern playfulness of *The Duppy* (which, for example, has a page "left purposefully blank as a convenience to [outraged readers who] now strongly desire to thump down this book" [p. 144]), consistent in his writings, beneath the level of humour and caricature, was an irreverence for established traditions, an impatience with colonialist values, and an irritation with America and American culture, resulting in a subversion of all such value systems. Also interesting to this writer was Winkler's consistency in the warmth and affection with which he portrayed his poor black protagonists, in contrast to the cynicism and frequent negativity demonstrated in the portrayal of his middle- and upper-class white and brown characters.

Winkler's relationship with his Jamaican publisher ended in 2004. In that year an anthology of short stories, *The Annihilation of Fish and Other Stories,*[9] was published by Macmillan. The collection demonstrates a continuation of his trend of writing exclusively about Jamaica or Jamaicans: most of the stories feature (black or brown) Jamaican protagonists, many of whom are migrants to America (such as Fish), with a few featuring (white) American visitors to Jamaica. The title story had previously sold film rights and been produced as a film starring prominent Hollywood actors (James Earl Jones, who plays Fish, Lynn Redgrave and Margot Kidder), which was released, briefly, in 2002. The film, suffering from distribution problems, failed commercially but was critically acclaimed. At the time of writing, two novels, *Dog War* and *The Crocodile*, are slated for publication by Macmillan.

Despite the size of his body of work, and possibly because of the commercial success of his novels, serious consideration of Winkler's work has been sparse. By undertaking a detailed reading of a number of his works, this book seeks to fill that gap.

The first part of the book explores Winkler's relationship to other white

West Indian writers. As a preliminary step, chapter 1 explores the meaning of whiteness in a West Indian, and particularly a Jamaican, context. Chapter 2 gives a brief, introductory overview of the works of a number of white West Indian writers, attempting to highlight and historicize the major tropes of discourse, and explores Winkler's relationship to these writers and this discourse. In chapter 3, by examining the social commentary, social satire and depictions of race and class in specific texts, I compare Winkler to three other, older white or near-white Jamaican writers; and in chapter 4, by examining their negotiations of racial identity, I compare Winkler to a number of contemporary white or near-white West Indian writers. My comparison suggests that while Winkler's work shares a number of tropological similarities with that of other white West Indian writers, there are significant differences, and that these differences relate to differing negotiations of whiteness.

The second part of the book uses the findings of part 1 as the background for a detailed exploration of Winkler's works. In undertaking this exploration I engage in close readings of specific texts. The works which I have chosen to analyse in detail are *The Lunatic, The Duppy* and *Going Home to Teach* – although Winkler's other novels are referred to for comparative or elucidatory purposes. (I have not dealt with Winkler's short stories in this study.) I have selected these three works because they are especially significant as markers in Winkler's development as a writer. *The Lunatic,* discussed in chapter 5, established Winkler as a popular writer, and is his best-known work. *The Duppy,* explored in chapter 6, is important in its relentless subversiveness. *Going Home to Teach,* the subject of the final chapter, is superbly rich in numerous respects, invaluable as an autobiographical record, and essential reading for anyone seeking an understanding of the writer behind the writing. These three books are also, in my view, his best works to date.

Ultimately, I hope, such a detailed reading will reveal that in many ways, and on many levels, there is much "at work" in Winkler's *oeuvre*: that there is a sobriety underlying the farcical humour and a richness underlying seeming superficialities which are often underestimated; that there is an artistry in the seamlessness with which these levels coexist; in short, that Winkler's books warrant serious consideration.

Part 1

White West Indian Writers and Winkler

"He's not one of us, you know."
– Morris Cargill, in reference to
Anthony Winkler

1

Winkler and West
Indian Whiteness

"Color has everything to do with this case, sah. Color and money."
– *The Lunatic*

EARLY IN THE BOOK *Going Home to Teach,* Anthony Winkler establishes himself as a white Jamaican, and also immediately establishes that fact as being problematic: "There was another drawback to going home [in addition to the country's turbulent political climate at the time]: I was white. And that was a graver problem" (p. 14). Throughout that book, Winkler frequently relates his experiences as a white Jamaican, addressing "the ambiguity of growing up white in a black country" (p. 170).

How significant is Winkler's whiteness in an assessment of his work? Indeed, what does the label mean? Winkler himself objects vigorously to such labelling in the context of this study. As he said in an interview, "I don't think of myself as white. I think of myself as a writer. The only thing white is my skin."[1] However, the appellation may be especially loaded in the Caribbean context, where a history of colonialism has left a lingering legacy wherein racial identity still carries particular connotations regarding social and economic status, social interaction and, critically, world view.

Why is it, then, that Winkler has often been taken by newcomers to his novels to be black? Is there a stereotype of a white Jamaican, or indeed white

West Indian, literary voice? And if so, to what extent would Winkler conform to, or depart from, such a stereotype?

Before these questions can be answered, more basic ones must be addressed: What do we mean by the terms "white Jamaican" and "white West Indian"? In fact, what do we mean by "white"? The question does not allow for easy answers. Racial classification has, of course, long been dismissed in modern mainstream scientific and anthropological discourse as biological fiction rather than biological reality, and such classifications as Caucasoid, Mongoloid and Negroid have been recognized to be but examples of pseudo-scientific, over-zestful Victorian categorization.[2] It is accepted that in the New World, the biologization of class distinctions was a manipulation by European settlers whose desire for slave labour encouraged them "to view, first, native Americans and later, African Americans as racially inferior people suited 'by nature' for the humiliating subordination of involuntary servitude".[3]

Furthermore, racial categorization is fluid. Sidney Mintz notes, "The same person can be perceived as being in different 'racial' categories, depending upon whether he/she is in Martinique, in Haiti, or in Jamaica, for example."[4] Mintz's statement supports Harry Hoetink's earlier observation:

> [P]erhaps the ultimate value of comparing race relations in different societies, an exercise to which the Caribbean region lends itself so well . . . [is that] it teaches us that the same word may have different meanings, and that *white, coloured,* or *black* do not always mean what our own experience suggests they should.[5]

In Winkler's *Going Home to Teach,* a brown-skinned man refers to himself as white; elsewhere in that book, Winkler relates being confused himself when a fellow Jamaican visiting him in the United States, someone whom he has always regarded as white, is labelled as black. Winkler notes that "in Jamaica, black is not always black, nor is white always white. One cannot find, as is true of America, a polarization of cultural opposites along racial lines. . . . Black in Jamaica is less a colour, and more like a way of being" (p. 78).

Black may not always be black in America also: a white-skinned person who is one-eighth Negro, for example, is considered black in an American context. "Americans see colour strictly as a consanguineous and physical quality," Winkler suggests, ". . . [but] Jamaicans, and West Indians as a whole, regard colour as inseparable from manners, behaviour, background, education, and culture – that whole constellation of traits the Englishman once labelled 'breeding' " (*Going Home,* 80). As the white-skinned Guyanese writer Pauline Melville points out, confusion arises "because there are over-lapping definitions of race: race is what you look like; race is your genetic heritage, whatever you may look like; race is a cultural concept that might or might not coincide with what you look like".[6]

Melville's own experience has shown that someone categorized as non-white in the West Indies may be called white in England. Much more commonly, someone categorized as white in the West Indies, such as the Jamaican writer Michelle Cliff, may well be called nonwhite in the United States. To complicate matters even further, as scholars such as Hoetink have pointed out,[7] labels differ between the Anglo and the non-Anglo Caribbean, within the Anglo Caribbean itself, or even within one small country: one may be classified as white by some (especially nonwhites) – "once you light you white", as a popular Jamaican saying maintains – and as nonwhite by others (especially whites).

"No person with a truly Caribbean identity . . . carries his or her own true name, just as his or her skin pertains to no fixed race," Antonio Benítez-Rojo observes in his essay in *Caribbean Creolization.*[8] Later in that essay he refers to the "multiple masks" of the Caribbean identity, whose reflections "will never be coherent images, but rather distorted ones".[9]

Racial categorization is dated, flawed, and ambiguous. Yet Winkler's racial identity still mattered to him when he went back home to Jamaica to teach in 1975, and it may still be significant in the context of this study. According to Glyne Griffith,

> The metaphorical inscription of race and racial difference in language is as mean-ingful as the scientific discourse invalidating categories of racial difference in the biological sciences. Each has similar claim to the ordering of human experience and reality, and independent if not equal validation in the realm of human knowl-edge. Paradoxically then, racial stereotypes and theories of race are not so much indicative of ignorance as they are evidence of a certain kind of knowledge given force and validity by Western discourse.[10]

If only as a social and political construct, race is real. Marxist analysis cor-rectly places race in class and economic contexts. The class paradigm of race, according to Michael Omi and Howard Winant, includes those approaches which argue that "social divisions which assume a distinctively racial or ethnic character can be attributed or explained principally by reference to economic structures and processes".[11] Alternatively, race can be seen as "a cultural construct, but one with sinister structural causes and consequences", as George Lipsitz suggests.[12] And whether one subscribes to Philip Curtin's historical concept of "Two Jamaicas", asserting the existence of two separate cultures – one black, one white – developing in Jamaica after slavery,[13] or to M.G. Smith's later analysis of Jamaica as a race-based plural society with separate cultures,[14] or to subsequent Marxist rejections of that analysis with their own substitution of social divisions based on economic divisions,[15] or to more current median positions embracing both views,[16] it is undeniable that race and class in Jamaica, and possibly in the wider Caribbean, are often difficult to distinguish – if only when it comes to whiteness. "In the colonies," Frantz Fanon pointed out in 1961, "the economic substructure is also a superstructure. The cause is the consequence; you are rich because you are white, you are white because you are rich."[17] Winkler's aforementioned confusion, related in *Going Home to Teach,* when a fellow Jamaican whom he considers white is labelled black in America, is partly due to the fact that his friend is from a prominent Jamaican family. This fact, combined with the friend's light skin and status as a law student, "emphatically meant 'white' " (p. 79).

In his study of the formation of working-class racism in the United States, David Roediger, while acknowledging the role of class in race, suggests that the privileging of class over race within Marxist and neo-Marxist analysis may be "damaging", because it allows for the possibility of overlooking the evolution of race as a construct which transcends class or economic considerations to embrace psychological and ideological ones.[18] Roediger's exploration of the development of working-class whiteness in North America builds on W.E.B. Du Bois's earlier exposition[19] which showed how

> the pleasures of whiteness could function as a "wage" for white workers. That is, status and privileges conferred by race could be used to make up for alienating and exploitative class relationships. . . . White workers could, and did, define and accept their class positions by fashioning identities as "not slaves" and "not Blacks".[20]

Whiteness, then, is defined in relation to, is dependent on, a construction of otherness. Similarly, Charles Mills has suggested that

> [b]eing white in the Caribbean cannot mean the same thing as being white in Europe, for being white in the Caribbean means, above all, *not* being black. Thus the ideas and values that develop in this so-called "cultural section" will be permeated by the necessity of defining itself against its despised and feared opposite.[21]

The words "despised and feared opposite" speak of a "terrified consciousness". The term, Kenneth Ramchand's adaptation of a statement by Frantz Fanon,[22] refers to a state of mind in which whites, driven in the twilight of slavery by a fear originating from an awareness of the fragility and vulnerability of their social position based principally on the sheer difference in numbers between them and the black majority, and justified by their perception of the intrinsic and natural barbarity of blacks, developed "an archetypal fear and repugnance: *'Maman, un negre, j'ai peur!'* "[23] As Anthony Maingot states, "[Whites] were governed by what Fanon called a 'manichean delirium': beautiful versus ugly; intelligent versus ignorant; civilized versus savage; white versus black; order (force) versus violence; white paternalism versus future Haitis."[24]

In the context of a West Indian society, then, as in any colonized society, an understanding of race is intricately interwoven with perceptions of self and other stemming from historical binarisms of colonizer versus colonized.[25] In the West Indies generally, in Jamaica specifically, the label of colour can refer not only to blood, and not only to phenotype, but also to behaviour and, most critically, to social class, and social and economic power. These latter indices figure almost as prominently in racial categorization as does skin colour. Racial categorization, in its fluidity, can be exclusive or inclusive, but is always highly manipulative.

"If you white, you rich. . . . If you white, you right," a popular Jamaican radio deejay joked recently.[26] Joking or not, he expressed a popular view of whiteness in Jamaica. In Jamaica, to the nonwhite person, whiteness tends to mean privilege. "It stereotyped you as a member of the ruling class, even if you were poor," Winkler recalls in *Going Home to Teach* (p. 98). As Lisa Douglass suggests in her study of the Jamaican elite, a white Jamaican is expected to belong to a well-to-do family with some historic if not current prominence and power. Some link to the old plantocracy is assumed, and if not actually present, may be invented by the whites themselves.[27] This link, Douglass continues, means that to the public eye the white Jamaican represents the plantocracy, with twofold, conflicting consequences: first, as past oppressor he incites resentment, and second, conversely, as past master he demands – and as Douglass suggests, receives – obeisance.[28]

This image is held as valid not only externally, by nonwhites, but internally, within the white group; hence, like the newly arrived Irish in America in the nineteenth century, white newcomer subgroups which do not (yet) fit the required profile of the white West Indian are othered. As Mintz observes, members of a subgroup such as the Portuguese in Guyana which satisfies the criterion of skin colour but not other cultural criteria are commonly labelled by whites and nonwhites alike, "in a way to set them apart from other 'whites' locally. . . . [It] seems to imply on social grounds that they are something less than white."[29] The same observation would, at least until recently, have applied to the Lebanese in Jamaica, who in the 1970 population census were still identified as a separate racial group, although by the 2001 census they had been absorbed into the category "white".[30] This may perhaps explain the reference by the plantocrat Morris Cargill to the half-Lebanese Winkler as being "not one of us, you know".[31] Meanwhile, Jews in Jamaica, who were not granted civil rights until 1831 (six months after free Negroes were granted such rights) and were up to the early part of the twentieth century similarly marginalized,[32] are now regarded as bona fide white by Jamaican whites and nonwhites because of their economic success as a group – and in fact, as Carol Holzberg points out, "have taken over the national entrepreneurial elite".[33] Bona fide whiteness, then, may be a reward for economic success.

For both those in the mainstream and those on the periphery, whiteness is what George Lipsitz terms "a possessive investment": "whiteness is invested in, like property, but it is also a means of accumulating property and keeping it from others".[34] Lipsitz is referring to American whiteness, but I suggest that the description holds for Jamaican whiteness. One way of investing in whiteness is to maintain a position of racial superiority, or of cultural or social exclusivity, in what Hoetink refers to as "the continuing aspiration of the white group to preserve its racial endogamy";[35] so some Jamaican whites such as Jameson the landowner mentioned by Winkler in *Going Home to Teach* prefer not to socialize with blacks (p. 48).

Lipsitz asserts,

> Whiteness has a cash value: it accounts for advantages that come to individuals through profits made from housing secured in discriminatory markets, through the unequal educations allocated to children of different races, through insider networks that channel employment opportunities to the relatives and friends of those who have profited most from present and past racial discrimination, and especially through intergenerational transfers of inherited wealth that pass on the spoils of discrimination to succeeding generations. I argue that white Americans are encouraged to invest in whiteness, to remain true to an identity that provides them with resources, power, and opportunity. This whiteness, is of course, a delusion, a scientific and cultural fiction. . . . Whiteness is, however, a social fact, an identity created and continued with all-too-real consequences for the distribution of wealth, prestige, and opportunity.[36]

I suggest that much of Lipsitz's argument about American whiteness applies in some Caribbean contexts, certainly in the Jamaican one, despite the fact that the ratio of whites to blacks in the population is entirely different (Jamaica is approximately 2 per cent white, 92 per cent black, according to the 2001 census,[37] while the US census for 2000 lists its population as being approximately 75 per cent white, 12 per cent black).[38] The poorest white still speaks from a position of privilege: "He may be poor, but he is white." The wages of whiteness are bountiful: a white skin entitles, privileges the wearer, allows the wearer access to mobility, to power.

So, whether the categorization is biological or social, political or cultural, race still matters. A white appearance makes a difference. The experiences of a white or light-skinned person will differ significantly from those of a black person because of the baseline of privilege which the former enjoys.

Conversely, in recognition of what Winkler terms "the ambiguity of growing up white in a black country", another reality is that in contrast to the white American, the white West Indian is a member of a tiny minority and as such, notwithstanding any baseline of privilege, is disadvantaged by this fact, suffering to at least some extent the stresses experienced by the members of any minority group in any society. These stresses are of course greatly magnified in the case of white West Indians because of their visibility. "A white skin made you conspicuous everywhere you went," Winkler says in *Going Home to Teach* (p. 93). And, "for the white Jamaican the feeling of not belonging is a cross he must bear even if he has never set foot out of his own country" (p. 76). In addition to a sense of unbelonging there may be a sense of vulnerability – possibly manifesting, in its most extreme form, as a "terrified consciousness" – caused by a perception of the black majority's resentment, whether in response to whites' assumed historical links to the plantocracy, as Lisa Douglass suggests, or to their assumed current wealth. "People hated us because we were white. . . . It was blind, rabid, seething" (*Going Home,* 159), and, "When you are white in a black land like Jamaica, you are no longer merely a man, or a woman, or a child. For good or ill, you are also immediately transmogrified into a living symbol of a detested colonial past" (p. 75). Such stresses must affect the individual's sense of identity, and must inform all expressions of that individual's identity.

So, despite Winkler's impatience with the label "white", and despite the instability of the term "white Jamaican", his whiteness is a useful starting point for an analysis of his work.

In seeking to identify common features among white West Indian literary voices, and to locate Winkler within and without, the remainder of the first part of this book will briefly examine the works of a number of white West Indian writers, focusing primarily on those of the twentieth century, but in the context of a historical overview of fictional and nonfictional works demonstrating discursive trends over the last three centuries. Writers to be examined include the Dominicans Jean Rhys and Phyllis Shand Allfrey; the Barbadians J.B. Emtage and Geoffrey Drayton; the Trinidadians Ian McDonald and Lawrence Scott; the Trinidadian/Bahamian brothers, Robert and Brian Antoni; and the Jamaican Morris Cargill.

Additionally, given the above discussion on the fluidity of the definition of "white", this part of my study includes a number of near-whites, or, in the case of Jamaica, "Jamaica whites". The term "Jamaica white", when used in this book (as opposed to Rex Nettleford's interpretation which suggests that any white Jamaican is a "Jamaica white"),[39] refers to those phenotypically white or nearly white Jamaicans whose ancestors included nonwhites, usually Africans.[40] These "Jamaica whites" are regarded as nonwhite by fully white Jamaicans, but as "functionally white" (to use Nettleford's term)[41] by both full whites and the brown/black majority; in other words, despite the "touch of the tar brush", they are accorded much of the status of full whites. "Jamaica whites" are therefore in many ways positioned similarly to such groups as the Lebanese in Jamaica, a group to which Winkler partly belongs. "Jamaica whites" in this study include H.G. de Lisser, a man of colour but one described by some (including Kenneth Ramchand) as a "White Creole",[42] and by Rhonda Cobham as being "'respectable' enough, due to his Portuguese Jewish name and ancestry and his excellent connections in England, to call himself White in a social situation not renowned for its logic or consistency on the question of race";[43] John Hearne (a relative of de Lisser)[44] and Evan Jones, both light-skinned members of the landed gentry; and Michelle Cliff, accorded in her formative years in Jamaica the privilege of whiteness because of her light skin, but now defiantly claiming her black side.

Cliff has considered the term "creole" in reference to herself.[45] And, as was noted above, the word has been applied to de Lisser. It has also been applied to Jean Rhys,[46] and, in one version or another, to other writers to be featured in this study.[47] It is useful at this point, therefore, to explore the term. As Judith Raiskin suggests, the word "creole" "defies easy definition, [and] the boundaries of this literary class are conspicuously, and usefully, elastic".[48] Raiskin continues,

> "Creole" generally refers to those of (some) European descent born in European colonies or in independent territories that once were colonies. However, depending on the time and the place of its use, the term can signify full European ancestry (implying a claim of "unsullied" whiteness), mixed "racial" ancestry resulting from colonialism (usually implying some European ancestry mixed with African, Amerindian, or other so-called racial groups, depending on the location), or syncretic cultural and linguistic practices (such as "creole" music, food, or language).[49]

Raiskin notes that "the plasticity of this term permits its usage as both broadly inclusionary and narrowly restrictive"[50] – a convenient plasticity which then allows her to consider writers such as Rhys and Cliff in the same category.[51]

The plasticity of the term may be problematic. In many cultures the attachment of one adjective or another to the word "creole" is necessary to convey specific meaning.[52] It is tempting, then, to extend the plasticity of the term "creole" to "white creole" in this study; so that "white creole" would embrace both those claiming "unsullied whiteness" and those with "a touch of the tar brush" – anyone of white appearance born and raised in the West Indies.[53] Such a label for all the writers being considered in this study would be convenient in one sense, but would be a contrivance. Raiskin's observation that "the conflicting meanings embedded in the term [creole] . . . cast the surrounding vocabulary of nationality and racial identity into confusion as well"[54] applies also, to some extent, to "white creole". Furthermore – and critically – the term "creole" is not commonly used in Jamaica, and therefore a reference to Winkler as "white creole" would be inauthentic. Despite their inherent limitations, this book will continue to use the terms "white West Indian" and, specifically in the case of Jamaica, "white Jamaican" and "Jamaica white".

Although the labels may sometimes be necessary or useful, they still smack of divisiveness, of a perpetuation of the old colonialist divide-and-rule approach which has so successfully crippled our Caribbean society for the last three hundred years. It seems that as we venture into the new millennium, half a millennium after the creation of a Caribbean creole society in the New World, one and a half centuries after emancipation and nearly half a century after independence, we are still struggling to come to terms with all the facets of our Caribbean creole identity. As individuals argue over cultural authenticity, the Caribbean melting pot remains a myth: rather than "out of many one people" (to use Jamaica's national motto) it continues to be, as Cargill suggests for Jamaica, "out of many only one sort of people",[55] or "we versus them", with the "we" in "a fi we time now" changing subject to location and time but with the confrontational element remaining. This colonialism-warped West Indian society still emphasizes polarity, not even plurality, much less the potential of a Caribbean potpourri. As Michelle Cliff says, "We are a fragmented people."[56]

Yet the potpourri is there, the mixing if not melting, or at least the plural coexistence of different ethnic groups and cultures in a way that is distinctly Caribbean. The concept of *"créolité"*, currently popular in Caribbean academic discourse, is attractive as a recognition of this reality. *Créolité,* or less prettily, creoleness, is at its best fluid in meaning but at its worst self-contradictory, and it may be more applicable to the seemingly less stratified non-Anglo Caribbean, where the concept originated, than to the Anglo Caribbean. Nevertheless it may usefully be applied here if one chooses an interpretation which broadly embraces hybridity, heterogeneity, symbiosis, synthesis, syncretism, mosaics, *métissage* in an attempt to understand Caribbean identity. *Créolité* acknowledges difference even as it celebrates commonalities. An embracing of *créolité* is an alternative to a perpetuation of divisiveness – although such an embracing, depending on who is promoting it, can itself be viewed as a perpetuation of divisiveness.[57]

Indeed, say the editors of *Caribbean Creolization,* "the issue of identity has been raised by every Caribbean writer who confronts the individual or collective question of memory, of belonging, and of being".[58] In confronting that question, especially given the fluidity, the politicization, and the manipulativeness of racial identity, we all make choices.

As Winkler has pointed out, one need not be phenotypically white to be socially white. Whiteness, in its socio-psycho-ideological sense as explored by scholars such as Du Bois, Hoetink, Roediger or Lipsitz, is by choice. Lipsitz states,

> I hope it is clear that opposing whiteness is not the same as opposing white people. White supremacy is an equal opportunity provider; nonwhite people can become active agents of white supremacy as well as passive participants in its hierarchies and rewards. . . . On the other hand . . . not all white people have to become complicit with white supremacy. . . . White people always have the option of becoming anti-racist, although not enough have done so. We do not choose our color, but we do choose our commitments. We do not choose our parents, but we do choose our politics. Yet we do not make these decisions in a vacuum; they occur within a social structure that gives value to whiteness and offers rewards for racism.[59]

And in *Going Home to Teach,* Winkler writes,

> To be a white man in Jamaica is to be constantly haunted with feelings of illegitimacy and dispossession. Against this the white Jamaican uses two stereotypical defences. If he is ignorant and callous enough, he revels in his whiteness and professes contempt towards the majority all around him to which he does not belong.

That he is not one of them, that he is not really part of this poor country in which misfortune has marooned him, are two lies he wears around his neck like a placard. He takes care that his children do not marry into black or brown families and professes to treasure the sense of dispossession with which he lives.

Whether or not he feels this way in his heart of hearts is another matter. But many white people in Jamaica have consciously walled themselves in with this way of thinking. Most of my mother's family have used it. One result is that their children are reared with no sense of patriotism or love for the land in which they were born and migrate as soon as they become adults.

The second defence is not as common. The white man simply surrenders to the superior forces that surround him and marries into the family of his heart's love – whether black, brown or otherwise – his skin becoming an anomaly belied by every other fact of his life. He is accepted in his own community where the conditions of his life choice are known, but whenever he ventures into the outside world he must still suffer the ambiguous consequences that result from his whiteness. (pp. 77–78)

I suggest in this study that Winkler chooses his commitments and his politics in an "out-of-order" way – one which distances him from many other white Jamaicans, and from many other white West Indian writers. A detailed examination of Winkler's novels, to be undertaken in part 2 of this study, will reveal that Winkler's relation to whiteness is, in one way or another, a critical issue in his writing.

Winkler and White
West Indian Writing

[T]here's no doubt that a certain wariness did creep in when I thought about the black people who surrounded me.
– Jean Rhys, *Smile Please*

IN KENNETH RAMCHAND'S seminal study *The West Indian Novel and Its Background*, the chapter entitled "Terrified Consciousness" discusses four novels written by white West Indians in the 1950s and 1960s: *The Orchid House*[1] and *Wide Sargasso Sea*[2] by Phyllis Shand Allfrey and Jean Rhys respectively, both of Dominica; as well as *Christopher*[3] and *Brown Sugar*[4] by the Barbadians Geoffrey Drayton and J.B. Emtage respectively.

The curious story of *Brown Sugar* (which Ramchand dismisses in a few lines) traces the career of Foggy Cumberbatch, a monstrous caricature of the black politician gone corrupt. This hideous contemplation of power in the hands of those who are incapable of handling it is thrown into relief by the counterpointing of an immensely civilized white planter family whose intervention narrowly averts a major disaster. Although the planter family is satirized in its excessive intellectualism (discussions of existentialism over dinner, for example), such satirization seems token, with the scathing incisions reserved for Foggy and the other black characters, who all wallow in one or both of the states of ignorance and evil.

According to Ramchand, the novel, "written by a West Indian of the old planter type, expresses in the form of political lampoon the extremist white reaction to the kind of situation pictured by [J.A.] Froude" wherein Froude, who visited the West Indies in the late nineteenth century, "indignantly foresaw" black majority rule. Ramchand quotes Froude's declaration: "No Englishman, not even a bankrupt peer, would consent to occupy such a position [of subservience to a black person]."[5] Emtage wrote *Brown Sugar* when Barbados was on the verge of independence and white Barbadians were extremely fearful about what this might mean, so much so that many had felt driven to migrate to countries such as Australia. Ramchand's comparison of Emtage's position to that of Froude therefore seems apt.

One is reminded of the type of white planter mentality which preceded that of the post-slavery English visitor Froude: principally, as exemplified by the virulent racism of the eighteenth-century planter-historian Edward Long,[6] whose views of the similarity of the Negro to the orang-utan are brought to mind by Emtage's depiction of Cumberbatch. Such a depiction also recalls W.P. Livingstone's turn-of-the-twentieth-century social Darwinist position that black Jamaicans were unable to govern themselves due to climactic influences which had retarded their evolution.[7]

In Ramchand's view, "the White West Indian's reactionary political stance interferes too often . . . to allow *Brown Sugar* to be a valid satire".[8] Emtage's authorial voice is not only reactionary but rampantly so; despite the elegance of the prose, and the occasional instances of wit, it is such excess that interferes with the validity of the work. Ramchand's statement, however, raises the question: Is the white West Indian's political stance typically reactionary? This is an essentializing claim. Without doubt, historically the white West Indian planters – especially the Jamaican ones – achieved infamy as reactionaries by their resistance, first to emancipation, and subsequently to an amelioration of living conditions for the masses. However, works by twentieth-century white West Indian writers which display such attitudes are not common.

Emtage's combination of racist superiority, sophistication and smooth wit reminds one of the worst of the late Jamaican columnist and author, Morris Cargill.[9] But Cargill has typically a somewhat more positive undertone to his writings. In his autobiographical *Jamaica Farewell* (1978),[10] as well as in the majority of his columns, a genuine if paternalistic affection for his countrymen is evident, which underscores his concern for the future of his country.

Cargill's politics were unapologetically conservative; nevertheless, his sympathies were, at least to some extent, with the poor. His paternalistic distancing is easier to forgive than the flagrantly racist arrogance displayed by Emtage.

Emtage's reactionary stance also recalls the earlier twentieth-century Jamaican author, the near-white H.G. de Lisser, who became increasingly conservative over the course of his twenty-plus novels. De Lisser's work, like that of Emtage and Cargill, is witty, hard-hitting in its satire, and increasingly cynical. Based on his personal antinationalist convictions, such cynicism has been read by some critics to be reactionary – a label supported by the racist stereotypes which dominate the immensely popular historical novels on which his fame has largely been based. This may do him an injustice, however, for his cynicism was all-pervasive: English visitors and residents, white Jamaicans and Jamaica whites, coloureds and blacks alike were all mercilessly ridiculed. For de Lisser, it seems, there were no heroes. What his works show is a willingness to display human foibles and weaknesses, a bitingly critical tongue that was, as Rhonda Cobham suggests, "adept at undermining the stuffy and hypocritical tenets of public morality"[11] – and he was quick to extend his cynicism to all members of the society, to anyone who deserved it.[12]

The disturbing arrogance shown in *Brown Sugar* is absent from the other novels examined by Ramchand in his chapter. What may be nearly as disturbing, however, is the existence of certain other elements in these novels which express negative views of the black population as other. Ramchand observes,

> [T]he elements of continuity between them are remarkable: attitudes of the White characters to landscape and to the other side represented by the Negro masses; the functional presence of long-serving Negro nurses, and of obeah-women; the occurrence of dreams, nightmares and other heightened states of consciousness; and references to an outer socio-economic situation that is recognizable as the fall of the planter class. These elements of continuity arise . . . involuntarily from the natural stance of the White West Indian. With differing degrees of intensity, the three novels reflect a significant . . . aspect of West Indian experience. . . . Adapting from Fanon we might use the phrase "terrified consciousness" to suggest the White minority's sensations of shock and disorientation as a massive and smouldering Black population is released into an awareness of its power.[13]

The existence of a terrified consciousness in these novels is indisputable. *Wide Sargasso Sea* most vividly, and hauntingly, portrays such terror, with this theme being established from the very first lines: "They say when trouble comes close ranks, and so the white people did" (p. 5). Antoinette and her mother, white plantocrats reduced to penury after emancipation, live in fear of the resentful black masses who surround them – a fear realized when the great house at Coulibri is burnt down by the ex-slaves, resulting in the death of Antoinette's younger brother. Neither Antoinette nor her mother ever recovers from this horror, Antoinette's mother retreating immediately into madness while Antoinette herself clings tenuously to sanity and eventually herself disintegrates.

The Orchid House and *Christopher* also portray white plantocrat families that are in a state of decay. Christopher, alienated from his planter father who is preoccupied with the economic woes caused by the collapse of the plantocracy, and from his weak and ailing mother, is a lonely, frightened child, terrorized by the sinister sound of drums from the surrounding black communities and retreating into the safe, tamed world of his garden with its flora and fauna. But tropical flora may not always be safe: in *Wide Sargasso Sea* the landscape can, for Antoinette's British husband, be wild, inscrutable or steaming with passion. *The Orchid House,* in its depiction of what Ramchand calls "the hot-house life of the white characters",[14] again speaks of decay, the decline of one planter family reflecting the decline of a class, with illness in the foreground (specifically, the Master's drug addiction and Andrew's tuberculosis) against a background of hatred and destruction.

The insecurity of a class that realizes it has lost, is losing, or is about to lose its power translates to vulnerability, and vulnerability to fear. This fear is especially compelling if the power that one is losing derived from oppression of those who are now taking control. Hence in the decades immediately preceding emancipation a terrified consciousness was clearly evident in the writings of the white West Indian population – a terror predictably magnified by the recent experience of Ste Domingue, which haunted the white West Indian consciousness, but a terror which had long been developing out of a history of violent slave rebellions. While this fear was experienced by white people throughout the West Indies, it was manifested in an extreme form in Jamaica. Historian M.J. Steel suggests that the Jamaican planters "had quite demonstrably and provably far more to fear" than their counterparts in the other colonies:

> By the 1780s Jamaica had one of the highest rates of servile rebellion in the New World, had an overwhelming majority of slaves to whites, had an impenetrable mountain interior which could (and did) harbour escaped slaves entirely beyond any hope of recapture, and even worse, was home to entire bands of escaped slaves in their hundreds (the Maroons) who could (and did) erupt in armed conflicts against the planters on such a large scale that they were called the Maroon Wars by the planters rather than "mere" rebellions. . . . . This provided them with a profoundly unsettling reminder that their slaves were not by nature either docile or harmless, but were perfectly capable of staging an armed rebellion that might prove impossible to stop, and engulf not a country or district but the entire Island.
>
> . . . . "[F]ear and loathing" – the two are often inextricably linked in the human mind – was the reaction of Jamaican planters to the slave *inside* the slave system, and their reaction to the possibility of the slave outside the system bordered on the hysterical.[15]

Terror can be seen in many of the early writings of white Jamaicans, and terror bordering on hysteria especially in those of the pre-emancipation period. Rejecting the liberal humanism of earlier visiting European writers such as Las Casas, Rochefort and du Tertre,[16] these writers translated their fear and loathing, as well as their recognition of their dependence on the slave-worked plantation system, into racism.[17] The most prominent Jamaican writers of this period would of course include the pro-slavery resident historian-planters Edward Long and Bryan Edwards.[18]

Such insecurities would have been easily passed on to short-term residents. Lady Nugent,[19] who in the first months of her four-year stay in Jamaica (1801–5) makes note of white planter barbarism (p. 51) to the poor little Negroes (p. 52), concludes in the last part of her stay that "the blacks are to be as much dreaded as the French" (p. 237), and speaks of terror in contemplation of the "savage . . . slaves . . . in the interior" (p. 240). Even the good-natured, paternalistic M.G. "Monk" Lewis,[20] a resident of Jamaica from 1815 to 1817, in noting that "the higher classes are all in the utmost alarm at rumours of Wilberforce's intention to set the negroes entirely at freedom", suggests that "the next step . . . would be, in all probability, a general massacre of the whites, and a second part of the horrors of St Domingo"

(p. 145). Such a terrified consciousness may have been parodied in the rollicking *Tom Cringle's Log* by Michael Scott, who lived in the island in the early 1800s: "An insurrection of the black population, mayhap" is the immediate assumption when the blacks start behaving boisterously – but no, this out-of-order behaviour is revealed to merely concern spruce beer.[21] Nevertheless, Scott's fun and jokes, and his mocking of the creole plantocracy and its paranoia, aside, this fear seems to have permeated the entire white society.

Inevitably, obeah was viewed as an index of the sinister threat that blacks represented. Obeah was seen to be mysterious, unfathomable, inexplicably powerful even to a rational mind such as Long's. And even the kindly "Monk" Lewis found it hard to ignore the not uncommon reports of slave masters being unaccountably taken ill after imbibing poison of unknown origin. So treachery, in the form of obeah, could invade the sanctuary of the home.

A century later in *The Orchid House,* as Ramchand points out, the sinister undercurrent is personified principally in the obeahwoman Majolie, who tries to poison the child Hel. It is an atmosphere which is reflected in nature: " 'Hel is not safe.' And I told her about the [poisoned] tamarind ball. I think she could not have believed me but for the menace of the storm, which made our island world dark and frightening" (p. 107). The obeahwoman, symbol of black evil and source of terror, appears also, as Ramchand notes, in *Christopher* in the figure of Old Rose, and in *Wide Sargasso Sea* as Christophine – although the view of this latter figure as negative is mostly from the eyes of the English "othered" husband of Antoinette, and less from Antoinette herself. Nevertheless, not only for Antoinette's husband but also for Allfrey's and Drayton's characters, obeah is evidence of black barbarity, as well as being the unknown quantity – unpredictable, irrational, uncontrollable, terrifying.

Obeah is also present in H.G. de Lisser's earlier historical novel *The White Witch of Rosehall* (1929), but with an interesting twist: the obeahwoman is white. However, Annie Palmer has learnt all her black magic skills from a black Haitian voodoo priestess, skills which she has sharpened with the help of local obeahman Takoo, and which she is using to control the "massive and smouldering black population" of slaves on her estate:

There were grumblings, plottings, and the belief was spreading that, at some date not distant, and at a given signal the slaves would rise, give the properties over to the flames, loot, murder their masters, and thus would take by savage means what they believed was being held from them.[22]

And one gets the impression that the author is somewhat ambivalent about the white witch's cruelty: some sort of control is necessary, after all, for a white woman running an estate singlehandedly: "[The] appearance [of the Three Footed Horse] had inevitably served to strengthen her hold on her sullen, discontented slaves. It was not only by bodily fear that she held them . . . but by far more potent spiritual terrors" (p. 119).

As has been suggested above, *The White Witch* and *Wide Sargasso Sea,* both historical novels, accurately portray the fear-filled environment of post-emancipation Jamaica. Whereas in de Lisser's work the portrayal seems tinged with more cynicism than terror, in the case of Rhys the subtext seems to read as the author's own fears, based on her childhood in Dominica – a reading supported by Rhys's autobiographical reflections in *Smile Please:*

[T]here's no doubt that a certain wariness did creep in when I thought about the black people who surrounded me. . . . Did they like us as much as all that? Did they like us at all? . . . This was hatred . . . and if you think that a child cannot recognise hatred and remember it for life, you are most damnably mistaken. . . . They hate us. We are hated. / Not possible. / Yes it is possible and it is so.[23]

So a hundred years after the societal upheavals of emancipation, the terrified consciousness remains, in the experience of young Rhys. And given the fear conveyed in *Christopher* and *The Orchid House,* it seems safe to suppose that for Drayton and Allfrey, growing up in Barbados and Dominica in broadly the same period as Rhys, their experiences as members of a white minority surrounded by hostile black people may have been similar.

More than thirty years after the publications of *Christopher* and *The Orchid House,* Anthony C. Winkler opens his novel *The Great Yacht Race* (1992) with a similar theme. It is the funeral of a murdered white Montegonian, and the mood of the mourners is one of doom: "No natural catastrophe, no pestilential disease could rival this murder for sheer horror. Bowen's slaying foretold of revolution and riot among the lower classes. Mayhem and rape, the mourners whispered to one another, lurked just around the corner" (p. 4).

Terrified consciousness – and we recall, first, that this novel is set in the 1950s, in approximately the same period that *Christopher* and *The Orchid House* were written; second, that the novel is based on the author's memories of growing up in Montego Bay at that time. Within a few lines, however, the author has clearly distanced himself from any such convenient academic analogizing, as he proceeds to make fun of the mourners, who spend the next few hours arguing about preferred methods of punishment for a mur-derer (for example, rack and thumbscrew versus piranhas – caricatures which nevertheless remind one of the excessive punishments outlined in great detail in the Jamaican slave laws, or of the obscene excesses in the punishment methods of the overseer Thomas Thistlewood),[24] and preferred methods for being murdered oneself (strangled versus cut throat). "Madness!" shrieks Mother Laidlaw in an argument about whether a black nanny should be allowed to wet-nurse a brown baby – again bringing to mind white attitudes of the past.[25] But the madness that reverberates in *The Great Yacht Race* is not the type that befalls Antoinette and her mother – a consequence of the hatred that has terrified them – but rather Winkler's view of the paranoid excesses of this colonialist society.

The black nanny – the long-serving Negro nurse referred to by Ramchand – is a persistent figure in the novels of white West Indian writers. For many white West Indians, living in an environment of social exclusivity, the nurse may traditionally have been their only close contact with black people. Consequently, in a large number of works by white West Indian writers, the nurse is the only black character which is developed.[26] Allfrey and Drayton give sympathetic depictions of unshakeable devotion in their respective portrayals of Lally and Gip, but these portrayals read as somewhat stereotypical, in an Aunt Jemima way: the good servant, or the "good Negro". Here one is reminded of the picture painstakingly painted by Mrs Carmichael[27] a century previously of the good Negro, who is "industrious, civil, with some sense of his own dignity, and a wish to retain a place in the good opinion of his master and all around him" (vol. 1, p. 31) as opposed to the more commonly encountered bad Negro (vol. 2, p. 272), who is dishon-est, deceitful, mischievous, wasteful, lazy and, most disturbing of all, treach-erous (vol. 2, p. 302). Rhys's Christophine is stereotypical to some extent as both types: unshakeably loyal to Annette and Antoinette, but also an unfath-omable, sinister, unpredictable obeahwoman – possibly based on Rhys's own memories of her own terrifying, sadistic nurse, Meta (mentioned in *Smile Please*).

The faithful nurse continues to feature as the only developed black character in more recent works. In Lawrence Scott's *Witchbroom* (1992) she appears as Josephine/Antoinetta,[28] and in Robert Antoni's *Divina Trace* (1992) as nurse-cum-obeahwoman Evelina.[29] In Brian Antoni's *Paradise Overdose* (1994) she appears as Evalina, one of two black characters.[30] In *Witchbroom* the stereotype proves to be that of both the good and the bad Negro: Josephine/Antoinetta is revealed to have a love-hate relationship with her mistress. And in *Divina Trace* the faithful-nurse stereotype is given a twist: Evelina is revealed to be the daughter of her hated master. In *The Great Yacht Race* there is an even greater twist: Winkler subverts the figure of the ever loyal, ever faithful, substitute mother-figure nurse to produce an eccentric caricature, the feisty "Mildred with black skin and no teeth" (p. 41), whose functions include clobbering her white master Fritzie on the head with a broom whenever he comes home drunk, and warding off his advances with similar weaponry.

In Robert Antoni's second novel, *Blessed Is the Fruit* (1997), the faithful nurse is once again featured, as Vel, one of two first-person narrators (the other being Vel's mistress Lilla).[31] Antoni's rendering of Vel stands apart from the other writers' depictions of nurses, in that it is the only one which accords her primary status as a protagonist (although Winkler's protagonist Missus Grandison, the housekeeper in *Yacht Race*, in many ways performs the role of nurse in her caregiving of Father Huck).

Vel is Antoni's only black protagonist to date. A number of other white West Indian writers over the last century have experimented with black protagonists as one-off efforts.[32] The early-twentieth-century white Jamaican writer "Tom Redcam" (Thomas Macdermot's pseudonym) devotes some energy to giving a sympathetic portrayal of the black child Becka and her family in *Becka's Buckra Baby* (1907),[33] but only sporadic attention to the black Fidelia in *One Brown Girl and –* (1909);[34] otherwise in that second work the principal characters are various shades of brown as well as white, while the blacks are caricatured and marginalized. De Lisser's first novel, *Jane's Career* (1914),[35] is centred around the life of the black servant Jane, and, as Ramchand observes, is "the first [West Indian novel] in which the central character, the one whose feelings and thoughts are explored in depth, is a

Negro".[36] De Lisser's second novel, *Susan Proudleigh* (1915),[37] again explores a black character with the predictable sympathy of one influenced by and eager to impress his Fabian Socialist mentor at the time, Governor Sydney Olivier. De Lisser's subsequent novels, however, discard a socialist agenda and relax into portrayals of the (brown and white) middle and upper classes.

Alice Durie's sole work, *One Jamaica Gal* (1939), follows the line of *Jane's Career* by tracing the life story of the black protagonist Icilda. Here, like the others, the author's tone seems sympathetic but detached, slightly condescending, interested mainly from an ethnographic point of view: here is one Jamaica gal, and here is the story to answer the question asked on the very last line: "Lawd, how she come here?"[38] "Here", incidentally, is death, a fate shared by Redcam's Becka. The fates of the other black women in these novels may not be as tragic, but are certainly not idyllic. For example, Jane in *Jane's Career* achieves material success and societal advancement, but the author implies that she may have compromised her integrity. Jane, de Lisser ironically notes, takes on the airs and graces of the same middle-class people who had snubbed her all along when she fulfils her dream of a white wedding and respectability.[39]

All of these (usually short-lived) efforts at portraying black protagonists focus on female characters. One cannot help but wonder whether black maleness is too threatening, too overwhelming, to be considered by these white writers – both male and female.

A similar situation exists in the second novel of the Portuguese Trinidadian writer Alfred Mendes, *Black Fauns* (1935).[40] While his first novel, *Pitch Lake* (1934),[41] is clearly semi-autobiographical and focuses on the Portuguese Trinidadian element, *Black Fauns* examines in great detail the lives of the black inhabitants – all female – of a barrack-yard. Mendes's desire for verisimilitude led him to live for an extended period in a barrack-yard, and his work is similar to Durie's in terms of its ethnographic leanings. However, there is no trace of condescension here; on the contrary, one finds a humble respect for the resilient working-class women who are featured. *Black Fauns* and Mendes's short stories demonstrate an ideological commitment to foregrounding the black experience, a realization by Mendes that "We were faced with the task of writing stories . . . which would have to be new and to be recognized, to some extent, as being Negro stories."[42]

This conscious political decision by Mendes and his *Beacon* partners in the mid-1930s to foreground blackness presages the development, some thirty years later, of a body of thinking which privileges those works which themselves privilege the black masses in the construction of a West Indian canon. Such a decision had clearly also been made in the 1930s by Roger Mais – who although he was not white was nevertheless a member of the ruling class, a "gentleman", an "aristocrat", as John Hearne termed it.[43] According to Hearne, Mais realized during the 1938 riots in Jamaica "that his position, the position of any contemporary man whose work might endure, was with the working class of the world, and with their desires and with their present agony".[44] Hearne relates elsewhere that this decision was greeted with concern by Mais's peers: "He was a sort of renegade . . . what he had already begun to write did not fit into the expected pattern. It . . . questioned the values which everyone in his class had been taught to accept."[45] Mais's interest in the poor black Jamaican may have coincided with the birth in the 1930s of a cultural movement led by Edna Manley and others which, in its promotion of a new nationalist pride of identity, encouraged a romanticization of the Jamaican peasantry and working class in creative work.[46] Mais's three novels of the 1950s, *The Hills Were Joyful Together* (1953),[47] *Brother Man* (1954),[48] and *Black Lightning* (1955),[49] were all concerned with the plight of the poor black Jamaican, male as well as female. As Sylvia Wynter said, "Mais . . . was near-white but he became perhaps, the Caribbean writer most closely identified with those who walked with hunger and destitution – the people of the shantytown jungles."[50]

Winkler follows in the footsteps of Mendes and Mais. Like Mendes's first novel, *Pitch Lake*, Winkler's first-written (though third-published) novel, *The Great Yacht Race*, is semi-autobiographical and deals with a group of brown and white middle- and upper-class people. Like Mendes, Winkler thereafter moves away from such subject matter, and in his subsequent works chooses to embrace the life of the black poor. Like Mais, Winkler is unafraid of the black male as a protagonist. The fisherman Zachariah in *The Painted Canoe* (1983), the madman Aloysius in *The Lunatic* (1987) and the shopkeeper Baps in *The Duppy* (1997) are Winkler's heroes. Zachariah and Aloysius are both from outside the mainstream of the society, both fighting against great odds to survive. Clearly, rather than being overwhelmed and intimidated by his black male characters, Winkler empathizes with them (although one might suggest that as representatives of black maleness, these are disenfranchised, unthreatening examples). The schoolteacher-turned-shopkeeper Baps is both less marginal and less of a hero, but he too comes out of the world of the black poor.

Zachariah overcomes a series of progressively more devastating blows: physical deformity, being lost at sea and, finally, miraculously, cancer. For Aloysius, nature provides not adversity but protection, both physical and emotional: a tree is his best friend, and the capricious bushes may be aggravating, but they also shield him from loneliness. Driven to lunacy by a life of severe deprivation, Aloysius manages, again miraculously, to end up in a respectable lifestyle – living with the village schoolteacher, who has taken him under her wing.

Such romantic, even fairy-tale depictions swing to the opposite extreme of the sinister Christophine/Old Rose black stereotype. The ever-faithful Lally type featured in other works is of course, in a sense, no more of a romanticization than Winkler's heroes. However, Winkler transcends the boundaries of such fiction because his characters, although they may sometimes come across as caricatures, are not stereotypes. And certainly Baps in *The Duppy* or even Missus Grandison, the priest's housekeeper and the only black principal persona in *The Great Yacht Race,* defy any classification other than as (stubborn) characters.

Where Winkler may retreat more into conventional stereotyping is in his depiction of brown people. Winkler's deep affection for the poor black Jamaican contrasts strikingly with his decided intolerance of the brown middle class, whom he has confessed to finding "selfish, mean and unfeeling",[51] and whose pretentious bumpkin mentality has been portrayed in nearly every book: from the brown-skinned doctor in *The Painted Canoe* who "lived up to the reputation of his colour. He acted as if he didn't care which patient lived or which one died" (p. 287); to the haughty teacher in *The Lunatic* who "walks through the village with her nose in the air" (p. 15); to people like Mother Laidlaw and Roxanne in *The Great Yacht Race,* who are incensed at the suggestion that they may have African ancestry: "I don't come from any damn Africa. I come from damn Trinidad!" (p. 156).

It is interesting how frequently the brown-skinned person is shown by the white West Indian writer to be an object of contempt. "I know that God meck two colour, black an' white, but it must be de devil meck brown people, for dem is neider black nor white!" says a domestic servant in de Lisser's

Jane's Career, in response to the miserable ways of her brown-skinned mistress (pp. 55–56). Ramchand notes that in the nineteenth century the coloureds "irritated their White neighbours by their want of meekness" and quotes Bryan Edwards as saying, "They are always proclaiming by their voice and their look, that they are as good as the white man; but they are always showing by their voice and their look also that they know that this is a false boast."[52]

Harry Hoetink observes that historically, in the non-Hispanic Caribbean,

> Where . . . racial violence erupted, the intermediate group . . . sometimes was internally divided about what position to take. . . . In its turn, the white group's intrinsic insecurity in such [frequent] times of crisis was aggravated by its nagging insecurity about the intermediate group's course of action.[53]

Such irritation with coloureds, whether or not it stemmed from either their want of meekness or their unpredictability – or whether in fact it originated from their being a constant reminder to the West Indian white of a shameful past of profligacy and miscegenation – is overwhelmingly apparent in white West Indian writing.[54] The brown-skinned Cornélie in *The Orchid House* does not consider the black Baptists to be worthy of her notice (p. 157), and similarly, like the other "coloured merchants, the educated people" in the island, callously dismisses the poor black majority: "We leave them to God" (p. 186). In *Wide Sargasso Sea* Antoinette's brown cousin Sandi seems to be the only person in her life who offers her protection, gentleness and love. But even Sandi's depiction is obscured by unanswered questions, and the coloured characters who linger more in the mind are the treacherous Amélie, the despicable, conniving, envy-ridden Daniel Cosway, and even, although briefly encountered, the hateful boy who along with a black girl frightens Antoinette on her way to the convent: "he had a white skin, a dull ugly white covered with freckles, his mouth was a negro's mouth. He had the eyes of a dead fish. Worst, most horrible of all, his hair was crinkled, a negro's hair, but bright red" (pp. 26–27). Pretentious, resentful brown-skinned people appearing in Rhys's short stories include Papa Dom in "Again the Antilles" (from *The Left Bank*)[55] and Mrs Sawyer in "The Day They Burned the Books" (from *Tigers Are Better Looking*).[56] It is only fair, however, to balance this observation with mention of the sensitive first-person portrayal of a coloured woman in "Let Them Call It Jazz" (from *Tigers*).

Another stereotype, that of the highly sexed and sensuous coloured woman, is prominent.[57] Brown Sugar in Emtage's novel is a precocious eleven-year-old ("Brown Sugar, they called her, but she did not like the brown" [p. 13]) who is continually trying to seduce the white planter's son. Cornélie in *The Orchid House,* who has seduced the ailing Andrew, is "of all the beautiful things . . . nearest to perfection . . . as frail and supple as bamboo. Her body filled the simple lines of the embroidered dress with a gentle narrow fullness" (p. 69). Amélie in *Wide Sargasso Sea* is the temptress whose seduction of the Rochester figure contributes to Antoinette's plunge into madness. Earlier, de Lisser's mother and daughter characters, both called Psyche in the novel of that title,[58] Millie in *The White Witch of Rosehall,* Elizabeth in *Morgan's Daughter,*[59] to name but a few of the mulatto female protagonists featured in his popular fiction, are all beautiful, tempestuous, impulsive, sensuous women who seduce white men with tragic results, as noted by Rhonda Cobham.[60] Such characterizations cannot be dismissed too easily, however. These women, dissatisfied with their restricted positions in society, are interested in liaisons with white men in order to elevate themselves; and often, as in the case of Psyche the daughter and Elizabeth Morgan, their failure to achieve such elevation, their continued exclusion from white society, causes them in their resentment to stir up trouble among the black majority. De Lisser thereby incorporates other mulatto stereotypes of ambitiousness and unpredictability in societal allegiances occurring as a result of frustrated ambitions.

In more serious works, de Lisser moves away from the sensational, sexual aspect of his stereotyping, but retains other stereotypes: in *Myrtle and Money* (1941),[61] for example, the bronze-skinned Myrtle is unapologetically, mercurially ambitious and determined to elevate herself, by any means necessary, above her more humble parents (her mother being a subdued version of the Jane featured nearly thirty years previously in *Jane's Career*).

Such determination to elevate oneself can have tragic resonances, in both its causes and its consequences. Repeatedly in the works of white West Indian writers one encounters the notion of the mulatto as doomed: fated because of white blood to achieve more than the black person, but doomed because of black blood to achieve less than desired; fated to aspire towards a white lifestyle, to reject the lot of the black person, but doomed to rejection by the white society because of the taint of black blood, and to rejection by the black society because of jealousy over the privileges accompanying the white blood; doomed, then, to frustration, dissatisfaction, unbelonging. Even Edward Long, although disgusted by miscegenation and convinced that the mulatto was a mule, nevertheless pointed out that

> it is impossible but that a well-educated Mulatta must lead a very unpleasant kind of a life here; and justly may apply to her reputed father what Iphricates said of his, "After all your pains, you have made me no better than a slave; on the other hand, my mother did everything in her power to render me free."[62]

In his brief study of the nineteenth-century antislavery novel, Gordon K. Lewis suggests that the theme of "tainted blood" is the leading one in the genre.

> All the other themes flow from that: the unwritten laws that socially exclude the colored person; love crucified on the altar of racial purity; the fear of sudden exposure and social disgrace; families fatally divided. . . . Not in and of themselves overtly antislavery tracts, they yet manage to describe how individual human lives are trapped within the constraints of the system.[63]

Among the works mentioned by Lewis is the anonymously published *Marly* (1828), which has "as its central figure the cultured Jamaican colored gentleman who, graduating from Edinburgh University, comes home to a 'white gentleman' society that rejects him and his type".[64] A century later, we see this same dilemma sensitively explored in Esther Chapman's *Study in Bronze: A Novel of Jamaica* (1928).[65] The coloured Lucea is a child "conceived in wantonness, born in apathy, reared in cynicism", according to her white father (p. 3), and the statement could apply to the lot of the coloured class as a whole. Lucea's exotic bronze beauty and European-style breeding bring her not happiness but frustration. Having moved away from Jamaica to the less restrictive society of London after her father's death, her horizons are expanded but not adequately so: the white Englishman with whom she falls in love, although at first willing to marry her, soon realizes that a legalization of the union would ruin his career. Lucea returns to Jamaica heartbroken, defeated, and doomed to a future of compromise – thereby fulfilling the earlier warning of her father: "Don't let Lucea suffer from the common delusion that she is any lighter in colour than she really is. It is a foolish attitude, and may lead to tragedy" (p. 57).[66]

Gordon Lewis commends the novelists of the nineteenth century who,

> by bringing both the black and the mulatto to the forefront as figures worthy of literary comment and analysis, . . . managed to compose a morally inspired social analysis critical of the slavery institution. *To have asked them to have done more would be to assume on their part a supernatural ability to transcend the limitations of the time and the society in which they had to live and survive.*[67]

Lewis observes that "merely to read the [nineteenth-century antislavery] Caribbean literature is to be made forcibly aware of the fact that every commentator, of whatever persuasion, had to come to grips with the existence of the mulatto class".[68] It would appear that, well over a century later, such a struggle has not yet been resolved in the case of many West Indian writers of all colours – and one wonders to what extent one can still excuse this as being due to the writers' natural inability "to transcend the limitations of the time and the society in which they had to live and survive". Ramchand draws our attention to the fact that "almost without exception . . . stereotypes of the Coloured person . . . appear in West Indian writing. . . . [This] is a creative failing of considerable social consequence".[69] In this area Winkler, too, fails.

It is particularly interesting to observe how the near-white or Jamaica white writers like de Lisser portray their mixed-race characters, since they are representing their own type. Evan Jones, in his novel *Stone Haven* (1993),[70] gives an unflattering portrayal of the family patriarch, Stanley (a portrait possibly based on Jones's own father),[71] who, in his determined othering of his blackness in preferring white wives for both himself and his son, is accused of wanting to become white (p. 135).

In a colonialist or post-colonialist society, where whitening means empowerment, wanting to become white is not of course surprising. And it is less surprising in the Jamaican context, where up to emancipation whitening was a legal process, officially possible for the descendants of a mulatto after four successive generations of marrying pure whites. When, therefore, de Lisser's coloured seductresses in his historical novels attach themselves to white men with such focus and determination, this is historical accuracy, showing part of the mulatto's socio-psychological heritage. As Rhonda Cobham says,

Clearly de Lisser understood only too well the racial tensions within his society. Had he been a writer of greater integrity he could have made through his novels an important contribution to his society's self-awareness in this respect. As it is, he shies away ultimately from examining the deeper social issues behind the miscegenation taboo, relying instead on clever coincidences to divert the reader's attention and round off his plots.[72]

In John Hearne's *Voices Under the Window* (1995), the light-skinned Mark Lattimer remembers when as a child he has referred to himself casually as white in speaking to the family servants and has been told dryly,

> "Missa Mark . . . *you* not white, you know."
> . . . [H]e had never thought of himself as anything but white, and the world he knew was only made for the values of being white.
> "What do you mean?" he asked angrily and desperately. "I'm not black. I'm not brown. I'm white." . . .
> "[Y]ou is not a white man, Missa Mark."
> "Then, what am I . . . if I'm not white? Of course I'm white. Look at me." . . .
> Terrified, now, and completely shaken. . . .
> Something he had was being carried and torn down so quickly and finally that he couldn't believe it.[73]

Hearne, then, shows the other side of the mulatto's dilemma – when the psychological process of whitening has been too successful – thereby revisiting the stereotypes portrayed by other writers, including Winkler. In the above excerpt we are reminded of Roxanne and Mother Laidlaw in *The Great Yacht Race,* and gain some insight into the reasons for their hysteria at being labelled as having African ancestry.

In *The Faces of Love* (1957),[74] Hearne effectively transcends another mulatto stereotype. The promiscuous, sensual Rachel Ascom is as mercurial and ambitious as de Lisser's Myrtle, and uses her sexuality for material advancement, but she is not presented as a type. As Ramchand notes,

> Hearne's vivid characterization and analysis interest us in Rachel as an individual from the first appearance. . . . [I]f we say that Rachel is the highly sexed, immoral Coloured woman, and the socially insecure mulatto buttressing herself with material possessions, it is necessary to recognize in the same breath that Hearne has fused and metamorphosed these two images in a broader study of the psychology of power working through an extraordinarily vivid character.[75]

The vividness of the characterization and the tragedy of Rachel's fate linger in the mind long after this book has been put down.

In rejecting such stereotypes and presenting his characters as people instead of types, Hearne in all his novels addresses human concerns: principles of love, honour, integrity. Yet, ironically, in so doing he chooses, in four out of his six novels – the Cayuna books – to immerse himself in an imagined world framed by a stable plantocracy, a plantocracy which he had experienced peripherally through encounters with relatives and friends, but of which he had no firsthand knowledge. In so doing, Hearne perhaps unintentionally underscores the tragedy of the near-white person's position of unbelonging, a position which he had addressed most directly in his first novel *Voices Under the Window* – as shown in the scene in which Lattimer, lying on his deathbed in a room above a street teeming with rioters, hears "a clamouring, deep roar of sound" and realizes,

> [T]hat's the sound I've always heard. It's the music I've moved to for so long. . . . The black people bellowing at me to get off their necks, and the whites too, screaming nervously, not so often, more refined, whenever I came nearer than a certain limit. Maybe someday I could write a book and call it *The Diary of a Racial Climber.* (pp. 27–28)

The dilemma of unbelonging recurs as a trope in more recent works. It is explicitly, and repeatedly, expressed in Michelle Cliff's writings of the 1980s. Cliff's anger at the distortions of her sense of identity caused by the warped societal values of her Jamaican colonial childhood, when she was taught the advantages of being able to pass for white, and the distinct disadvantages of acknowledging any connection to blackness, is most forcefully enunciated in the novels *Abeng* (1984)[76] and *No Telephone to Heaven* (1987).[77] And her position can be most succinctly summed up in the title of her poetry/prose collection: *Claiming an Identity They Taught Me to Despise* (1980). Unlike Hearne, whose Cayuna novels imply a yearning for the stability of the plantocrat life, the younger Cliff – child of the 1970s with their political awakenings – rejects the position of privilege into which colonialist society has placed her, and instead embraces blackness, that previously denied part of herself.

Honor Ford-Smith, another near-white Jamaican only a few years younger than Cliff, also embraces the black part of herself in an awakening of political consciousness, as shown in *My Mother's Last Dance* (1997).[78] The near-white and very white-looking Guyanese writer Pauline Melville prefers to embrace the notion of hybridity rather than any narrow racial classification – of being, to borrow the words of her compatriot Wilson Harris, "born from a close fantasy and web of slave and concubine and free, out of one complex womb".[79] Nevertheless she agrees, albeit wryly, to have herself included in *Daughters of Africa,* an anthology of black women writers (1992).[80]

Such contemporary embracing of blackness or hybridity contrasts with the stereotypical near-white and white West Indian positions of a total rejection of blackness, of the type demonstrated by the French Creole Monagas family in Lawrence Scott's *Witchbroom* (1993), who are obsessed with proving that there is no black blood in their ancestry, with some "refusing to linger in the sun more than was absolutely necessary, lest they be mistaken for being black" (p. 168); or by another French Creole family, the Angosturas in Brian Antoni's *Paradise Overdose* (1994), who keep "the heavy dose of Indian blood securely in the closet" (p. 47).

In the West Indies, it is of course difficult for most people to be absolutely sure of their ancestry; the white West Indian is often suspect in terms of racial purity, so that the divide, for example, between white Jamaican and Jamaica white becomes very difficult to distinguish. Black blood may be lurking somewhere. A modern embracing of hybridity, or of the romantic concept of *créolité,* contrasts with Jean Rhys's earlier questioning of the dark skin of her great-grandmother: "I was told that she was a Spanish countess from Cuba but even then I doubted that" (*Smile Please,* 34). Rhys appears to be ambivalent about a possible touch of the tar brush in her ancestry, and about blackness generally. In *Voyage in the Dark* (1934), her protagonist Anna yearns for blackness: "I wanted to be black. Being black is warm and gay, being white is cold and sad."[81] These sentiments are echoed repeatedly in the autobiographical *Smile Please*; for example, "Once I heard [my mother] say that black babies were prettier than white ones. Was this the reason why I prayed so ardently to be black, and would run to the looking-glass in the morning to see if the miracle had happened? . . . Dear God, let me be black" (p. 42). But her awareness of black hatred eventually teaches her to hate too, and her final position is one of alienation – rejecting and being rejected by both blacks and whites.

Anthony Winkler's embracing of blackness decades later is less ambivalent. His novels, by their contrasting portrayals of their black and white characters, repeatedly demonstrate that being black is warm (Missus Grandison, Aloysius and Baps, for example) and if not gay then any number of other positive attributes such as good-natured (Missus Grandison, Aloysius, Baps), generous (Aloysius), brave (Zachariah), determinedly positive (Zachariah), respectful of God (Zachariah), affirming of God's goodness (Zachariah, Baps), or compassionate (Aloysius). By contrast, being white is cold (Mr Saarem in *The Lunatic,* the English doctor in *The Painted Canoe*) and if not sad then any number of negative attributes such as anarchic (Inga in *The Lunatic*), bigoted (Busha in *The Lunatic*), nihilistic (the doctor), atheist (the American philosopher in *The Duppy*) or bloodthirsty (the Americans in American heaven in *The Duppy*). His discomfiture with his whiteness and his empathy with the poor black Jamaican majority are explicitly expressed throughout *Going Home to Teach:* "I, who had been born white, had internalized a black [identity]," he says (p. 79).

In both Rhys and Winkler, one reason for a stated desire to be black is evidently a distress at being marginalized, at not being regarded as a "real" West Indian because of the fact that one's skin colour is not that of the majority group. One is therefore both disturbingly visible and invisible. As Rhys says, "I loved the land. . . . I wanted to identify myself with it, to lose myself in it. (But it turned its head away, indifferent, and that broke my heart.)" (*Smile Please,* 81). And in Winkler:

> The feeling of inauthenticity, of being a bogus Jamaican that had haunted me as a child, grew in force and intensity. I longed to say to the public: Look! I am one of you. My heart is your heart. Your blood is my blood. . . . It is only the skin that's wrong, that's different. But I am of you. (*Going Home,* 162)

This frustration at not being recognized as belonging is common in the works under discussion, for example in Brian Antoni's *Paradise Overdose*: "I was on this island before there was even a Freeport. . . . I fucking belong here!" (p. 105).[82]

The pain of rejection by one's compatriots might conceivably be reduced by the white West Indian's historical tendency to regard Europe, in particular England, as home.[83] This stereotype of the traditional white West Indian attitude of cultural exclusivity and alienation has been reinforced by numerous visiting white writers over the centuries. In 1838, for example, Michael

Scott observes in *Tom Cringle's Log:* "All Creoles speak of England as home, though they may never have seen it" (p. 238). Anthony Trollope, visiting Jamaica in the 1850s, marvels at the fact that a love for England and things English, such as food, is a predominant characteristic of the white inhabitants.[84] A century later, another visiting resident, the Englishwoman Mona Macmillan, notes a comment of a member of "the Jamaican-born white class": "We were brought up to believe that there was nothing worth while in Jamaica, we were only marking time in the island, and saved our money and our hopes for the visit to Europe."[85]

However: "Now these same people," Macmillan adds, "are ready to fight for the right to be called Jamaicans" (p. 194).[86] One reason may be that the white West Indian has endured centuries of being regarded as inferior by the European – especially the English. Michael Scott has fun commenting on the bad speech of the creole whites: "Cousin Taam, what you bring we?" ask Tom Cringle's young cousins, described by Scott as "little creole urchins" (*Tom Cringle's Log,* 506). Lady Nugent comments similarly on creole speech – "dis, dat, and toder" (*Lady Nugent's Journal,* 76) – and continually despairs about the lack of breeding and culture of the creoles with whom she is forced to socialize: "Find a sad want of local matter, or indeed, any subject for conversation with them. . . . I mean in future not to attempt anything like a conversazione, but to have Friday dances" (p. 14). Visiting some eighty years later, J.A. Froude, although he feels sorry for the poor struggling post-slavery whites, nevertheless finds them somewhat pathetic, and prefers to fraternize with his fellow Englishmen.[87] John Henderson, visiting the island at the turn of the twentieth century, finds the creole men arrogant, and the women idle.[88] The disdain may be mutual: the Englishman is in turn satirized by the white West Indian. De Lisser's humble Cockney Swiffles in *Under the Sun* (1937) comes to mind;[89] and Winkler's relentless attack in *Going Home to Teach* on the English, "slavish devotee[s] of inheritance" (p. 66), and in *The Duppy* on Americans, who are "always giving [God] a hard time" (p. 76), continues this trend.

Meanwhile Jean Rhys's white West Indian female protagonists in *Voyage in the Dark* and, more gothically, in *Wide Sargasso Sea,* discover that the England about which they spent their childhood fantasizing is very different in reality. For both it reads rather as a bad dream – for Antoinette, a horrible nightmare from which her only awakening is death.

For Winkler, migrating to America at the age of twenty, fifty years after Rhys arrives in England, his new homeland also reads as a bad dream, as shown in *Going Home to Teach:* Southern California is "the geographic equivalent of a salesman's soul: fretful, insomniac . . . and once in a while on a full mooned night, slightly demented" (p. 20). For Morris Cargill, who has a short-lived stint as a migrant to America in the 1970s, Americans are "a strange people", and he confesses to "try[ing] to leave Jamaica three times, but it's never worked. I always end up getting homesick."[90] America is foreign, strange, alien. Jamaica is home.

So the rejection by one's compatriots because one's skin colour is different becomes all the more painful. Sometimes this pain expresses itself in a desire for anonymity. In Ian McDonald's *The Hummingbird Tree* (1969), for example, Alan, the protagonist, is excited at the prospect of playing mas in a disguise that leaves "no gaps of white skin. . . . I felt a balm of confidence that all my actions would be anonymous. The pleasure of feeling safe from having to be careful and mannered in the sight of others all the time rose in me."[91] In the case of Rhys, this sense of unbelonging, of alienation and displacement, carries into other aspects of her life, and it pervades her work.

In contrast, Winkler rejects any crisis of unbelonging. As *Going Home* demonstrates, he knows where he does not belong: America. "Many immigrants carry within them always . . . a gnawing sense of things not being quite right. . . . Jamaicans do not see the world the way Americans do." And he is equally clear about where he does belong: Jamaica. Jamaica has "recognizable and familiar types of people" (p. 115). All his writing is firmly rooted in Jamaica. Winkler's concern is to prove where he belongs.

Both Rhys and Winkler demonstrate that their yearning for blackness is in part caused by their discomfort with belonging to a group whose history is distasteful. Rhys's view of the plantocracy's cruel treatment of slaves, with the consequent justification of black hatred for whites, is implied throughout *Wide Sargasso Sea.* And Winkler relates, "I was often set upon by swarms of street urchins and beaten in the streets for no other reason but that I was white. . . . [I]n my heart I felt I deserved their abuse" (*Going Home,* 16).

Such guilt is a condition commonly expressed in the fiction of other white West Indian writers. It is significant in Allfrey's *The Orchid House* (and partially assuaged by the figure of the socialist Joan). In Drayton's novel, young Christopher is horrified when he gradually becomes aware of social injustices. Cliff's anger is partially caused by guilt about the position of exclusivity thrust upon her. Mentioned both in *Abeng* and *The Land of Look Behind* is an episode in school when one of the few black students had a *grand mal* seizure and the only woman who came to help her was the black gamesmistress: "Were the other women unable to touch this girl because of her darkness?" (*Land of Look Behind,* 61). Discomfort with a position of privilege is clearly shown in Brian Antoni's *Paradise Overdose,* especially in the relationship between the rich white protagonist, Chris, and his black best friend, Shark, who is continually reminding him, "I am black. . . . I got noting to lose. You white and got money" (p. 14).

Guilt is the central theme in Ian McDonald's *Hummingbird Tree,* where the protagonist's betrayal of his Indian servant friends, Kaiser and his elder sister Jaillin, due to his family's disapproval of their class and race, is an act of treachery for which he will seemingly never forgive himself:

> So opinion changed me, and I changed friends. Life got much easier to live. The pressures building up before died down. . . . It didn't occur to me that the formula so many people used to solve the problem might involve a deep corruption of principle. I drew apart from the world of brown faces. . . . I entered the white colonial world which from birth I had belonged to, but from which I had walked away for a time. (p. 148)

Alan's understated self-recrimination, and the sadness of his loss, contribute to making this one of the more poignant pieces of West Indian fiction.

Guilt also resonates strongly in Lawrence Scott's *Witchbroom,* where the author's revulsion at the role of whites in a Caribbean history of colonialist carnage and oppression translates to the view of a white society which is diseased and inevitably doomed. The fungus witchbroom which in the novel slowly eradicates the island's cocoa crops, and which in actual fact caused the late nineteenth-century decline of the French Creole group who were heavily dependent on the cocoa industry, is symbolic of the poisonous past which contaminates the present: "Within the laughter there is pain, a pain reaching up from the former century, a guilt choking at the throats of the children as the witchbroom chokes the cocoa estates" (p. 154).

Other authors extend this pessimistic view to the entire society. Emtage is cynically fatalistic in his depiction of black rule. The negativity displayed by de Lisser in his historical novels, which describe a corrupt, immoral West

Indian society, is succinctly summarized by the close of *The White Witch of Rosehall:* "Do you think you will ever come back to the West Indies?" asks the parson who has come to say goodbye to the Englishman who is returning home after a disastrous stay in Jamaica. "Never," is the reply, and one feels that the preceding text has established this response as being fully justified (p. 255). The general tone of de Lisser's other works is only slightly more moderate, as he paints an overwhelming picture of societal pettiness, hypocrisy and intellectual dishonesty.

For Rhys, "everything gets twisted in the West Indies" (*Smile Please*, 85). For Allfrey, "Beauty and disease, beauty and sickness, beauty and horror: that was the island" (*Orchid House*, 77). The cause of such societal disease and distortion is colonialism. Of the twentieth-century writers in question, only Emtage does not acknowledge this. De Lisser, even with his antinationalism, shows clearly in his historical novels whence the society's illnesses originated. Most of these illnesses relate to race, class and identity; social polarization; alterity; hatred of others and of self.

In *Wide Sargasso Sea,* the consequence of living in a hate-filled colonialist society is shown to be madness. Scott in *Witchbroom* suggests, "You have to be mad to live in this place" (p. 218). Cargill's view of the insanity of Jamaican society is familiar to anyone who used to read his newspaper columns, a piece entitled "It's All a Bit Dotty" being but one example: "When we consider our economic situation it's rather like living in a kind of madhouse."[92]

Winkler's view of the insanity of Jamaican society is most clearly established in *The Lunatic,* at the end of which one concludes that the madman Aloysius may be the sanest person in the book.[93] In this lunatic society, pretentiousness and hypocrisy abound – so that in a sense one is reminded of de Lisser's vision. But this is in one sense only, because de Lisser's overall vision, like that of most other white West Indian writers, to varying degrees, is of hopelessness.

Winkler is never hopeless. In *The Lunatic,* pretensions, hypocrisy and societal madness are overcome by Aloysius's compassion. In *The Painted Canoe,* the cruelty of fate is overcome by Zachariah's stubborn determination to live, and his faith in God. In *The Duppy,* the true meaning of life is revealed as Baps is given a second chance in life, an opportunity to reform his ways and to tell the world about God's goodness and forgiveness. One reason for this hopefulness may be that Winkler is one of the few white West Indian writers who distances himself from the white world which the other writers have shown to be fragile – distances himself from the terrified consciousness, the angst, the unbelonging, the eroding exclusivity. By embracing his poor black characters and their world, Winkler disinvests in, subverts, his whiteness, and he may be able to do this because he is one of the few white West Indian writers who seem able, or willing, to identify fully with the black majority.

Transcending the
Planter Legacy

So isolated were they in their Caribbean backwater and so carefully conditioned,
they could only mumble the catch phrases of more-English-than-the-English
loyalty on the one hand or London School of Economics parrot cries on the other.
– Morris Cargill, *Jamaica Farewell*

ANTHONY WINKLER'S RETURN home from the United States to the turbulence of Manley-led socialist Jamaica in 1975 was viewed as a most unusual
move, as he recalls in *Going Home to Teach*. "Everyone going, and you coming," his brother greeted him incredulously at the airport (p. 33). For this
was the time of panicked migration of the communism-fearing middle and
upper classes. Among those leaving was another white Jamaican, the late
Morris Cargill, whose book *Jamaica Farewell* is an account of his life in
Jamaica in those final months before he took the decision to migrate to the
United States. A comparison of that book with *Going Home to Teach* reveals
interesting parallels.

On one level, *Going Home to Teach* may be read as an explanation, first, of
Winkler's decision to leave the United States, and second, ultimately, of his
decision to return to the United States after only a year in Jamaica. *Jamaica*

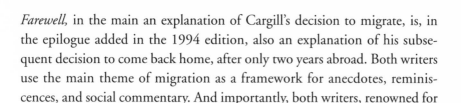

Farewell, in the main an explanation of Cargill's decision to migrate, is, in the epilogue added in the 1994 edition, also an explanation of his subsequent decision to come back home, after only two years abroad. Both writers use the main theme of migration as a framework for anecdotes, reminiscences, and social commentary. And importantly, both writers, renowned for their humour, continue in these works to discern the comic in any situation.

Such parallels are intriguing in view of the fact that Cargill and Winkler are two completely different personalities. Cargill, in his mid-sixties in 1976, "was born a member of the old plantocracy" (*Jamaica Farewell,* 105); he is a British-rooted upper-class gentleman whose family, landed and wealthy, has been in Jamaica for three hundred years (p. 232). Winkler, nearly thirty years younger, is the lower-middle-class descendant of Lebanese and Hungarian merchants who migrated to Jamaica less than a century ago. Cargill's reminiscences at times read like a who's who, with mention of celebrities of the likes of Lawrence and Gerald Durrell, Ian Fleming, Noel Coward and Blanche Blackwell, to name but a few. Winkler's colleagues at the teacher-training college and relatives such as his mad Aunt Petulia or his uncle the embezzler are not quite in the same category. Cargill's every humorously dry word exudes his aristocratic and sophisticated breeding; Winkler is down-to-earth, occasionally downright vulgar, and his brand of humour might more appropriately be described as hot and juicy.

Such differing personalities contribute to different perspectives. Cargill's identity with and love for Britain are clear; Winkler is virulently anti-British. Cargill's ancestral roots in Britain make that a second home to him; Winkler, although his family has been partly rooted in America for generations, is uncomfortable there, and defiantly Jamaican. Different circumstances also contribute to different perspectives: Winkler thinks and writes like the novelist he is, while Cargill thinks and writes like the ex-lawyer, ex-politician columnist that he is.[1] More critically, at the time of writing *Jamaica Farewell,* Cargill has been living in Jamaica uninterruptedly for some twenty years (after a ten-year stint in London) and has been in close proximity to what he views as sinister developments in his country. Winkler has been living away from Jamaica for more than a decade, and has only second-hand knowledge of the horrors of the 1970s. This partly accounts for Cargill's sense of foreboding, a certain gloom and pessimism about Jamaica's future, in contrast to Winkler's overall elation, notwithstanding certain frustrations, at being back in the land of his birth. Perhaps as critically, Cargill as Tory landowner must inevitably feel more threatened than Winkler, who with his working-class sympathies or sensibilities has relatively little at stake.

On the other hand, it soon becomes apparent that the views of Jamaica held by these authors are similar in many respects. Winkler's views of the insanity of Jamaican society, well established in his novels, especially *The Lunatic,* are reflected in *Going Home,* in the form of an insane bureaucracy which Winkler encounters, as for example when he attempts to sort out his salary adjustment at the Ministry of Education and ends up being told that it is he who owes the government money: "But this is madness!" he yelps (*Going Home,* 235). Similarly, Cargill's encounters with bureaucracy force him to the conclusion that "there are . . . many situations in which it is essential to stretch, even to break, the law", and cause him in one instance (when, in order to have a mentally ill woman hospitalized, he resorts to breaking windows on her behalf) to rightly exclaim, "But this is insane!" (*Farewell,* 12, 13). (And in fact this is one of many instances in which Cargill's eccentricity borders on madness, as does Winkler's from time to time.)

The issues of racism, race relations and self-image are treated with some soberness – and returned to time and time again – by Cargill as much as Winkler. Both writers despise and ridicule the racism of their own families – Winkler, his mother's family who "would rather a child of theirs had been stillborn than grow up to marry into a family that was not white" (*Going Home,* 11); Cargill, the likes of his Uncle Sidney, whose black servants "stood exactly on a par with his Cocker spaniels" (*Farewell,* 94).[2]

Winkler relates that his maternal grandfather's occupation as dry goods merchant

> required him to rub elbows with the very class of Jamaicans he professed to despise – the poor black people – and this experience seems to have fuelled his hatred of them. Whenever he got vexed at his customers, he had the bad habit of raging out loud for all the world to hear that the "negro is a monkey without a tail". (*Going Home,* 10)

Cargill is appalled at the behaviour of his class: "I was soon to learn that this habit of downgrading and insulting the Negro race in general in the hearing of Negro servants was very widespread among Jamaican Whites" (*Farewell,* 94). Cargill continues,

> I wondered . . . why the Blacks of Jamaica had not long ago arisen and slit the
> throats of their white masters. . . . I . . . came to understand that the barrage of
> belittlement to which the Negro was subjected . . . was what in fact kept the
> Whites safe. It made the Negro doubt and despise himself; and people consumed
> with self-hatred have little time to spend upon hatred for others. (p. 95)

Cargill notes succinctly the Jamaican saying "Nayga . . . can't bear to see
Nayga prosper", and also states that "the great wound [of slavery], exceeding
any wound which could be inflicted by the ship, was to [the slaves'] self-
esteem" (pp. 167, 177). Winkler voices similar concerns:

> [I]t is a commonplace belief among black Jamaicans that their own kind are not
> gladdened by a neighbour's triumph but would, instead, move heaven and earth
> to thwart it. . . . [O]ne does get a little weary of trotting back to slavery days with
> every national idiosyncrasy. But this one definitely came off that dirty shelf.
> (*Going Home*, 189)

Whether black self-hatred is manifested in petty acts of maliciousness by
blacks against other blacks (such as Winkler's college principal's last-minute
decision to prevent two students from sitting their A-level exams), or in the
more literal sense of despising one's own features (for example, the notion of
"bad hair" which Cargill has to address with his adopted black daughter –
whose adoption, incidentally, elicits "unpleasant or catty comments" only
from "black or coloured people" [*Farewell*, 167]), or in the denial by obviously black people of their blackness (Cargill's very dark-skinned worker
refers to himself as being Scottish; a dark-brown Miami refugee trying to dis-
courage Winkler from going home calls himself white), it is, both authors
suggest, a problem which has stunted the entire society.

The complexities and contradictions of the issue of race in Jamaica, for
example, the dislike of brown people for black people, and the preference of
black people for white people over brown people, are explored over and over
in Winkler's novels, and are again seen in *Going Home:* "Gimme a white man
any day," says an impatient black traveller waiting for the brown customs
officer to fill out his quadruplicate forms. "[N]o matter how him wicked . . .
him can't be any more wicked dan brown man" (p. 35). These issues are also
addressed by Cargill: for example there is the "probably apocryphal" story of
the well-educated brown man who rails against the prejudice of whites but
does not want his daughter to marry a black man (*Farewell*, 171).

The ambivalence and confused signals take many directions: white Jamaicans are viewed equivocally. "When negar man thief, him thief a dollar. When white man thief, him thief de bank," Winkler hears – making him feel "oddly vainglorious about [himself], like a master swindler among lowly pickpockets" (*Going Home*, 168). Cargill is disturbed to find that one of his workers has drunk a mug of insecticide. "Good God!" he exclaims. "Why?" The response is: "[He] say if Backra tell you something bad for you that means it is good nourishment" (*Farewell*, 46). In the antiwhite political climate of the 1970s, when some of Winkler's more militant colleagues at the college grow to like him they are quick to assert that he can't be white: "White? . . . Who say Tony white? . . . White, my foot!" (*Going Home*, 170).

This love/hatred of self/other is, both authors agree, rooted in three hundred years of colonialism. Winkler's suggestion that "a people who were brought here as slaves . . . grew into nationhood simultaneously clinging to the passive resistance mentality of the enslaved while unconsciously admiring and aping the ways of the English master" (*Going Home*, 35) is echoed by Cargill:

> The white upper classes had on the whole no expectation that [the black man] could ever be anything else but inferior. Such was the cultural dominance of the white man's world that the black man came to share the same opinion. Of course, he did not wholly share it. Half of him did, and half of him didn't.

As a result,

> The half of the Jamaican black man that does not share the low opinion of his own colour is always understandably eager to hear opinions which will release him from the condemnation of inferiority. The other half makes him prone to mistrust his own judgment. So he tends to withhold appreciation of anything unless someone else, preferably from abroad, makes the judgment for him first. (*Farewell*, 178)

Winkler expresses great impatience with the black-skinned, white-masked pseudo-Englishman, who, having been influenced by the Englishman's "excessive emphasis on rightness in ceremony and grammar", comes to confuse "accoutrement with accomplishment" (*Going Home*, 70, 204). "[T]his mistaken belief [gets] translated into educational axioms," says Winkler, ". . . and our educators [are] too preoccupied with aping the Englishman's obsolete and backward ways to devise a better system for students" (p. 205). Cargill notes that "every accepted idea, every accepted attitude in Jamaica, was at least fifty years displaced in time. To this day the people tend to be like flies encased in amber" (*Farewell,* 107).

Cargill's distress about the predicament of his countrymen reminds one of Winkler, who observes that "as a people Jamaicans are hobbled by a streak of self-hatred and suspicion against their own . . . an engrained sense of self-worthlessness acquired in a demeaning colonial history" (*Going Home,* 164). "All Jamaicans," says Cargill,

> are suffering the consequences of all the Uncle Sidneys who ever lived – of the people who regarded blacks as nonpersons – and the consequences, too, of self-hatred and the concomitant hunger for significance which has led our people down blind alleys, following demagogues who sing so sweetly but perform with such incompetence and lust for power. (*Farewell,* 182)

And elsewhere: "Once again, as they have been for three centuries, our good people have been betrayed" (p. 180).

Betrayal, in the opinion of Cargill as much as Winkler, has been personified in the sweetest-singing demagogue of all: Prime Minister Michael Manley. Winkler does not object to Manley's basic socialism since it addresses the "obscene" inequalities in Jamaican society (*Going Home,* 14). Cargill's sympathies are decidedly not with socialism, or at least the Jamaican brand of it, but throughout the book – and in fact all his writings – there is evidence of a genuine concern for the welfare of the poor black majority, "the majority of people [who] lived at subsistence level to service a minority of masters" (*Farewell,* 107). This concern separates him from the mainstream plantocracy represented by his Uncle Sidney, notwithstanding the implicit condescension of his observations and his telling use of "they", as opposed to Winkler's "we", when referring to the people.

Cargill's paternalistic distancing, a possible placement of his concerns in the context of "upper-class obligations", is not unexpected, given his generation and social background. In contrast is Winkler's embracing of, and identification with, the black poor Jamaican – he has internalized a black identity (*Going Home,* 79): "My heart is your heart. Your blood is my blood. . . . I am of you" (p. 162).

Here, then, is the key difference between the two writers – one which accounts for the opposite directions in which the two are travelling on the outgoing legs of their migration journeys in the mid-1970s. Cargill, thrice threatened with prosecution "for being critical of the government", his water cut off because he is a "wicked capitalist oppressor" (*Farewell,* 176, 173), reacts as a typical upper-class Jamaican and flees. Winkler, a young progressive who identifies with the black poor and wants to help to improve their lot, comes home to help the cause.

What, then, accounts for the return legs? Cargill claims in his 1994 epilogue that he returned to Jamaica to join in the fight to save the country by ousting Manley and the People's National Party. In his book Winkler suggests that it was his disgust with the treachery of the principal of his teacher-training college that caused his abrupt departure. Neither story is fully believable. Cargill, one may surmise, may well have been too old to adjust to a foreign culture which he clearly disliked (his irritation with America and Americans was expressed explicitly in an interview with this writer);[3] and less charitably one may guess that for a white Jamaican used to a privileged lifestyle in a small society, the harder, more anonymous life in the United States may have been difficult to get used to. Winkler, on the other hand, though white, was never used to being a big fish in the small pond of Jamaica. His real reason for leaving, a close reading of *Going Home* may suggest, was his wife's unhappiness – an unhappiness at least partly caused by her discomfort at being white in a black society.

Cargill, then, it may be speculated, left Jamaica partly because as an upper-class (white) person he was frightened of the possibility of communism with its curtailment of his freedoms, and possibly came back at least partly because as an upper-class (white) person he missed his privileged position and so decided to fight for it. Winkler came to Jamaica partly because as a socially conscious person who empathized with the black poor he wanted to be part of the socially progressive movement that he thought was taking place in the country; and left partly because he found that movement to be not progressive but destructive, one which was in fact, among other things, intensifying racial tensions and making life difficult for whites.

In short: Colour and class, then, are, inevitably, prominent triggers in the mid-1970s migrations of Cargill and Winkler. Notwithstanding a seeming similarity of social consciousness and social analysis, the differences in identity between the two men contribute to the difference in the direction of their migrations. Cargill goes and comes back partly because, unconventional and critical of his society though he is, he is nonetheless upper-class white, with a possessive investment in his upper-class Jamaican whiteness. Winkler comes to Jamaica partly because he has internalized a poor black identity, and leaves in part because no matter how identical his heart and blood may be to that of the black Jamaican majority, his (wife's) skin is white.

So, finally: In a time of tremendous socio-political turbulence, the older, more conservative landowner Cargill goes home, though not to teach, and the younger, more progressive Winkler bids Jamaica farewell.

Like Morris Cargill, the writers Herbert George de Lisser and Evan Jones share a number of characteristics with Winkler. By dint of their skin colour and/or social status they could all be classified as members of Jamaica's elite. Unlike Cargill, however, de Lisser, Jones and Winkler are in various respects located only on the periphery of Jamaican whiteness. These three writers, all novelists unlike Cargill, are also all better known for the popularity of their work than for its serious literary merit. With de Lisser being born in 1878 (he died in 1944), Jones in 1927 and Winkler in 1942, the three writers represent three separate generations. An examination of three novels – de Lisser's *Under the Sun,* Jones's *Stone Haven,* and Winkler's *The Great Yacht Race* – may help to determine the extent to which these three writers have a shared vision, one which crosses over boundaries of time.

Under the Sun, published in 1937, is one of some twenty-plus novels written by de Lisser. It is subtitled "A Jamaica Comedy", and could in some ways be described as a comedy of manners. While the majority of de Lisser's works of fiction were historical, *Under the Sun* was set in contemporary times (the 1930s), and is a cynical study of the Jamaican middle and upper classes.

De Lisser's family, according to W. Adolphe Roberts, was of "very old Jamaican ancestry, Portuguese-Jewish on the paternal side with a modicum of African blood".[4] His family being of "very old ancestry" did not, however, mean that de Lisser grew up as a pampered child of the elite; his father suffered financial difficulties from early on and died when de Lisser was fourteen years old, leaving the family practically destitute. Rhonda Cobham states that de Lisser thereafter fought hard and ruthlessly "to avoid his father's fate. . . . [In 1904] he became the [*Gleaner's*] youngest ever editor-in-chief, a position he was to hold unchallenged for the next forty years".[5] De Lisser married the daughter of a well-established white Jamaican family in 1909. By the time of his death in 1944 his family had fully regained its financial footing and was firmly placed within the ranks of the Jamaican upper middle class.[6]

Evan Jones's *Stone Haven,* published in 1993, and the author's only published novel to date, is the saga of a Jamaican family that rose to prominence over three generations and fifty years (circa 1920–70). The novel reads as a thinly veiled biography of the author's family, and as such it is revealing in its portrayal of the author's perceptions of his own ancestry.

Jones, born nearly fifty years after de Lisser, is, like de Lisser, near-white, but unlike de Lisser, not of old elite stock; the ascent of his family into the ranks of the landed gentry occurred in his father's generation. Jones's actual family history, as gleaned from an interview with the author by Laura Tanna,[7] differs only insignificantly from that of the protagonist in *Stone Haven.* Jones's Welsh missionary great-grandfather (grandfather in the novel) moved to Jamaica in 1842. The novel tells us that the goodly reverend fathered a number of children with his black housekeeper before finally marrying her, leaving the church and purchasing a piece of property; however, according to Tanna it was actually his son who "chose agriculture over the ministry, leased a ruinate property in 1872 and married a Jamaican, a Burke from Portland".[8] The reverend's grandson (son in the novel) married a white American and expanded the family holdings, so that their offspring, young Evan Jones and his siblings, grew up as members of the landed gentry.

Winkler, born fifteen years after Jones, is regarded by many as a Lebanese or Syrian white because of his Lebanese mother and despite his Hungarian great-grandfather. Lebanese (the name indiscriminately given to immigrants from the Middle East) are Jamaica's most recent white immigrants and as such, despite being elevated by the society at large because of their white skins, and despite their success in trade, are still at the margins of the Jamaican elite.

Winkler's third novel, *The Great Yacht Race,* is semi-autobiographical, based on the author's recollections of life among the middle and upper classes of Montego Bay in the 1950s, when he was a teenager. Many of the characters in the novel are sketched from memories of family friends. Notwithstanding a brief period of prosperity, Winkler, like de Lisser, grew up in straitened circumstances, one of a family of eight children, supported by a father whose success as a businessman fluctuated wildly.[9] Winkler's father, like de Lisser's, died suddenly when the writer was a teenager, leaving the family penniless. Forced to move in with a relative, the family struggled for years, supported by Winkler's mother, older brother and himself, until gradually, one by one, the family migrated to the United States. So Winkler's categorization as elite would be strictly in terms of colour and – as he would readily volunteer – not of class.

In her ethnographic study, *The Power of Sentiment: Love, Hierarchy, and the Jamaican Family Elite,* Lisa Douglass suggests that the upper-class historical consciousness incorporates a "myth of origin" wherein "an invented tradition attempts to establish continuity with a suitable historical past".[10] For example, unlike Cargill's family, most of Jamaica's powerful elite families today were neither slaveholders nor estate owners but are "descended from urban-based traders and merchants" who established themselves only two or three generations ago; nevertheless they have "inherited the planter legacy"[11] with its accompanying behavioural patterns of exclusivity.

To compound the myth, many of the white Jamaican families who have in fact been in Jamaica for two or three *centuries* and are thus regarded, and highly respected, as the old elite, are actually Jewish – like de Lisser's ancestors – and as such were regarded as second-class citizens by the original plantocrats.

To compound the myth even further, many of Jamaica's elite are not fully white but Jamaica white, that is, to use Douglass's definition, "those apparently white people whose ancestors included Africans".[12] These Jamaica whites (like de Lisser and Jones) are, as noted in chapter 1, regarded as non-white by fully white Jamaicans but as white by the brown/black majority. According to Douglass the "touch of the tar brush" (usually introduced by a female ancestor) is often de-emphasized, with emphasis instead on the series of great white men who formed the family dynasty. This othering of blackness is successful, as often with succeeding generations the touch becomes progressively fainter, with family members marrying fully white people and thus enabling future generations to "become" white.[13]

Douglass refers to a parallel myth of origin among the middle class: here, the myth tells us that "the nonlegal union of a white male master and a black female slave . . . produced an illegitimate brown offspring of status midway between slave and master".[14] The truth, of course, is that most white immigrants were not planters. But such a myth validates the existing status quo. For both middle and upper classes, Douglass suggests, the past begins when the white ancestor arrives in Jamaica.[15] Both classes, then, create their own past – ancestry as *choice* – in an attempt to justify and hold on to their minority positions of power. Such myths of origin speak ultimately of a society with a power base of dishonesty, deception and pretence.

All three writers explore the issue of "whitening" the family by marriage. In *Stone Haven* Stanley Newton, the brown-skinned bastard turned banana planter, determinedly woos and eventually wins over Grace, the Quaker missionary posted at a local girls' school. Although Stanley's attraction to Grace's whiteness, with its accompanying long-term benefits, is not explicitly stated, his subsequent dalliance with Grace's fellow missionary Esther makes his preference clear: "She had an over-powering jaw. . . . But she had a good figure, she was young, and she was white" (p. 168). And indeed, Stanley Newton's marriage to Grace proves to be but the first step in a steady rise towards plantocrat status, as he acquires, first, legitimate ownership of his father's property, then more and more land, with the epitome of his success being the purchase of a property owned by Jamaica's wealthiest landed family – "as close to [aristocracy] as the country could produce" (p. 314). And his brother's accusation rings true: "You want to . . . become a white man! You're into property and morality and all of that" (p. 135).

So all-pervasive is Stanley's othering of his blackness, his determination to become white, that he is genuinely dismayed at his son's choice of a brown-skinned wife – "She's not of good colour" (p. 308) – and has to be reminded by Grace, "She's the same colour as you are. . . . You haven't changed your skin by going to Ascot every year!" (p. 309).

In *The Great Yacht Race* the brown-skinned magistrate Angwin, attending a summer institute in Glasgow as a young barrister, finds himself shunned

> just because he was brown – a prejudice which deeply shocked him since his Jamaican experience had led him to believe that his shade of brown was superior to all others and only slightly inferior to the most pristine white. Moreover, he had always believed himself to be firmly upper-class. . . . [The magistrate's] ances-

tors had been as white and as British as possible for nearly a hundred years. Then in 1890 a profligate outcast of a son . . . sullied the family's bloodline by marrying a Bajan black. . . . [T]he magistrate had been unremittingly bitter in his denunciation of his grandfather's folly, and very early in his life he made up his mind to marry a white woman and begin the process of restoring his blood for the benefit of his descendants. (pp. 120–21)

Angwin is delighted when Charlene, a barmaid, seems impressed by him, and he soon proposes marriage. On Angwin's return to Jamaica with his Scottish bride, he receives "a tumultuous welcome from his family, their hearty congratulations ringing with a meaning his foreign wife could not quite fathom" (p. 124).

Such pictures are reminiscent of one painted over fifty years earlier. In *Under the Sun,* the light brown but lowly clerk Christopher Brown is amazed when, on holiday in England, he succeeds in attracting and subsequently marrying Amy, a beautiful white woman: "Here was he, with a beautiful girl beside him, a sort of girl whom he could only meet in Jamaica in the relation of salesman to customer. It was wonderful. It was intoxicating. It was proof that the age of miracles had not passed" (p. 38). When he brings her back to Jamaica, others are equally astonished: "How had it been done? Why, why . . . this would make him a man of mark among persons of his social standing, and among those of a higher standing also" (p. 67).

But unlike those of the later novels, Christopher Brown's marriage to Amy in *Under the Sun* turns out to be disastrous – at least for Christopher, who finds himself forced into social groups and settings in which he is decidedly uncomfortable. Furthermore, he eventually realizes that "persons of wealth and position were treating Amy to pleasure trips and parties while quietly ignoring him" (p. 182).

For Amy, on the other hand, the marriage has opened up all sorts of vistas:

In London she would have remained eternally obscure. . . . She had had no scope as a girl-cashier in a shop. . . . But now, in a new environment entirely, in a land where most of the faces were dark, where a beautiful white woman moved like a kind of goddess amongst plainer-looking people and against a romantic background – here indeed such a one . . . might make something of her life. (p. 109)

De Lisser appears to demonstrate some admiration for Amy's ambitiousness, similar to the admiration he demonstrated some twenty-four years earlier for the resourceful heroine of *Jane's Career*. The lies which Amy tells about her background in order to insinuate herself into Jamaican upper-class society appear to be forgiven by the author for being *white* lies. On the other hand, de Lisser is singularly impatient with Christopher's early ambitiousness which drove him to the folly of marrying above himself, and makes sure that he is suitably punished for some time before allowing him to marry his childhood, middle-class, sensible but somewhat ordinary brown sweetheart at the end of the novel.

There is less impatience in *Stone Haven* and *Yacht Race*. Generally, Jones seems more sympathetic than de Lisser to his brown male protagonist, and shows admiration for Stanley's quiet, plodding but determined amassing of wealth and status. However, the angry thoughts of John, Stanley's elder son, when he confirms his father's infidelity, are telling: "Now he could resent him without guilt . . . knowing . . . that this loathsome, self-important bastard had betrayed his sainted mother" (p. 244). And Stanley's daughter-in-law's denunciation of him as "just an illegitimate half-breed trying to become a gentleman, a nouveau riche not half as rich as he thought he was" (p. 337) may be an opinion held by many.

The only person venerated by Jones in *Stone Haven* is Grace. There are hints that Grace's marriage to Stanley is a sacrifice, and when his infidelity with Esther is discovered, a sacrifice in vain: "Her mistake had been . . . to give up the purity of service for the joy of raising a family. Her husband had betrayed her and what would become of her little brown children? There was no way back" (p. 195). Grace's portrayal as sacrificial victim is shown unequivocally in her later outburst to Stanley: "I married you to prove a black man could be a gentleman" (p. 309).

The author's evident sympathy for her position, and his corresponding impatience with her manipulating predator husband, seem to be echoed in Winkler's obvious distaste for the pompous magistrate in *Yacht Race*, in contrast with his fond portrayal of the good-natured, dimwitted, bovine Charlene, whom the magistrate regards as "simple but delightfully good in the natural way of the Jamaican peasant" (p. 122), and who, at the Yacht Club one afternoon, tramples on brown middle-class sensibilities:

> "You have to be careful with domestics," [the magistrate] said heavily. "Many of them practise obeah." . . .

"Witchcraft?" Charlene exclaimed, looking astonished. . . .

"Charlene," the magistrate chided, "you must remember that these people originally came from Africa."

"Well, so did your grandmother, William," she replied innocently.

The magistrate scowled.

"Whose grandmother came from Africa? Look here, woman, my grandmother
did not come from Africa!"

"Well, then your great-grandmother did," Charlene said cheerily. . . .

"My great-grandmother came from May Pen," the magistrate hissed through
clenched teeth. . . .

Fritzie guffawed. Laidlaw chuckled. . . .

"I don't see what you find so funny, Peter," Charlene said to Laidlaw.
"Obviously your ancestors are also from Africa."

Laidlaw stopped laughing and looked savagely at her. . . .

"I don't see what all the fuss is about," Charlene clucked. "It's obvious that . . .
you all came from Africa at one point or another. . . ."

"Africa?" Roxanne looked furious. "I don't come from any damn Africa. I come
from damn Trinidad!" . . .

The table lapsed into a sullen silence. (pp. 154–56)

The difficulty of the brown middle class in coming to terms with both
sides of its ancestral heritage is an issue which has been explored in all but
one of Winkler's novels to date (the exception being *The Duppy*), where the
brown-skinned characters cry down and disclaim any connections to "ole
negar". We see a similar pattern in *Stone Haven,* particularly as expressed by
the light-brown Mavis, Stanley's daughter-in-law, who was greatly distressed
during her stay in England at finding out that she could never be fully
accepted by white people because she was "not what they call white" (p.
296). Mavis is very clear about her views: "The niggers were incapable of
self-government, incapable of democracy! They came from Africa under
whip and gun, and whip and gun was the only rule they could ever understand!" (p. 337).

The depiction of Mavis is an ugly one. Although Jones's character John
Newton is at first captivated by her freshness and unpredictability, such
attributes are soon overwhelmed by a spreading coarseness and vulgarity.
The reader's final image of Mavis is of a woman who is deranged: "She was
still on the verandah, talking at him, shouting at him. . . . He looked behind

and saw her on the verandah in the light from the drawing room, screaming her head off, like a witch in a bonfire" (p. 338).

This last image is similar to the final images of Cynthia, Stanley's brown-skinned sister-in-law, who starts out pert and pretty but soon degenerates into coarseness, and eventually, stark lunacy: "A high, babbling cry attracted his attention. . . . It was . . . Aunt Cynthia who had gone quite mad and now fancied herself as a prophet" (p. 362). The rather sudden descent into madness of both Cynthia and Mavis seems a fitting fate for two characters for whom the author appears to have little sympathy.

In striking contrast is the figure of Miriam, John's sister, whose intelligence and ever-increasing social awareness make her an isolated voice, in an environment of colonialist complacency: " 'Why isn't there a history of Jamaica?' she asked her father. . . . 'There's no Jamaican history at school, not even a book in the library' " (p. 249). And elsewhere, "I'm writing poetry now. I've decided Jamaica needs a literature of her own, or somebody to recognize what literature there is. If you look at the pattern of consonants in Carry Me Ackee go a Linstead Market . . . it's easily as good as Chaucer!" (p. 272).

Such examples of progressive thinking from Miriam's early years – which remind one of the author's determination in his own early years to demonstrate "what West Indian poetry should be",[16] hence the creation of the classic poem "The Song of the Banana Man"[17] – make it no surprise that she ends up being the revolutionary of the family, turning socialist and deciding to have a child for a Rastafarian reggae musician.

But Miriam is the exception. It is significant that the ill-fated Mavis and Cynthia are the only other brown-skinned female characters in the novel – both reminding one of the husband-bashing, squawking brown-skinned Roxanne in *Yacht Race.* Such parallels are not immediately evident in de Lisser's *Under the Sun,* where Gracie Seawell, Christopher Brown's brown-skinned true love, is one of the few characters not subjected to biting satire. (However the author's apparent boredom with Gracie's ordinariness has been indicated earlier.)

There is an abundance of hypocrisy and bigotry in *Under the Sun.* The overall thrust of the novel is its satirization of the near-white upper middle class, to which de Lisser himself belonged. The society has been warped by colonialism, is full of pretension and dishonesty, believing its own myths about itself, full of mimic men and women who have accepted the worst of the British class system, knowing that the lower orders must be kept in salutary check: "For while . . . we might all be equal in heaven, there was not the slightest necessity to hasten such a socialist condition of affairs on earth" (p. 111). The humble Cockney Swiffles, brought in from London to start a tailoring department in the store in which Christopher Brown works, has his status elevated from tailor to English Director of Tailoring in order to attract the necessary clientele. Amy, enjoying the luxuries of the privileged life in Jamaica, realizes soon that if she wants to continue enjoying them she must make a few amendments to her own ancestry: in a fitting tribute to the credo of ancestry as choice, her father is elevated from sergeant to captain and her mother from washerwoman to lady of leisure. Such society is prepared to overlook Swiffles's inappropriate pronunciation ("I" becomes "oi" and "hot" becomes "ot") and credibility gaps in Amy's family history, since they are both white and English, but is certainly not prepared to overlook Christopher's combination of lowly status and the fact of being "a bit coloured" (p. 123).

One recalls the depiction of Mrs Mason in *Jane's Career* – what Kenneth Ramchand has referred to as the "remorseless" satire against Mrs Mason and her class which presents "the author's intuition that more and more, the exploiter of the West Indian peasant . . . is the West Indian middle-class or lower middle-class".[18] W. Adolphe Roberts recalls the observation of a friend of de Lisser that "he had no bump of reverence, but . . . 'a passion for reality, a love of the fact and of truth' ".[19] And Ramchand has pointed out that "de Lisser's revelation of the gap between the West Indian middle-class and West Indian mass is remarkable because he had arrived at a position whose consequences West Indian writers would only begin to explore and understand almost fifty years after his original probe".[20]

As a comedy of the middle and upper classes, *Under the Sun* deals with blacks only peripherally. For the most part the same can be said for *Stone Haven*. The one notable exception here is the author's treatment of the black grandmother, who is dismissively mistaken for the cook by the innocent Grace at their first meeting, but soon establishes herself as a down-to-earth figure of strength. So when Grace asks Cynthia why she eats alone and is told, "It's her teeth . . . she takes them out to eat. . . . She just don't want to wear them out", the person degraded in this exchange is not Mama Newton but Cynthia, who is dismissed even by her sister Mavis: "Oh lawd . . . you're a terrible liar" (p. 36). Jones's brief but positive portrayal of Mama Newton brings to mind his two classic poems, "The Song of the Banana Man" and "The Lament of the Banana Man",[21] which convey the voice of the poor black Jamaican with credibility and resonance.

In Winkler's *Great Yacht Race,* whose focus, like that of *Under the Sun,* is a biting dissection of the brown and white middle and upper classes, blacks are again somewhat peripheral, with the significant exception of the lovable Missus Grandison who is a no-nonsense, matter-of-fact figure, a tower of strength as well as a source of comfort, and ultimately, the voice of principle, common sense and reason to the tortured, equivocating Catholic priest, Father Huck. But Winkler's other novels all have black protagonists, and consistently demonstrate love and respect for the poor black man – with the first two novels, as suggested in the previous chapter, perhaps even romanticizing their black heroes: the fisherman Zachariah in *The Painted Canoe* and the madman Aloysius in *The Lunatic.*

Winkler's satirical vision is clearly shown in all of his books, which in their hilarious outrageousness reduce various aspects of Jamaican life to the level of the absurd, especially any areas of self-aggrandizement or self-righteousness. Such a focus necessarily means that the principal butt of his satire, like that of de Lisser, is the middle class. Winkler follows his predecessor in wringing the humour from that class's societal dishonesty and self-deception. However, while de Lisser's satire reads as having a subtext of anger and tension, with no forgiveness and no granting of exceptions, Winkler's laughter, in his books generally, is softened by an underlying note of affection and warmth – not so much for the pretentious middle class, but for those oppressed by that class: the poor black Jamaicans. And, as *The Great Yacht Race* shows, the affection, muted as tolerance, extends to the upper classes with which he dallied in his adolescent years in Montego Bay.

At the end of *Under the Sun,* one feels some impatience with the young protagonist Christopher, and suspects a boring, tedious, humdrum petit bourgeois future for himself and his wife. In contrast, the novel seems to applaud the conniving Amy for her focused, driving ambition to raise herself out of the middle-class morass. De Lisser's decision to make Amy successful in her manipulation of Jamaican society, then, is an indictment of that society.

De Lisser's sense of both past and present is overwhelmingly negative. Overwhelmed by the pettiness, immorality and intellectual dishonesty that he sees in his own society, he takes an antinationalist stance: how can such a society be capable of self-government?[22] On the other hand, nearly sixty years later, both Winkler and Jones are less negative and more forgiving – possibly due, at least in part, to the fact that some social progress has occurred in the intervening period. In *Stone Haven* Evan Jones demonstrates, despite any negativities, a love of country and family, and a pride in the achievement of his ancestors.

What of the present and the future? Jones seems to make Miriam the voice of today and tomorrow: progressive, commonsensical, unconventional, sometimes shocking. Change is often sad but inevitable. And while one may be tempted to shut one's eyes, like the image of the house at the end of the book, which appears to have "ceased its contemplation of the sea" (p. 409), it seems clear that one will ride the waves instead. Similarly, the nostalgic recollections of Gary Hawkins at the end of *The Great Yacht Race* linger in the mind, and despite any cynicism about the past, the final feeling is one of love. Past follies explain present excesses, and one must weep over them both.

Perhaps this is why *Stone Haven* and *Yacht Race* may stand above *Under the Sun* as works of some significance. De Lisser's evident ennui in *Under the Sun* may result in the reader's final dismissal of the novel itself. The engagement of the authors in the other two works encourages a similar engagement on the part of the reader.

Yet, ultimately, none of the three novels stands out as an especially compelling work. In contrast, de Lisser's *Jane's Career,* Jones's early poems "The Song of the Banana Man" and "The Lament of the Banana Man", and Winkler's *The Painted Canoe* and *The Lunatic,* in which the authors engage with their black protagonists, linger in the consciousness long after they have been read.

Unfortunately, neither de Lisser nor Jones sustains an exploration of the black voice. De Lisser, as indicated in chapter 2, retreats from a portrayal of the black Jamaican protagonist after his first two novels, while Jones directs his energies to international scriptwriting. Only Winkler, the most white and least upper-class of the three writers, has remained rooted in Jamaican blackness in all his novels since *Yacht Race.*

As peripheral, or newly admitted, members of the Jamaican white elite, these three writers have evidently been able to maintain a critical distance from the class to which they have gained acceptance, as has Cargill, a long-established, though maverick, member of the upper class. As members, associate or otherwise, of this elite, all four writers have benefited from an economic and social security that allows them freedom not only of expression but of enjoyment. But in the four books considered in this chapter, de Lisser, Jones and Winkler, and to a lesser extent Cargill, transcend any assumed limitations of elite self-interest in their critical depictions of their society. In their deconstruction rather than reinforcement of exclusivity, they also transcend the planter legacy that they, as white or near-white Jamaicans, may have inherited.

Winkler, however, goes further. By immersing himself fully into the world of black Jamaica in all but the first of his novels, demonstrating a consistent commitment to this world as opposed to a temporary one, he not only transcends the planter legacy that may have been thrust upon him because of his identity as a white Jamaican. Winkler subverts that legacy.

4

Claiming an Identity
We Thought They Despised

It is not a question of relinquishing privilege. It is a question of grasping more of myself. . . .
  – Michelle Cliff, *The Land of Look Behind*

GOING HOME TO TEACH, Anthony Winkler's autobiographical account of a year spent in Jamaica, expresses the dilemma of a white Jamaican marginalized by the black majority because of skin colour. Winkler's account is set in the mid-1970s, a time of heightened black consciousness and racial antagonism in Jamaica. However, Winkler's book makes it clear that his fight to prove his Jamaicanness has been lifelong.

Thirty years after Winkler completed his teaching stint in Moneague, the legitimacy of the white Jamaican's claim to Jamaicanness still seems very much unresolved. At election time in late 1997, as the press recorded, the question of whether one's leader should be able to merge with the crowd in terms of colour became a key issue,[1] one which has resurfaced from time to time since then. In his 1998 Grace, Kennedy Lecture, Professor Don Robotham bemoaned the fact that while in the 1970s the class struggle divided the tribes, in contemporary Jamaica another division is being drawn in terms of colour:

Many people, especially light-skinned Jamaicans, perceive that there is a not particularly subtle move afoot to sideline them, to make them feel that they are not

"true" Jamaicans and to promote a chauvinistic Black Nationalism as the ideology of Jamaica today. Many people perceive this with great bitterness in private but fail to denounce it publicly for fear of being labelled racists or because they think serious public discussion of the issue of race is taboo and not possible in Jamaica.
. . .

On the other hand, the majority of Black Jamaicans in the inner cities feel that they are stigmatized as violent, criminal and worthless. . . . There is also the very strong sentiment in the Black middle classes and Black sections of the business community that they have been discriminated against all their lives in the establishment and expansion of business activities of their own. . . . For many of them, the whole point of having a Black Prime Minister is for the power of the State to be used to right . . . historic wrongs.[2]

In recent years, white newspaper columnists such as Christine Nunes, Diana McCaulay and the late Morris Cargill have been accused of distancing themselves from the masses by their choice of subject matter,[3] while on the other hand they have indicated discomfort with (or in Cargill's case, drawn attention to) their marginalized positions as white Jamaicans – in a number of instances referring to *Going Home to Teach* in support of their views.[4]

"Look! I am one of you", Winkler longs to say to the public in *Going Home to Teach* (p. 162). The complaints of marginalization by white columnists bring to mind not only Winkler's cry, but similar cries heard over and over again in white West Indian literature, as discussed in chapter 2. We recall the defiant proclamation of Brian Antoni's protagonist in *Paradise Overdose:* "I fucking belong here!" (p. 105).

Meanwhile the discussions persist about the white West Indian's location within the West Indian literary canon. Such academic positions as Kenneth Ramchand's seemingly grudging inclusion of white West Indians in *The West Indian Novel and Its Background* (1970), or Edward Kamau Brathwaite's controversial 1974 statement that "White Creoles" cannot "meaningfully identify or be identified with the spiritual world on this side of the Sargasso Sea",[5] have since been modified but not, it would seem, significantly; hence such recent dialogic crossfire as Brathwaite vs. Hulme in *Wasafiri,*[6] followed by Evelyn O'Callaghan's outraged response[7] – all in the continuing debate of "Where do we locate Jean Rhys?" and, by extension, other white West Indian writers.

It has been suggested in previous chapters that characteristic tropes of the literature of white West Indians might include not only a sense of unbelonging and anger at marginalization, but also guilt over the colonial past, guilt at one's own racism and at the racism of one's fellow white West Indians, guilt at one's privilege, a terrified consciousness (that is, a fear of reprisals from the resentful black majority), and a sense of the decay of one's social group, the plantocracy (being smothered by witchbroom, for example). Undeniably, history has burdened the white West Indian with his own peculiar set of baggage: as past oppressor and present threatened minority, saddled with collective guilt but still holding the reins of power, resented but envied by the black majority, rejected but still elevated and aspired towards by that same majority, visible but invisible.

In this scenario of dichotomies and contradictions, in this society of confrontation and confusion, where race is a power construct, the manipulation of one's identity may be, and most often is, an external imposition, but to some extent it is an internal manipulation, a matter of personal choice. This freedom to choose, to claim an identity, is of course more limited the darker one's skin colour is: the whiter the skin, the more one's options are expanded. The choices that have been made by a number of contemporary white or near-white West Indian writers then become all the more interesting.

The Jamaican writers Michelle Cliff and Honor Ford-Smith may be classified as near-white, or red ("a term which signified a degree of whiteness", says Cliff [*Land of Look Behind,* 59]), or as Jamaica white. The fair-skinned Cliff and Ford-Smith are both the daughters of a white man and a brown woman. Cliff has referred in her books to the polarized realities of her Jamaican upbringing, in which she was able to "pass" for white ("Passing demands . . . silence" [*Claiming an Identity,* 6]) and thereby benefited from many of the privileges accorded to whiteness, in contrast to the treatment of those with darker skins around her. "You're lucky you look the way you do," her mother tells her, "you could get any man. Anyone says anything to you, tell them your father's white" (*Claiming an Identity,* 47). As she observes, "Those of us who were light-skinned, straight-haired, etc, were given to believe that we could actually attain whiteness", and "The light-skinned person imitates the oppressor . . . [and] becomes an oppressor in fact" (*Land of Look Behind,* 72, 73).

Cliff's response to such a warped upbringing is, first, to experience rage: "As a light-skinned colonial girlchild . . . rage was the last thing they expected of me" (*Land of Look Behind,* 15); second, to reject whiteness, and instead – to use the title of her poetry/prose collection – to claim an identity they taught her to despise: blackness. "To write as a complete Caribbean woman," she says, ". . . demands of us retracing the African part of ourselves, reclaiming as our own . . . a history sunk under the sea . . . or trapped in a class system . . . [dependent on] a past bleached from our minds" (p. 14). *Abeng* and *No Telephone to Heaven,* her first two novels and the only West Indian ones, mirror, through the growth of the protagonist Clare Savage ("Her name, obviously, is significant," Cliff has said),[8] Cliff's own personal journey to racial, moral and political self-awareness.

"You callous little bitch," says Clare's father shortly after her mother's death in *No Telephone to Heaven.*

> "I suppose you have more feeling for niggers than for your own mother."
> Clare breathed deep. . . . "My mother was a nigger –"
> His five long fingers came at her, as she had expected. . . .
> "And so am I," she added softly. (*No Telephone to Heaven,* 104)

For Clare's father, love for Clare's mother means respecting her enough to raise her above the level of "nigger". For Clare, love for her mother means recognizing and foregrounding her blackness as her true identity. As Cliff states in *The Land of Look Behind,*

> It is not a question of relinquishing privilege. It is a question of grasping more of myself. . . . To be colonised is to be rendered insensitive. . . . The test of a colonised person is to walk through a shantytown in Kingston and not bat an eye. This I cannot do. Because part of me lives there. (p. 71)

This conscious decision to foreground her blackness is again symbolized by the blackening of the West Indian mulatto Annie Christmas's skin in Cliff's third, and first American-based, novel, *Free Enterprise,*[9] in which the author expands her identification with blackness to politically embrace American blackness.

Cliff has now lived in the United States for over thirty years, and has not visited Jamaica since 1975.[10] But her collection of stories published in 1998, *The Store of a Million Items,* indicates that the scars of her early warped upbringing are still present in her memories: memories of social injustice and an indifferent middle class (for example, in "Stan's Speed Shop": "We originated in a place where the sun never set and the blood never dried. . . . Whatever happened, we weren't to blame, nor were we to make any change");[11] of an isolated, decaying plantocracy surrounded by resentful blacks ("Contagious Melancholia"); and of the peculiar loneliness of the white Jamaican, most hauntingly portrayed in "Transactions". In this story, a childless, white Jamaican travelling salesman impulsively "adopts", or rather purchases, a dirty, animal-like roadside waif, just because she is white – "Like is drawn to like" (p. 10), and "Now he thinks he'll never be lonely again" (p. 11). Warped motives have warped consequences: the child turns out to be a vampire, sucking the life out of him – perhaps just as his warped values have previously drained him of the ability to find fulfilment.

Cliff's embracing of her black side is readily understandable, and not only in terms of her political sensitivities and moral conscience. The disparagement apparently accorded near-white people by fully white people in her childhood may have urged her to go to one extreme or the other: as Clare is warned, "Only sadness comes from mixture. You must remember that" (*Abeng*, 164). Additionally, her formative teenage years would have coincided with the blooming of the Black Power, Black Is Beautiful and Caribbean socialist movements. Third, and critically, living in the United States as she has since her early teens, she would in any case be categorized in that country as black.

Honor Ford-Smith, on the other hand, although currently based in Toronto, grew up in and has spent most of her life in Jamaica. Yet her rejection of claims to the privileges of whiteness is in many ways similar to Cliff's. In her beautiful, moving tribute to her mother, *My Mother's Last Dance*,[12] Ford-Smith relates her own rejection of what whiteness represents – privilege, insensitivity – and this contributes to the mother-daughter conflict so sensitively portrayed:

> MOTHER
> Formed by all I fought so hard to earn
> She styles herself the opposite of me,
> Says she's ashamed by privilege.
>
> . . .

The little boonoonoonoos who cried
When I went back to work in the afternoon
Has become Lady Bountiful of the suffering masses.
. . .

DAUGHTER
She doesn't like my friends – wrong class.
. . .

Wrong colour too.
. . .

Now, ask her what colour she is.
She can't say it. Afraid to say it.
Had to go to North America to find out.
. . .

BOTH
Once our hearts beat in one body,
MOTHER
Now this strange white fruit has burst from my flesh. . . .
("Amputation for Two Voices", 70–73)

Ford-Smith's embracing of blackness is, like Cliff's, primarily political. Her rage at social injustice has caused her to reject the privileged background that her mother represents (represented to Cliff by her father), and to become "Lady Bountiful of the suffering masses". Like Cliff, her rage develops through an understanding of history, and again like Cliff, she explores much of this history by exploring her brown mother's family background, as opposed to the unfamiliar background of her white father from whom, like Cliff, she has long been estranged. Again like Cliff, Ford-Smith relates the trauma of a light-skinned person being trained to pass for white: "They just kept her in the house, till she took house colour. Till she learned she was different from them. She was not to speak patwa like them. Not to bathe in the river like them" ("Shame-mi-lady. Shame", 40).

One is taught to be ashamed both of one's partial whiteness (due to miscegenation) and of one's blackness: "STOP RUBBING UP YOURSELF WITH THE PICKNEY CROSS THE RIVER" (p. 41). The reproach is haunting: "Shame-mi-lady. Shame / Shame-mi-lady. Shame / Shame-mi-lady. Shame" (p. 40). One is also taught, as Ford-Smith recollects elsewhere, in her life story "Grandma's Estate", that whiteness is not straightforward:

> "You must remember" [her grandmother tells her] "you are not white; you only
> look white."
> I looked at myself in the mirror. . . . I peered at my nose – it was dead straight.
> My lips were thin. . . . I checked my hair – it was brown and long and soft. Yet I
> was not white. I concluded that white was not a colour.[13]

The confusion, pain and shame of the near-white person's position of
unbelonging cause Ford-Smith to relate, in that same piece, her outrage as
a schoolgirl at the othering of the creole Bertha Mason in *Jane Eyre:* "I
couldn't stomach the way I had been relegated to the attic" ("Grandma's
Estate", 185). Cliff, in *Claiming an Identity,* also relates directly to the
Bronte figure: "To imagine I am the sister of Bertha Rochester. We are the
remainders of slavery – residue: / white cockroaches / white niggers /
quadroons / octoroons / mulattos / creoles / white niggers" (p. 42). And in
her essay "Clare Savage as a Crossroads Character", she states that her protagonist Clare Savage is "an amalgam of [her]self and others", "a crossroads
character, with her feet (and head) in (at least) two worlds" and that
"Bertha Rochester is her ancestor".[14]

Ford-Smith's many years of dedicated involvement with the Sistren
Theatre Collective of working-class women, as opposed to the life she could
have led (with "a gun toting stockbroking BMW driving husband, / a four
bedroom house in Norbrook with two starched helpers, / a gardener, security
guard" and so forth ["Dinner at the Apartment in Toronto", 85]) is but one
proof of her determination to reject the privileged but unbelonging Jamaica
white lifestyle. This straying from the path of expected behaviour is lonely,
causing anguish in her mother ("when I see her coming / I have to take a val-
ium. / I just start to tremble all over" ["Amputation for Two Voices", 72]),
and anger from her family:

> it's all a lie.
> And you know it.
> Grandma never spoke patwa
> and you know it.
> Why do you have to keep on
> calling your mother
> a brown woman?
>
> . . .
>
> Nobody would know.

> But you have to keep on bringing it up!
> . . .
> you have it
> like some ole cross to bear.
> You are just obsessed with race.
>
> You just want to be black.
> That's all.
>   ("Disputed Truths", 67)

The result is alienation both from her family ("Yuh can't even go back to your risto yard. Yuh too soiled with the sex of old neaga") and from some of those she is seeking to assist, who will never accept her fully: "History say yuh can take yuh chances, but yuh can't hide. . . . Your skin glitters bright in the dark. . . . Dutty gal. Sodomite gal. . . . Yuh notten more than a mule" ("History's Posse", 26–27). It takes much strength to persist, but Ford-Smith shows that she is finally able to overcome such disabilities, and "head out for the open road" (p. 29).

Yet such expansion of frontiers is precisely what her mother herself achieved in her own time, Ford-Smith demonstrates, as she resisted the restrictions imposed on a young woman of colour, and determinedly pursued the unheard-of goal of becoming a physician, thereby revealing that she could "loom suddenly secretly at night, / a black flower white with rage" ("Aunt May at Carron Hall Orphanage", 7). Just as Ford-Smith has, in turn, revealed herself to be a white flower black with rage. Ultimately, however, *My Mother's Last Dance* is not rage, but resolution; in this tribute to and reconciliation with her mother the writer dissipates the rage generated by societal injustice, and in coming to terms with her familial and personal past, she also reconciles with her own identity.

However poignantly or beautifully expressed, Cliff's and Ford-Smith's struggles for identity as white women of colour are weighed down by anger, pain, conflict, sadness. A refreshing contrast is provided by Pauline Melville. Self-declared Guyanese/British, the most white-looking of the three women, Melville has no time for angst over her ambivalent, indefinable status: "Pinning down my identity is not what interests me most about life", as she says in her essay "Beyond the Pale".[15]

Melville has a white English mother and an African-Amerindian-

European father, and among her siblings is the "whitey in the woodpile". In Guyana, no one calls her white ("You're not white. I know your family"), but in England where she is anonymous and judged only by her appearance, the idea that she could be anything but white is viewed as ridiculous: "You're not black. That's crazy. You're as white as I am" (p. 740). Melville's situation, then, is different from Cliff's and Ford-Smith's in that Melville passes for white more successfully in the metropolitan environment. She does not have blackness thrust upon her; she has more freedom of choice to claim whatever identity she chooses.

Such freedom of choice extends even to a decision as to whether she wants to be included in an anthology of black women's literature:

> I hesitate. "Do you think I'm black?"
> "That's for you to say."
> Well, it's an odd thing to have a choice about. (p. 741)

An odd thing indeed. Melville eventually accepts, partly through "an unwillingness to disinherit [her]self . . . mainly through fear of betraying [her] father". Here, then, she is obviously faintly uncomfortable with such attempts at labelling, just as she acknowledges that she is "faintly uncomfortable when people insist that [she's] white". She does not want to be identified with the oppressor, or rejected by the black community, "[a]nd simply, for me, it does not feel like the whole truth" (pp. 741, 742).

But Melville brushes aside such moments of discomfort, and generally views modern society's preoccupation with the quest for identity as somewhat extraordinary: "When questioned about my identity, I would wish to echo Clark Gable in *Gone With the Wind*: 'Frankly, my dear, I don't give a damn.' In my interior landscape, the South American jaguar and the English chaffinch live easily together" (p. 742).

Melville compares her position to that of the Yoruba trickster god who loves to "cause confusion" (p. 739). "I am a champion of mixtures and hybrids," she declares (p. 742). She enjoys Carnival because "it is a masquerade where disguise is the only truth. . . . Death comes in the guise of uniformity, mono-cultural purity, the externals of the state as opposed to the riot of the imagination" (pp. 742–43). In her rejection of narrow labelling, what Melville is celebrating is the ambiguous, ambivalent, multifaceted creole identity, with its multiple masks, as referred to by Benítez-Rojo.[16]

Such a celebration is hinted at, more subtly in the content than in the title, in *Shape-shifter,* Melville's first collection of short stories, which moves from hot, rotting Guyana to cold, crumbling England and features black, brown, white and anonymously hued protagonists and narrators. In the Guyana-based stories, Afro-Guyanese characters are generally depicted as especially corrupt or otherwise unpleasant – although this may be explained (if not forgiven) by the fact that the Burnham regime which was evidently a nightmare for Melville was primarily supported by blacks. And to balance this observation, her depictions of black working-class Londoners are sympathetic, insightful and poignant. Melville's perspective is primarily fixed on life's victims, from the naïve, do-good English missionary in Guyana to the cantankerous, lonely black Londoner with a disabled child; their pain, loneliness, frustrations and simple pleasures are universal. Only in one story, "Eat Labba and Drink Creek Water", does she address her own racial ambiguity. The story suggests that Melville's current comfort with hybridity was not always there: as a child in Guyana, where the narrator is both envied and resented for her white skin, she is embarrassed when children taunt her by calling her "ice cream face"; but when in England she is also embarrassed by her brown father, whose appearance subjects her to another type of taunting: "Mum, Keith says Daddy looks like a monkey. And I think so too."[17]

In *The Ventriloquist's Tale,* her first novel, Melville immerses herself in an Amerindian Guyanese world, with its magic, lore, and very non-Western realities. As with her first book, the title promises more than it delivers: by far the most exciting, powerful moments in the book are to be found in the Prologue and Epilogue where the mischievous, irrepressible, elusive narrator makes his voice heard: "Ah, secrecy, camouflage and treachery. What blessings to us all. Where I come from, disguise is the only truth and desire the only true measure of time."[18] This may be double ventriloquism, because although it is the ventriloquist speaking, Melville could be projecting her own voice: "White present, black past, a good position for breaking down preconceptions, stirring up doubt, rattling judgements, shifting boundaries and unfixing fixities. I am also well-placed to survey the ludicrous."[19] This is precisely how the ventriloquist narrator locates himself in *The Ventriloquist's Tale,* when he is allowed to speak. Multiple voices, multiple masks, the creole identity. What a pity Melville opts to suppress her creole voice thereafter; what a pity she succumbs to the misguided notion that "sad though it is, in order to tell these tales of love and disaster, I must put away everything fantastical that my nature and the South American continent prescribe and become a realist" (p. 9), for by comparison the rest of the novel falls flat.

This is not to suggest that *The Ventriloquist's Tale* does not make absorbing reading. It is engaging, in a somewhat static, linear, conventional way – despite the unconventionality of the subject matter. But it is in the brief encounter with the ventriloquist's fantastical voice – reminding us of that other fantastical narrator, Lavren in *Witchbroom,* the novel of Caribbean creole complexity written by white Trinidadian Lawrence Scott – that we catch a glimmer of the fantastic, explosively rich potential of the creole identity. It is in such displays of multiple-identity, ambiguous creoleness that Melville is most rewarding.

The fantastical voice returns, again too fleetingly, in the story "The Parrot and Descartes" which appears in Melville's second collection of short stories, *The Migration of Ghosts.*[20] Here again we taste the richness of the creole experience as we move from jungle to European palace, from century to century, taking the perspective of a parrot whose cockiness reminds us of the ventriloquist. The other stories are technically competent but, again comparatively, creatively unexciting. Still, following the trend of her first collection, Melville takes on many voices, in many settings, crossing boundaries of geography, race and culture in ways that few other writers do.

"The imagination," says Melville, ". . . is where boundaries are crossed and hybrids fertilized. . . . The imagination is effortlessly trans-national, trans-racial, trans-gender, trans-species."[21] In her disclaiming of any narrowing identity as expressed in her essay "Beyond the Pale", in her claiming of hybrid creoleness in that essay, in her tentative explorations of the rich creole imagination in her fiction, and especially in her unfettering, all too briefly, of this imagination in the ventriloquist's voice, Melville fertilizes not only the hybrid Caribbean identity, but also a newly sprouting, potentially rich hybrid Caribbean literature. Thus her work takes the journey in quest of self embarked on by Michelle Cliff and Honor Ford-Smith a step or two further along the road from linear, fragmented divisiveness to inclusive creole cohesion.

❧

Melville's claiming of hybrid *créolité* is similar to that of another white-looking West Indian author: Robert Antoni. The Trinidad-born, Bahamas-raised, French Creole Antoni is, like Melville, irritated by the restrictive and, in his view, inaccurate labelling of him as white, and is quick to point out his multinational and multiethnic roots, which he says include African, Amerindian, Indian, Spanish, Italian and a host of other constituents.[22]

Robert Antoni's first two novels, *Divina Trace* and *Blessed Is the Fruit,* both take place in the fictional Caribbean island of Corpus Christi. *Divina Trace* is a novel of creolization on many levels, using "creolization" in the sense that depicts ambiguity, ambivalence, multiple levels of meaning as well as multiple voices, multiple identities. The mysterious Divina Magdalena is perceived in seven different ways by the seven different narrators. Saint or whore? Black or white? All of the above? As Jane Bryce notes, Magdalena is "the true syncretic object embodying all the Caribbean's manifold differences".[23] And as Benítez-Rojo observes in his essay "Three Words Toward Creolization", the mirror playfully placed in the centre of the book, through which readers see a disfigured reflection of themselves, is "part of the novel's double performance: in the mirror, the western reader will read a joke or an irony or a mystery, but the Caribbean reader will see any one of his/her multiple masks". Benítez-Rojo continues,

> These reflections, invested with the political and social ideas of the observer, will never be coherent images, but rather distorted ones; they will be images in flux or, rather, images in search of their own images. Therefore, the mirror of *Divina Trace* . . . in the end . . . reflects an identity in a state of creolization, a reflection that oscillates between history and myth; that is, a paradoxical mask launched into the distance by the explosion of the plantation.[24]

This vision of the paradoxical, imprecise Caribbean identity reminds us not only of Melville's briefly encountered fantastical ventriloquist narrator, but again of the ambiguous, ambivalent, multiple-identity narrator Lavren in Lawrence Scott's *Witchbroom.* In both *Divina Trace* and *Witchbroom,* the richness and complexity of the author's vision of Caribbeanness stimulates us intellectually. But complexity sometimes tends to obscurity, intellectuality tends to self-consciousness, and at the end of both books one gets the sense that in their quest for the elusive Caribbean creole identity, the authors may be trying too hard.

On the other hand, Antoni's second novel, *Blessed Is the Fruit,* approaches the issue of identity from another direction, and the results are intriguing. The story is related by two narrative voices: the near-white but "highwhite" French Creole mistress of a decaying colonial mansion (p. 107), and her black servant. In the first half the voice of the white woman, Lilla, takes us from the present, where the two women are together, back to Lilla's past. In the second half Vel, the black woman, relates her life story. In between these two narrative accounts, in a brief section in the middle, the heart of the book, the two voices interweave and intersect in stream-of-consciousness verse, with the actual point of intersection marked by a sheet of plastic at the centre of this section, signifying the transparency of the division between the two lives. Antoni at play again.

Despite such instances of postmodern playfulness, the structure is a relatively simple one – unlike that of *Divina Trace.* Lilla's and Vel's stories are also relatively straightforward, and the primary message of the novel seems unambiguous and, indeed, possibly overemphasized: it is that, despite their different skin colours and their different backgrounds, Lilla and Vel have equally tragic pasts and overlapping histories, with hope for a brighter future (personified in Vel's unborn child, which has survived against all odds) if they unite and work together. Lilla and Vel, in other words, possibly unlike Antoinette and Tia (if one agrees with Brathwaite)[25] can indeed be friends. In fact, the echoes of *Wide Sargasso Sea* resonate frequently and determinedly throughout Lilla's narrative as, surrounded by decay and disappointed by her lover, she too descends into madness – although a much milder and seemingly more remediable, and generally less interesting, type than Antoinette's.

What makes this novel intriguing is how unsatisfactory the first half of this book is, and how much more successful the second. Lilla's half reads as contrived (witness the *Sargasso* parallels), self-conscious, stilted prose. The character of Lilla seems unclearly defined and inconsistently portrayed, with early signs of reclusiveness disappearing completely and inexplicably from the narrative voice when she leaves school, to be replaced abruptly by a seemingly superconfident extroversion and strength, as shown in her spirited encounter with her future husband on the night of her debut:

> "I've just realized," I said, "that you look exactly like my first love."
>
> "And you find that comical?"
>
> "Quite, if you consider that my first love affair occurred with a chicken!"
> (p. 116)

Dysfunctional behaviour only reappears again abruptly when her husband leaves her, at which point her rapid descent into madness seems extreme. Furthermore, her voice is irritating, especially the constant emphases in her speech ("all her dresses hideously *bosomy* . . . tottots out to *here!* . . . All Vel's dresses hideously *short*. The two of us giggling again at my *insistence* at trying on her little minidress" [p. 16]). Not to mention her addiction to masturbating as she rolls her rosary beads, an activity which moves from curious to tedious after, say, the tenth occurrence.

In contrast, Vel's narrative, which follows, engages us from the first page. In fact, in the bivocal, interwoven middle section which serves as a prelude to Vel's narrative, we find ourselves skipping over Lilla's self-indulgent lines, which only repeat what we just endured reading, and focusing instead on Vel's lines, which not only provide new information but also sound a lot more interesting. Vel's narrative is fresh, flows smoothly, develops naturally, reads realistically, and Vel is three-dimensional, convincing in that we understand her motivation and purpose, likable and, most of all, compelling:

> Now begin the scourge and blight. The second session. I just look at granny granny look at me. Wasn't nothing to say. We did know wasn't nothing to say. Them few dollars that I had saving from the canes, them dollars finish before the month out. Wash from my hands before the month out. Wasn't no food left now. No more money and no more food. All we could do is scrape by best we could. (p. 299)

One wonders why a white writer, himself of a presumably plantocratic background, should have such difficulty in constructing a white character of a similar background, and such obvious ease in constructing a black one of a background with which he has no firsthand experience. The observation that the book's dedication is to Lilla and Vel gives us a clue to the fact (later confirmed in an interview with the author)[26] that these characters are based on real people. Is he too close to the subject matter of Lilla, but with Vel has attained a distance that enables? Surely this is not the full answer.

White West Indian fiction, as discussed in chapter 2, traditionally features the female black servant as the only significant black character, presumably because this is the black figure with whom the white author would have had principal contact – but usually the nanny portrayal lapses eventually into two-dimensional clichés, be it of faithfulness (like Allfrey's Lally or Drayton's Gip) or the ominous unknown (Rhys's Christophine). Antoni transcends such limitations. He undoubtedly romanticizes the hardworking, fate-battered Vel, but also seems to have enjoyed creating her. On the other hand, the creation of Lilla, in its studied deromanticization of the plantation belle, its relentless subversion of the chaste, devout Catholic, its dogged revisiting of the Antoinette story, appears to have been fraught with difficulty and discomfort.

Whatever the reasons, whether consciously or subconsciously, deliberately or accidentally, in *Blessed Is the Fruit* Robert Antoni effectively disengages from his white character, and embraces his black one. In so doing, he subverts his own conscious agenda of promoting interracial sister- or brotherhood and envisioning a new creole, creolized interracial unity, by privileging blackness. And so he claims an identity one thought he, as white West Indian, as French Creole, as elite minority, would have despised.

Such privileging reminds us of Winkler's novels. Indeed, in the voice of Vel, Antoni achieves the freshness and spontaneity of many of Winkler's works. In particular, *The Painted Canoe* and *The Lunatic* project poor, suffering black men as heroes of humanity in the face of adversity – Zachariah the deformed, cancer-ridden fisherman, Aloysius the lunatic. Zachariah and especially Aloysius are likable, engaging characters – a feat for the author, given that Zachariah is an obdurate old man "of unyielding pride" (*Painted Canoe,* 1) and Aloysius is a madman who has conversations with bushes. Winkler's affection for the black Jamaican, and Jamaican foibles and eccentricities, is conveyed in his warm, hilarious, romping novels, which generally read as fresh and unpretentious, not to mention out of order and outrageous, and thus are immensely popular with Jamaicans of all colours and creeds.

Indeed, Antoni's problems with Lilla bring to mind Winkler's admittedly less severe problems with *The Great Yacht Race,* the only one of Winkler's novels that does not have black protagonists and is not told from a black point of view. *The Great Yacht Race,* his least popular novel, reads as much more self-conscious, stilted, and effortful than the others (and in fact it was his most effortful, going through many drafts before the final published version was arrived at). The first draft of this work was Winkler's first attempt at a West Indian–based novel (although the novel was finally published after two others, *The Painted Canoe* and *The Lunatic*), so its laboriousness may be partly attributed to this fact. But one wonders, in addition, whether Winkler may be unable to achieve the necessary distance from his subject matter because the protagonists in this novel are mainly white and brown, or whether, to the contrary, he is alienated, or has alienated himself, from his subject matter. As Winkler says in *Going Home to Teach,* "[T]here were only periodic and welcome interludes of relief when I was not made painfully aware of being clothed in a loathsome skin" (p. 111).

Winkler's description of his skin as loathsome is not merely a projection of the assumed view of the black majority surrounding him. As he says earlier in *Going Home to Teach,* "if I had been born black and poor in one of Jamaica's mephitic slums, I too would have hated the sight of a white skin and been just as inclined as [some street urchins who attacked him] to kick and thump and abase me on the street" (p. 16). His obvious endorsement of any hostility held by blacks towards whites is evident in his negative depictions of white people in all the novels other than *The Great Yacht Race:* for example, the mad, nihilist doctor in *The Painted Canoe,* the sexual fascist Inga and the racist Busha and his wife in *The Lunatic,* the narrow-minded American philosopher, the fanatical American students and indeed the entire demented, racist white population of America in *The Duppy.* Very often the adversity that is fought against by Winkler's black heroes, who represent the compassionate side of humanity, is embodied in these white characters. (One is reminded of the picture painted by Antoni, through Lilla's narrative in *Blessed Is the Fruit,* of the bigoted "highwhites" of Corpus Christi.)

Do contemporary white, or near-white, West Indian writers need to escape, in one way or another, from whiteness, from "being clothed in a loathsome skin", in order to shed all the white man's burdens of guilt, angst, marginalization and unbelonging that may be weighing down their works? If so, is this dilemma yet another manifestation of our schizophrenic, polarized Caribbean identity?

Yes and no. In the case of *Blessed Is the Fruit,* Antoni's presumably unintentional subversion of his conscious agenda of interracial unity by the privileging of blackness in fact subverts the subversion. As we celebrate the white person's celebration of the black one, we inevitably celebrate the coexistence of both – returning eventually and indirectly to the vision of a creole cohesion – one that we glimpsed briefly in Melville's writing, one that was trying not to be submerged by intellectual weightiness in Antoni's *Divina Trace* and Scott's *Witchbroom,* one that may generally be in short supply in Caribbean works.

Brathwaite concludes his 1971 study, *The Development of Creole Society in Jamaica 1770–1820,* with the following:

> It remains to be seen whether the society will remain conceived of as plural – the historical dichotomy becoming the norm – or whether the process of creolization will be resumed in such a way that the "little" tradition of the (ex-)slaves will be able to achieve the kind of articulation, centrality, prestige and influence . . . that will provide a basis for creative reconstruction. Such a base . . . could well support the development of a new parochial wholeness, a difficult but possible creole authenticity.[27]

By privileging the "little" tradition of ex-slaves, Antoni (however unintentionally or perversely) in *Blessed Is the Fruit,* but most especially Winkler in nearly all of his works, may be helping to support the development of this difficult but possible creole authenticity. And they may be doing this more successfully than Cliff and Ford-Smith have done in their own privileging of blackness, during their often painful, sometimes (in Cliff's case) laboured quest towards an understanding of their hybrid creole selves, and perhaps more so than Melville, the self-proclaimed "champion of mixtures and hybrids", has so far achieved in her multicultural yet slightly static fiction.

Part 2

Reading

Anthony Winkler

"White? . . . Who say Tony white? . . .
White, my foot!"
– *Going Home to Teach*

5

Writing the
Black Protagonist

"White people don't go mad in Jamaica. Only negar go mad here."
– *The Lunatic*

THE LUNATIC IS by far Winkler's most popular novel – somewhat to his bemusement: "Funnily enough, the book that everybody seems to like the most is the one I personally feel is the weakest," he once said in an interview.[1] Notwithstanding such authorial reservations, it is easy to understand why the novel is the most commercially successful. More so than the others, it is hilarious, bawdy, outrageous, and thoroughly out of order – "the funniest and most scandalous novel ever written by a West Indian", according to Wayne Brown[2] and "perhaps the most unorthodox novel in Jamaican literature", according to Barbara Lalla.[3]

It also reads as his most effortless work, and the history of its creation may support that impression. Winkler says that he wrote *The Lunatic* as a relaxing diversion while working on a computer science textbook.[4] Unlike his other books, he finished *The Lunatic* in a few months, and was asked by his publishers to do only minimal rewriting. Publication of the novel brought him immediate recognition in the United States (where it had been copublished) and in Jamaica. Although pleased by the American attention, it was that of his fellow Jamaicans that mattered most to him. As he said in an interview in *Lifestyle* magazine,

> [W]ho wants to be a world-known name? I don't particularly want to be a world-known name. . . . I have always said that I would like absolutely nothing more than to be a prophet with honour in my own country. My country is Jamaica. . . . And anywhere else I live other than Jamaica, I will automatically be an expatriate, because my home is Jamaica. . . . There are only two things in life that I think you really need. One is to do the best work you can. The other is to get that certain smidgen of recognition by the people you care about.[5]

In fact, notwithstanding any boredom with computer science, it was the desire for such recognition that, he says elsewhere, was a driving force behind his writing of *The Lunatic*: "I felt the majority of Jamaicans don't like white Jamaicans. So I said to myself one day, 'You fuckers, you have to like me one day whether you like it or not.' "[6]

Winkler succeeded – so much so that *The Lunatic* is easily Jamaica's most popular work of fiction. On its publication many readers expressed disbelief and seemed somewhat at a loss when they found out that he was white. *The Lunatic,* in a *raw-chaw* (coarse), raucous Jamaican way, is Jamaican to the core – and by writing it Winkler proved that he too, despite being white, was "a Jamaican to the core. My essence is Jamaican, and I will never be anything else than a Jamaican."[7]

The novel is obviously Jamaican in terms of its language. Most especially, its indecent language is unequivocally Jamaican, and the liberal usage echoes the way in which many if not most Jamaicans actually speak when in an informal forum – thus generating a delighted popular reader response in appreciation of this verisimilitude. "It sounds like us," one pleased reader said.[8] Outrageously, the novel is peppered with colloquial references to bodily functions (wee-wee, doo-doo) and body parts: hood, and most of all, pumpum. Winkler's naughtiness in his unabashed and frequent usage of such vulgar Jamaican terms undoubtedly contributes to the novel's popularity.

It is not only the indecent language, however, that makes the novel sound Jamaican. Lalla's observation about *The Painted Canoe* applies to Winkler's other works, including *The Lunatic*: "The lexis . . . is distinctively Jamaican even though most of its words are derived from English."[9] Lalla highlights

Winkler's use, in *The Painted Canoe,* of words and phrases such as "john-crow", "boastiness", "ignorant" and "out of order", which have specific Jamaican meanings in addition to their standard English ones. Some of these Jamaican meanings, such as that of "out of order", become pivotal to the reader's full understanding of *The Lunatic.*

This is not to say that the non-Jamaican reader cannot appreciate *The Lunatic.* But, as Mervyn Morris suggests about a poem by Dennis Scott, "it communicates more fully to readers who have learnt in more specific detail about the language and culture in which it is grounded".[10] The line between international accessibility and cultural inauthenticity is always, for the Jamaican writer, a fine one, as has been implied by Morris.[11] Winkler has acknowledged this difficulty in his approach to the tonal creole:

> One major problem I see facing the West Indian writer is how to write in his mother tongue's idioms and native dialect while at the same time making himself comprehensible to a wider audience. He has to write in his native tongue or he will lose the dramatic context for his stories and fumble about unconvincingly.
> . . .
>
> The way I have faced this problem is with asides and with a stooshing up of the dialect. Take . . . the sentence, "What are you doing?" This phrasing is likely to pop out of the mouth of an upper-class or well-educated Jamaican but seldom out of the mouth of someone like Aloysius. . . . "A wa oonu a do?" . . . is comprehensible only to a Jamaican and if used by a writer will doom his work to a smaller audience than a writer wishes for – we all have a secret craving to write for the world, for the universal reader. . . .
>
> When I first started writing about Jamaica, I evaded the problem by relying mainly on narrative and with very little dialogue. . . . But I've noticed that I'm gradually moving towards trying to inflect my character's worldview with an increasing taste of Jamaican idioms mainly because that is how I myself see the world and because I feel more confident that that is how my characters also would. . . . Note, however, that this usage is dictated not only by the need for verisimilitude – the need runs deeper than that. It is necessary because if I am to write from the heart my heart must speak the language of its childhood that it learned at its nanny's bosom.[12]

The evolution of Winkler's Jamaican tone can be seen in a comparison of *The Painted Canoe* and *The Lunatic:* while most of the "Jamaicanisms"[13] in the former are restricted to dialogue, in the latter they infiltrate into the omniscient third-person narrative voice, which uses words and expressions such as "rockstone" (p. 128), "thief" as a verb (p. 199), or "drinking beverage" (p. 73), omits prepositions, as in "like goat kid" (p. 218), and regularly neglects to pluralize, as in "when donkey hood drop" (p. 69), or "having more parson than mongoose" (p. 87). (In *The Duppy* Winkler employs the useful device of making his first-person narrator an ex-schoolteacher, thereby giving the author "the validation, when solemnity requires it, to have him sing to the world in standard English, and when his mood changes to have him speak of it in his natural idioms".)[14]

The Lunatic sounds creole in an easy, comfortable, natural way that few other works have achieved – including those by white or near-white West Indian writers. The attempts of H.G. de Lisser, Jean Rhys and John Hearne to give voice to their black protagonists in *Jane's Career,* "Let Them Call It Jazz"[15] and "At the Stelling"[16] spring especially to mind: here, despite the overall validity of their efforts, there are inevitable moments of slippage – the black voice cannot be sustained – a problem which occurs also in other works where black voices make occasional appearances, such as Morris Cargill's *Jamaica Farewell.*[17] Indeed, such a comparison between Winkler and other white West Indian writers reminds us of Cargill's earlier quoted statement: Winkler is "not one of us".[18] Winkler's voice does not sound like a contrived effort; it sounds authentically black.

The Jamaicanness of the novel extends further than its language. In its sketch of rural Jamaican life, the novel successfully and hilariously conveys many of the nuances of the Jamaican society – executed, of course, with the exaggeration typical of Winkler. The lunatic Aloysius has conversations with flora, fauna, inanimate objects. He is befriended by a German tourist, Inga, who becomes his sexual partner and companion – much to the horror of all and sundry, including bushes and stray dogs, who agree, undoubtedly with the reader, that this combination of madman and white woman is definitely out of order (p. 45). This unlikely twosome is expanded into an even more unlikely threesome when the sexual services of the local butcher (aptly named Service) are acquired by the insatiable Inga to supplement those provided by the lunatic. Meanwhile Busha, the local landowner (and owner of the land on which the out-of-order *ménage à trois* build their house) and one-time employer of Aloysius, supposed pillar and patron of the community, actually devotes most of his energies to a morbid obsession about his ignominious future should he be buried at the local cemetery, where he would be victim to the out-of-order excretory practices of the local cows and goats. "Too much damn slackness!" he complains of their behaviour (p. 61). It is a quarrel about cemetery-related matters that causes Busha to cut short a Sunday afternoon drive with his wife, Sarah, as a result of which they catch Inga, accompanied by an unwilling Aloysius and a willing Service, in the act of burgling Busha's house. When the lunatic is eventually acquitted of the charge of attempted murder, he is adopted by the respectable though flatulence-plagued Widow Dawkins who, by bathing, clothing and feeding him, and censoring his conversations with bushes and all, converts him into an acceptable sexual partner.

The strong farcical elements in the plot contribute to the novel's popularity. The use of the word "popular" when used to describe fiction often implies a lightness of weight, a lack of substance, a deficiency of seriousness. However, even the most cursory reviews of *The Lunatic* have acknowledged at least one serious level, which Morris Cargill refers to as the "hard cutting edge of first-class social satire" – a level which the reader may realize exists, Cargill suggests, only "after one has laughed heartily at the surface situations".[19] Winkler pokes fun at various aspects of Jamaican society – a most refreshing change for Jamaican fiction. In fact, the presence of such satire makes the book's popularity all the more interesting, since one characteristic of the Jamaican audience may be a tendency to take itself too seriously, and to react badly to criticism. On the other hand, *The Lunatic*'s tone is so good-natured that it defers offence. Against Naipaul's cynicism and the cold, "hard-won simplicities of his classical style", Wayne Brown contrasts the "pure pleasure with which Winkler takes in his Jamaican characters, matched by his ebullient prose".[20] Furthermore, *The Lunatic*'s satirical focus is so broad that it may allow each reader to find someone to laugh at other than himself. As Bob Shacochis notes, "Perceptions of female and male, black and white, developed and undeveloped, the mad and the sane, are acid-stripped to their original surface of moral ignorance."[21]

Indeed, the main driving force behind the writing of *The Lunatic* may have been a serious meditation upon one aspect of the acid-stripped Jamaican reality. As Winkler said when he was in the process of writing *The Lunatic*,

> I am trying to understand that part of the poor Jamaican's character that I have never fully understood – the enduring, forgiving, compassionate part. I do not have much of that part in me and if I had been born poor and wretched in Jamaica I am sure that I would have been hanged by now.[22]

The lunatic Aloysius is a poor black Jamaican who is barely eking out an existence. Aloysius lives in the woodlands of Moneague; the trees and bushes are his shelter, as well as his companions. In a sense Aloysius is not lonely – the flame heart tree is his best friend, and the irritating, gossipy bushes are always there to give their opinions whether or not he wants them – but, of course, these demented imaginings, if one accepts them as such, underscore his isolation. Aloysius is starved for love and human companionship as well as for food.

Aloysius has known nothing but hard times. An orphan, he was raised by his aunt, who felt that he had the brains to become a barrister, but "God never give me de chance to reach me ambition in life. God take me outta school before me learn to read and write" (p. 147). Since then, his life has deteriorated significantly, and he has been homeless for an indeterminate time, forced to forage for food in the bushes except when the occasional opportunity to earn a few pennies arises, such as diving for coins in the Ocho Rios harbour when the tourist ships come in. "Me is a negar man. Me used to hard life and wicked treatment" (p. 145): the comment, made by Service, is self-pitying, but it applies unreservedly to Aloysius.

Despite his hard life, Aloysius refuses to blame God. "God do me plenty injury. . . . But me not raising me hand against God. Him is still me Daddy" (p. 148). Such faith despite great odds reminds one of that earlier poor black "unlikely hero",[23] Zachariah the Portland fisherman in Winkler's first published novel, *The Painted Canoe*. Zachariah is poor and "unspeakably ugly", "horribly disfigured" by a swollen and elongated jawbone (p. 1). His life, too, has been one of hardship from the start. Yet he is "a man of unyielding pride" (p. 1), and also a man of unyielding stubbornness. It is around this trait of obduracy that the story revolves: despite its hardships and against all odds Zachariah clings stubbornly to life. He manages to survive being lost at sea for twenty-eight days and being attacked by a hammerhead shark, only to discover that he has terminal cancer. The fates continually conspire against him, yet Zachariah is determined to live. In this depiction of one man's battle against the forces of nature, or against fate, and ultimately against the inevitability of death, the predominant theme of *The Painted Canoe* is determination versus determinism – a stubborn, unreasonable determination to defy the inevitable forces of heredity and the environment.

And in fact, as one reads *The Painted Canoe,* at first there seem to be strong naturalistic resonances: where humans are victims of instincts (especially hunger and sexuality) as well as social and economic forces beyond their control; where the focus is on the lot of the poor; even where the action in the story would appear to follow a "heroic but losing struggle of the individual mind and will against gods, enemies and circumstances".[24] Any similarity to naturalism is, however, countered by the seemingly miraculous turn of events wherein Zachariah survives not only the twenty-eight days adrift at sea, and the shark's attack, but, most incredibly of all, the cancer.

Such miracles may read as contrived. Zachariah's suddenly finding his way back to Charity Bay, for example, seems a bit abrupt – and the information that Winkler's original ending to this story had Zachariah dying at sea, but that a friend encouraged the author to make the ending a happy one, is not surprising.[25] But these miracles introduce resonances of magical realism which are explored further in *The Lunatic.* More importantly, the novel's message is an affirmation of faith in God. For all along, in all his troubles – being lost at sea, having his leg nearly severed by the hammerhead shark – Zachariah has refused to pray to God for help. He believes that "God have plenty on him brain, and when you run to him over every little thing, soon him don't know when you truly need him or when you just bawling over little fool-fool hardship" (p. 6). "A man," he believes, "should wait until his trouble was dire and beyond all hope. And he was not yet beyond all hope. The canoe was not foundering. . . . His heart was still strong. What, really, were his present troubles?" (p. 78). "When me go to de Almighty again," he has declared from early on in the book, "you know me on death doorstep" (p. 6). It is only when he is literally on death's doorstep, ravaged by the cancer which has now riddled his body, that he goes back to sea to pray.

Such brave and illogical clinging to life is, for Winkler, characteristic of the island's black poor: "Nobody love life more than a poor man" (p. 198). As the English doctor's woman in *The Painted Canoe* says scornfully, "Ole negar . . . love de earth too much. . . . [Dem] cling to life like weed" (p. 251) – reminding one of the East Indian canoe owner in *The Lunatic* who complains that Aloysius is not successful enough in his diving for coins because "Damn negar man breathe too damn much" (p. 33). And as Zachariah himself says to the "vast, shuddering ocean", "Negar not so easy to kill" (p. 183).

The resiliency of Zachariah is developed in Aloysius, whose existence is in many ways even more precarious than that of the fisherman. Aloysius is more vulnerable than Zachariah because he is more child-like, innocent, trusting. Winkler quickly establishes Aloysius's position as what Wayne Brown terms "a child of nature",[26] and Lalla refers to as "essential man".[27] His purity, goodness and innocence ("Vhy must one person be boss?" [p. 116]); his sense of decency and propriety; his upholding of traditional values (not only does he not want to kill Busha, but to him Inga with her wanton licentiousness and her foul mouth is definitely out of order); his vulnerability (he has nightmares [p. 22], he is afraid of the sea [p. 32]); his loneliness (he has not shaken a hand in twenty years [p. 41]) and need for love and family (he never knew his parents [p. 14]); all of these characteristics make him lovable to the reader. They also contribute largely to the "extraordinary grace and tenderness throughout *The Lunatic*" observed by Shacochis.[28] Aloysius, in his refusal to kill Busha, his insistence on loving him, represents compassion.

In all of this, as the reader easily becomes attached to Aloysius, Winkler succeeds in a rapid deconstruction of stereotypes, contributing to an overall deconditioning of the reader, as noted by Lalla.[29] The reader's initial assumption, that this is a book about a lunatic in a sane society, is rapidly altered to the point that one soon questions whether the supposedly mad lunatic may not be saner than the supposedly sane individuals, or indeed the entire supposedly sane society, surrounding him.

As part of Winkler's deconstruction, the lunatic's reality is portrayed as an ordered and consistent universe: the bushes have predictable responses, the flame heart tree has a clearly defined character. So the most obvious indications of lunacy – his conversations with trees, bushes, animals, inanimate objects – very quickly cease to strike the reader as signs of raving madness, and become viewed instead as a harmless and amusing eccentricity, if not as an enviable ability, a gift from God, whom Aloysius refers to as his "Daddy" (p. 148). Aloysius is the innocent child of God. Aloysius may indeed be, as the green lizard suggests, "de only sensible man in dese parts, who have ears dat listen" (p. 28). "This is Winkler's ingenious device," Brown suggests:

to body forth an animist's Creation . . . and then to bestow upon Aloysius, alone . . . the key to that voluble kingdom. The device reverses at a stroke the vagrant's "madness", making it synonymous, not with alienation from reality, but with an integration into reality deeper by far than that available to those of us who pass for sane in the world.[30]

Meanwhile the supposedly civilized world, which has ostracized the lunatic, features persons such as Inga, a convention-defying, hate-mongering "sexual fascist and a Nazi of the Left"[31] with "a maniacal, frenzied laugh, laughter such as Aloysius had never heard outside of the madhouse" (p. 39). Winkler's establishing of Inga and others as madder or at least as mad as Aloysius is direct. Aloysius's logic is hard to find fault with:

> He could not tell her when he had first gone mad because he had never gone mad. He could say when the world had first proclaimed him mad and why: it was because he had gotten into a heated roadside argument with a Trinidadian don-key. . . . He could tell her what it felt like to be draped up by a constable . . . and driven to a madhouse in Kingston, while the donkey, who had started the argu-ment, incurred no punishment. This was the unjust state of affairs in Jamaica. (pp. 47–48)

In contrast, Inga displays what Aloysius regards as "foolish reasoning", a judgement which the reader may initially question, until he continues, "Me sleeping in de bush, me not troubling anybody. You creeping pon de ground taking picture o' me hood. Which one is de madder one?" (p. 38). The hotel manager echoes Aloysius's question: "I don't know which one of you is de madder one" (p. 87). It does not take Busha too long to come up with the answer: "Dis woman is even madder dan you," he tells the lunatic (p. 106).

Among the leading community figures in this supposedly civilized world are a "stuck-up" (p. 15), "vain" (p. 16) teacher who is not only insensitive but misguided; a doctor who has the urge to examine all the pumpums of his female patients, even if, as in Sarah's case, the ailment is an ear infection ("she asked him to his face if he was mad" [p. 95]); a hypocritical parson whose favourite sermons are those which blast rum and pumpum but in whose belly "the rum juice [sits] sweet" (p. 92); a self-delusionary, infatu-ated inspector of police whose obsession is the batty of his friend Busha's wife; and, as the pillar of the community, Busha himself, who is not only cemetery-obsessed but also racist, best demonstrating, Lalla suggests, the "decadent, morbid and grasping fixations of a threatened (propertied) class".[32] The Widow Dawkins suffers not only from severe flatulence but also severe prudishness – and still loves hood. Shubert the village shopkeeper (and predecessor of Baps in *The Duppy*) remembers not his customers' names, but their credit balances – hence, for example, Mrs Sepole is $78.59 (p. 172). Service the butcher is a nihilist who loves to kill. In one way or other, these individuals are all clearly out of order: first in the sense which Winkler uses both frequently and fondly, that is, the colonialist sense of displaying inappropriate or (in Winkler's words) outrageous, indecent or improper behaviour (p. 12); second, in the sense of being dysfunctional; and third, ultimately, in the sense of representing a world of disorder.

Even the bushes and animals, which from early on have established themselves as the voice of Jamaican country folk and are quick to identify any out-of-order behaviour (such as the lunatic's grinding of the ground, or Inga's photographing of Aloysius's hood), are themselves shrill, raucous and disorderly – reminding one of the villagers in *The Painted Canoe* who, as Michael Thelwell suggests, are "resilient, randy and stubborn as goats; as quick to laughter as to anger, to violence as to tenderness; capable of meanness and great generosity".[33] This "populous pastoral scene", then, as Brown notes, is "hardly paradisal".[34]

Madness, in various shapes and forms, invades all areas of the society, even courtrooms ("lemme outta dis damn madhouse" says a juror [p. 213]), although some expressions may be more permissible than others: talking to bushes and trees, for example, may not be "the kind of madness appreciated in such high places" as a government ministry (p. 213). Madness may be even more widespread: Busha declares that "you have more madman in the United States dan in any odder country on de face o' de earth" (p. 98); and, in Inga's opinion, "if God vere a human being ve vould say that he vas mad" (p. 146).

Such direct authorial means of questioning established definitions of sanity and lunacy are combined with indirect ones: at an early point in the book, for example, two villagers agree glumly with Aloysius that "Jamaica bush always chat too much" (p. 24). Later, when Busha is angry with Aloysius for "telling [his] cow story about movie in de bush . . . [thereby ruining] de best milch cow with [his] damn talking", one has a disconcerting suspicion that Busha may feel it is not the talking *per se,* but Aloysius's choice of subject matter, that has "mix[ed] dem up" (p. 66).

Yet no matter how widespread lunacy may be, in another way Winkler never denies that the lunatic is, plainly, a lunatic. Although Morris Cargill suggests that Aloysius's "thousand names and a craving for pum-pum" make him "not, after all, so very different from the countless males in Jamaica who parade long words, the meaning of which they do not understand, crave pum-pum constantly, especially from tourists, and end up nicely dressed in church",[35] nevertheless Aloysius's claiming of a thousand names confirms his madness – which is why Barrister Linstrom uses it as the key to his defence.

However, this claiming of a thousand names warrants further investigation, beyond the level of Cargill's comment as well as the presumed authorial teasing with regard to the Jamaican working-class tendency to give one's children impressive sounding, but often misspelt, names. This collection of highfalutin words is literally meaningless to Aloysius who does not understand them, and nonsensical to the sane observer who does understand them. But in another sense the collection means the world to the lunatic. He has accumulated this collection by eavesdropping outside the village schoolroom window because he – illiterate but with a brain that he has been led to believe could have allowed him to be a barrister had he had the opportunity – is desperate to learn. It is his only claim to dignity and respectability: like the village teacher who drills words by rote into the minds of young schoolchildren, he knows that a mastery of words signifies a mastery of education and that such a mastery would be the only way in which he could better himself. Words mean power, which is why a white man has "twenty names for a tame dog while a poor black child [has] only one" (p. 16). Words access respect – hence his being overcome when Inga records his words. Ironically, his babbling of such words defeats this very purpose, as it confirms his distance from "normal society", a society which includes the white man who gives his dog twenty names and the white woman who diligently records Aloysius's madness in her book.

And Winkler suggests that, with his deprived background, madness may have been hard to escape. Deprivation leads to depravation; after all, "White people don't go mad in Jamaica. Only negar go mad here" (p. 76). In the autobiographical *Going Home to Teach,* Winkler's accounts of his mad aunts show that this is not true: the times are indeed "hard on every man" (p. 28).

In *The Painted Canoe* the white doctor's sanity is first questioned, then eventually proven to have disintegrated. However the figure of the poor black street madman seems to be an especially haunting one in Winkler's consciousness, and a recurring one in most of his books published to date. In *Going Home to Teach* he refers to a disturbing encounter with one, and in his fiction the madman appears first as the psychopathic murderer in *The Great Yacht Race* (Winkler's first-written novel), then in hilarious vignettes as the wacky, mooing Lascelles or the more pathetic Seahorse in *The Painted Canoe* – in which that other poor, struggling black man, Zachariah, fights not only for survival but for sanity – before being developed fully in *The Lunatic*. For Winkler, the black madman is the ultimate symbol of a madly and maddeningly difficult Jamaican existence.

This lunatic society suffers the effects of colonialism, among them the creation of a social structure where power and wealth are in the hands of the few, usually white, landowners like Busha, and ignorance, backwardness and poverty are the lot of the black majority (represented by Aloysius as well as by the bushes); where opportunities for advancement are few; where the majority are exploited by the minority. It is a society where black, brown and white people are divided. White people are racist: Busha would hate to "spend de rest of [his] life thinking dat every breath [he] drew was because of some old negar" (p. 223). "Brown-skin" people are unsympathetic, pompous and arrogant – like the doctors at the asylum (p. 48); or the jeering doctors and nurses at the hospital (p. 79); or the schoolteacher; or the Barrister Linstrom who turns up his nose at the bumpkin mentality but ultimately, in his inability to understand the scope of Aloysius's charity and forgiveness, proves himself to be possessed of the same bumpkin mentality. Blacks are occasionally resentful of whites – such as in the days of the Socialists when "the Prime Minister so roused the rabble with firebrand orations that urchins and vagrants used to scream 'pork' at white people in the streets" (p. 57). More often, however, they are self-deprecatory: with their constant derogatory references to "ole negar" (as in "ole negar never satisfy" [p. 72], or "once ole negar got started on a point, only Almighty God knew when he would stop" [p. 225]); or their use of "negar" as the ultimate abusive adjective (as in "damn nasty negar cow" [p. 63] or "rass negar bee" [p. 73]); or their eagerness to abandon as much of their "negarness" as possible – shown, for example, by a claim that sex makes "kinky hair turn straight" (p. 128), or, most tellingly, by Aloysius's boast that "me not whole negar. Me is only half" (p. 45).

It is a society with fixed and often bizarre notions of what is in order and what is out of order.

> Out of order: a parliamentary phrase that Milud and Milady of the fallen British empire might use to scold one another at Whitehall. Yet after three hundred years of colonialism by the ancestors of Milud and Milady, it is a phrase that Jamaicans of all walks of life use to signify outrage, indecency, impropriety – even a woeful madman such as this Aloysius. (p. 12)

In order means with appropriate dignity, as in "wearing a mien of effortless imperturbability like a colonial English governess making doo-doo on the potty" (p. 124). In order means an upholding of "right principle" (p. 25), about which even a lunatic like Aloysius is very clear: for example, no one should address anyone else as "Lord" because "Dere is only one Almighty Lord" (p. 25), "pum-pum must be seen and not heard" (p. 27), and "no foreign woman should beat a Jamaican" (p. 50). Out of order, on the other hand, means such outrageousness as grinding under a stop sign ("Dat is out of order. You can't grind under stop sign in Jamaica. Dat's why de sign say stop. It means everything must stop" [p. 80]), tying up a local madman on a bed in a north coast hotel (as opposed to, say, on a bed in the madhouse in Kingston [p. 87]), dying when one is good and ready (as opposed to when one is supposed to [p. 138]), or having a naked-batty angel (as opposed to a covered-batty angel [p. 169]) on one's mausoleum. Aloysius, the bushes and all Jamaicans in *The Lunatic* cling to their warped versions of original colonialist notions of order and disorder, which themselves may have been warped, as a means of retaining dignity and pride: for "poor might be dirty and poor might be ramshackle and stink like fat Queen Victoria in a crinoline, but poor was not nasty" (p. 77).

It is a society not independent long enough to be convinced that the Queen does indeed doo-doo, but independent long enough to have suffered a series of incompetent governments mismanaged by demented politicians – especially, in Busha's view, the Socialists. Busha can never forget the insane days "when the Socialists were raving in Parliament about idle land and threatening to confiscate private property all over the island" (p. 57). A government form, especially one in the hands of a "holdover Socialist from the previous government, a man who took perverse delight in inflicting the intricacies of government document on the lives of innocent citizens", is expected by Busha to "ask imponderable, insensible questions about everything under the sun" (p. 68). Busha suggests that it is no mere coincidence that Aloysius went mad "during the budget debates, when the damn Prime Minister chat for eight hours non-stop" (p. 94). As Busha speculates, "the torment of socialism . . . was more than enough to drive any man mad" (p. 94). Busha's views are echoed by another white character, Mr Saarem, whose view it is that during the years of the socialist government "Jamaica went temporarily mad" (p. 167). Such condemnation of the years of socialism is predictable coming from the white characters, but their cynicism about politics is not restricted to those years: Sarah advises Busha that if he thinks there is an advantage to having a madman on his cricket team, then he should "go to Parliament and get all de ministers to come bowl for you. For dem all mad" (p. 98). Nor is the cynicism restricted to the white characters: a villager also recognizes madness in politics, comparing the carryings-on of a raving lunatic to a minister without portfolio (p. 11); and a bush is objective: "From Socialism to Capitalism to Pum-pumism . . . Lawd Jesus God, what now on de head of poor Jamaica?" (p. 117).

As a result of all this historical and political madness, life is hard – especially for the black man. The social infrastructure is awry. The legal system provides "an unjust state of affairs in Jamaica, as any poor man could testify to" (p. 48). And Inga's eventual escape from the hands of the law, obviously enabled by bribery (which itself would be enabled by Inga's father's wealth and skin colour) certainly underlines this fact. Education is substandard due to inadequate resources, as illustrated by the village school with six classes of fifty-odd students each, all sharing one room, resulting in the need for a learning method of competitively loud, mindless recitation of facts (p. 16). The health services are not much better: even Busha with his wealth must suffer the consequences of overall inefficiency and out-of-order machines (p. 137). And those like Aloysius who are condemned to Bellevue are subjected to silly American experimentation (p. 213) or otherwise senseless treatment: "they locked you in a room whose walls were padded with rubber and they forced you to eat chicken behinds for dinner" (p. 48). Religion provides no relief, its zealots being extreme and excessive, not to mention ignorant, especially in their incessant, fanatical (and of course hypocritical) railing against rum and pumpum. As Service says, "no matter what woe and trouble in dis world, parson say pum-pum cause it" (p. 183). "Oh, Babylon," shrieks a bush who has taken a correspondence course from an American seminary, "what will become of this Babylon dat we call Jamaica? . . . What will happen to Babylon in dese wicked times? Woe unto ye, Oh Jamaica! Pum-pum and rum gone to your brain and make you giddy!" (p. 55). Given such inequalities, inadequacies and excesses, no wonder an indignant stone, expressing the sentiments of most real-life Jamaicans, proclaims, "Dis is Jamaica for you! Where man treat man like dirt! God strike me down dead if I don't migrate to America next year!" (p. 154). (Or, as the juror, we recall, will say at Aloysius's trial, "Lemme outta dis damn madhouse!" [p. 213].)

Winkler's satirization of tourism in this "sinful paradise, carefree Babylon",[36] on which the sad economy is sadly dependent, is relentless: Inga's relationship with the ragged madman is an extreme caricature of the "rent-a-dread" phenomenon, where female tourists vacation in Jamaica with the express purpose of seeking exotic, black male companionship – the Quest for the Big Bamboo. Inga is possibly sarcastic but definitely blunt: "I stay vith [Aloysius] because he has a big cock!" (p. 106). The German's liberal "Sinsemilla" smoking, sensation seeking and sexual insatiability are stereo-typical of the infamous hedonism of a particular species of tourist which causes some concern among conservative locals: "What is dis, Oh Lawd, dat Jamaica come to? See how de damn slack foreign woman dem go on nowa-days?" (p. 37). Of course, Winkler is also playing with the stereotype of the black man's eternal quest for white pumpum (as touched upon by the village doctor's yearning to touch upon that particular type): so some are equally alarmed because "for a madman who lived like an animal in the bush to sud-denly find himself shacked up with a tourist woman only encouraged other men to go mad" (p. 97). Tourism is necessary, as the whole population has been taught, but the licentious liberties taken may stretch one's tolerance to the limits: "Is me country dis!" Aloysius says to Inga. "You come and visit me country, and you is very welcome like de Prime Minister say 'pon de radio. . . . De Prime Minister say no call white man no name in de street, so me no call you no name. . . . But you is out o' order" (p. 38). "Damn out of order, man!" Busha agrees. "Dis Jamaica is de only country in de world where even when a man dead and in him grave him must still pose for tourists" (p. 124).

Inga, like many European tourists, is hungry for factual knowledge of the island. It is a hunger for possession, for control. She devours statistics, place names, sites and sights; her camera "gnaws at the land" (p. 50). In her determination "to see the real Jamaica" (p. 49), she sets about this task with typical German thoroughness, efficiency and detailed planning ("Why white people love so much plan, eh?" Service asks later on when she applies this approach to the burglary of Busha's house [p. 158]), and soon succeeds in knowing more facts about the land than her undereducated Jamaican guide:

> Aloysius knew his land the way a poor man knows it. . . . But Aloysius did not know Jamaica the way the white woman knew her. She knew the land the way a teacher knows a schoolbook . . . she knew it better than Aloysius to whom the land had given life. It was a way of knowing that galled Aloysius so that he could hardly stand to talk with her and be told about the country, about the names of mountains and villages and towns. (pp. 70–71)

Aloysius's distress causes him to cry out, "De darkness cover me mind and me eye! . . . De darkness o' everlasting ignorance" (p. 71). And the cry sadly attests to the state of existence of most Jamaicans: "Life hard here" (p. 45).

But of course Aloysius, to whom the land has given life, knows much more about the country than Inga. To Inga, the land

> was the most beautiful she had seen, to which Aloysius always replied with dour memories: here was a tree under which he had once huddled against a driving rain . . . through a long fretful night. There was a pasture where he used to sleep once . . . before the bushes drove him away with nasty gossip. . . . At the foot of that mountain he had once spent a hungry week. . . .
>
> The woman saw none of these things . . . she saw none of the misery and pain in the empty land. (p. 70)

Aloysius's vision, then, is in one sense distorted by hardship and in another sense made clearer.

Aloysius loves the land.

> The land put food in his belly and it gave him a place to sleep and in the morning when he woke up and stared around him, the land was always there, waiting for him like a faithful nurse. . . . He could reach out and touch the land, and feel its warmth during the night, and imagine that under his touch lay the flesh of a beautiful woman. (pp. 28–29)

After the rain, "the smell of the moist earth rose up around him like the odor from a freshly bathed woman" (p. 49).

But nature is hostile. "Tree grapples tree for room in the sun. Perched high on limbs like carrion birds, parasite plants suck life and sap from everything that grows. Wild vines and lianas ooze menacingly out of the dark earth to seize and entwine the trunks of towering hardwoods" (p. 19). The sun "lick[s] greedily" at the pale skins of tourists "like a hungry dog licking meat off an old bone" (p. 44). The "rocky bay of Ocho Rios yawn[s] open and chew[s] on the gristle of the wreathing sea" (p. 45). When Inga sees the bay she exclaims, "Vhat a lovely island this is," but Aloysius's response is, "Life hard here, ma'am" (p. 45).

In fact, this particular response as quoted above is incomplete: it is given because despite Aloysius's love for the land, nature has scorned him. Aloysius's sense of the land as woman drove him in his state of sexual frustration to "grind the ground" (p. 29), but not only did nature disappoint him – "De ground hard" – but also its elements turned against him: "Bush talk too much" (p. 45). "Life hard here, ma'am . . . de ground hard. Bush talk too much." Indeed, the scandalized bushes won't stop talking about this out-of-order behaviour: "Kiss me Granny, him fuck de ground" (p. 45).

Aloysius, then, the child of nature, struggles for survival in a land that is brutal, an existence that is hard. He struggles against a nature that has both nurtured and fought against him.

Inga enters his life and eases this particular struggle, providing him with food, shelter, sex, companionship and, as the novel eventually reveals, genuine affection and friendship. Brown's suggestion that she "gets herself spirited out of the country"[37] to escape punishment is misleading; she is spirited out of the country by her father, and her letter to Aloysius from Italy suggests that she left against her will and that she genuinely misses him. Yet at the same time she is undeniably another negative force: the exploitative white person, the destructive foreign interloper. In this role she follows that of the English doctor in *The Painted Canoe* – another intrusive dark force, whose sanity is also put into question: "Now here . . . was a white man unlike any other on the island, a foreigner with such strange, perverse ways that . . . everyone . . . called him 'mad' " (*The Painted Canoe*, 91). According to Brown:

> This is Winkler's theme, as it has been Naipaul's . . . the disruption of old rever-
> ences by the coming of the self-seeking stranger. . . . Winkler, however (and it is
> the source of his buoyant faith) inverts the Naipaullian equation. In *The Lunatic*
> the native culture, while "backward" in the usual senses of the word and not with-
> out its old iniquities . . . is not frail, as it would be in Naipaul, but robust, ani-
> mated, resilient and (its author clearly implies) ultimately on the side of the
> human spirit. By contrast, the intruding European perspective is emphatically
> denied authenticity.[38]

Attesting to what the bushes refer to as the "wickedness of foreigners" (p. 39), Inga is what the parson calls "a foreign temptress": "He speculated about the heinousness of foreigners in general who came to innocent islands such as Jamaica and spread moral turpitude all over the land" (p. 93). She is immediately a disruptive force: "Only two days now the woman had been in the bushland but already there was not a minute's peace" (p. 91). She is a dangerous defier of convention: "History is shit" (p. 72), although "Shit has deep meaning" (p. 101). She is disrespectful of morals and mores: she yells filthy, unspeakable Jamaican words at respectable people, she commits an act of presumably unspeakable filth with a young village boy, she demands "at least two, three, maybe four lovers" (p. 54), she insists on having sex in out-of-order positions and places.

But there are more sinister elements. Inga is "no ordinary woman": she is "strong and violent" (p. 40), boasting that as easily as she can chop the limb off a tree, "so easy I kill a man" (p. 38) and, later on, that "One time I put a bomb in a Paris restaurant that killed fifteen people" (p. 144). In her distorting, darkness-covered eyes, Service's slaughter of animals is art, which causes even the naïve Aloysius to have "a mounting sense of foreboding" (p. 111). To some she is the legendary White Witch of Rose Hall reincarnated – a comparison invited by her appetite for young black men, and by her evil. Violence and death are not foreign to Jamaica – they have long been a shadow hovering in the nature of even one as good as Aloysius who, when teased mercilessly by a bush about "fuck[ing] de ground", chops it down, "and when the first chop of the machete rang through the darkness the silence of night and death fell on the bushland" (p. 30). But certainly Inga brings a new strength of the dark force of evil into the community, "some nameless, palpable and ancient thing", and into the environment of the *ménage à trois*: "It was like death, this thing that had come among them" (p.

150). Yet the evil that she introduces is disguised, twentieth-century style, as social justice, and inspired at least partly by genuinely good intentions (combined, of course, with more pragmatic self-seeking concerns). Thus Inga, "clear-eyed avenger" of the radical left, "assassin of the status quo",[39] may in fact be even more dangerous than the original White Witch:

> "I think I know vhat is wrong with this island," she said softly . . . "Too many lies. Not enough hate. . . . There is reason for hate. Poor people everywhere you look. A few rich people. There should be hate. . . . That is vhat wrong with this place. . . . In Europe, ve have lots of hate. This is why [*sic*] Europe is strong and rich. This is vhy Jamaica is poor." (p. 108)

Much of the evil that Inga introduces is facilitated by Service, who "love death too much", Aloysius observes. "It was in the eyes of this butcher that Aloysius saw love of death – the black eyes that tunnelled, like two worm holes, into a dark place" (p. 121). Of all the characters in the book, Service as representation of evil is the least ambivalent. His nihilism – "Mud is God. . . . Dere is no God and dere is no coming back. When you dead you dead and gone back to mud" (pp. 143–44) – reminds one of that other destructive foreign interloper, the doctor in *The Painted Canoe:* "Slowly, surely, over the passage of time, the doctor came to be on the side of death . . . the one thing the doctor believed in . . . was inevitable death" (*The Painted Canoe,* 251). (Yet even here, in his indictment of Service, Winkler introduces shades of grey: " 'He vas a beaten child,' Inga said to Aloysius one day" [p. 121].)

This evil is introduced under the rule of pumpum. Indeed, pumpum rules in the novel, figuring predominantly not only as word but as key plot element: Aloysius is as hungry for it as he is for food when Inga encounters him, and it is the evidently long-standing nature of his deprivation that draws her attention to him. It is her eagerness to provide pumpum that causes him to bond with her emotionally. It is her voracious sexual appetite that causes her to engage a supplementary Service, and the *ménage à trois* is established under the strict rule of pumpum. Inga's dispensation of pumpum causes dissension among the male ranks; however, it is the power of pumpum that keeps the unlikely *ménage* together, and ultimately persuades Aloysius to participate in the burglary of Busha's house. Later, when the Widow Dawkins decides to take the lunatic under her wing, it is less an act of charity than a practical solution to her own sexual needs – and so pumpum rules again.

And here Winkler again displays ambivalence. Pumpum is a natural and inevitable force, "for Almighty God put pum-pum between the legs of women and then he put dreams about it into the heads of men" (p. 11). As a natural force it is a law unto itself, especially when combined with hood – "the parts utterly ungovernable by religion or preaching, the parts that obdurately pay no collection in church, endure no hymn singing . . . the hood and pum-pum whispered to one another in a private tongue like two lawyers outside a courthouse" (p. 51). Hood may mingle with pumpum, but pumpum rules. Hood is helpless against pumpum. Hood rises immediately to attention when pumpum displays itself (p. 91). The eyes of men dart "like moths around the pum-pum" when it is unsheathed (p. 116).

The power of pumpum casts a spell over mankind. It lures Aloysius and then Service into Inga's lair. It persuades the two men to participate in Inga's careful planning and rehearsing of the burglary. "Why oh why oh Lawd," a bush screeches plaintively, "you invent pum-pum to torment men so? Why you put pum-pum in dis world to make honest man turn thief?" (p. 163).

Winkler seems to suggest that pumpum is maligned, as indicated by the following:

> "[I]s de parson dem fault, for dey is de one dat preach dat pum-pum must lurk inna crotch like rat in a tree!"
> "Must tie up like bad dog!"
> "Eh ah! And why? Who pum-pum ever bite?"
> "Who indeed? Since when pum-pum have teeth?" (p. 123)

And frequently in the novel Winkler ridicules the absurd fixation of parsons with pumpum.

Nevertheless, the course of the novel suggests that pumpum does after all have teeth. Pumpum becomes evil and frightening, "gaping wide like fish mouth" (p. 184) – reminding one of the goat's throat slit by Service: "The wound gaped as vulgar and gaudy as the painted red mouth on a whore" (p. 110). So the constant railing of parsons against pumpum may in fact be justified – as implied inadvertently by Service when he suggests the contrary: "Me Daddy was a parson. When I chop him he say, 'Is pum-pum make you chop me.' Dat's how parson mind work. Everything is pum-pum fault"

(p. 183). Who knows, could the parson have been right about the cause of his son's deviance?

And in an earlier exchange:

> "Everybody love preach in Jamaica," Aloysius grumbled. . . .
>
> "Bee, you bumbo!" yelled the tree. ". . . Is too early for pollination!"
>
> "Preaching from ignorance," Aloysius mumbled sleepily. . . .
>
> "Rass negar bee grind me blossom before de sun even rise!" the tree yelped.
>
> "Bee, you blood!" (p. 73)

The juxtaposition seems deliberate: There may be too much preaching about pumpum, but there may also be too much pumpum (or pumpum-related activity).

Later the tree makes up a "raucous vulgar hymn . . . about crossing the River Jordan to the heavenly Land where no Pum-Pum abounded and no Hood abided. The refrain was something about 'Hood and Harp keep no Company among the Heavenly Ewes' " (p. 149). Here the foreshadowing of one of the principal themes later to be developed in *The Duppy* is evident – all the more interesting as again, in this case, one suspects that Winkler may not entirely disagree with the tree, whereas in the later book he seems to resolve this ambivalence, becoming celebratory of the rule of pumpum in a Bakhtinian way (see chapter 6).

In *The Lunatic*, then, pumpum may be a necessary evil, or a package of mixed blessings. Such a view may extend to other parts of the body of womanhood. The fact that Inga becomes Aloysius's "only family" (p. 149) is positive for this desperately lonely man, but at the same time puts him in a tremendously vulnerable position as a dependant of a violent, anarchic madwoman – so that one has to wonder if he was not better off with the tree as his best friend. This question persists, if only as a niggling doubt, when he is "rescued" by the Widow Dawkins, thereby entering a new phase of the rule of pumpum. This is not a happy-ever-after ending, because Aloysius must toe the line by concealing his madness if he wants to keep on benefiting from the free food, shelter and pumpum that was provided first by Inga and now by her replacement.

The depiction of the dominant black Jamaican woman may be uncommon in the literature of the region[40] but it is common in Winkler's novels, and the strength is usually associated with the power of pumpum: Carina always wants to be on top and Zachariah must suffer the indignity of being ridden, Missus G persuades Father Huck to abandon his vow of celibacy, Miss B practises "fatty power" on a helpless Baps. In *The Lunatic,* Winkler extends this view of pumpum-ruling womanhood to embrace a white woman – as an extreme caricature, and in a new disguise, but a familiar entity all the same.

So Inga (who tells Service that she must do "one better" than him because "I am a voman and you are only a stupid man" [p. 144]) is not in reality a "new kind of woman", as the bush suggests (p. 39), but a new colour variant of the typical Winkler woman, and a new departure from the type of white woman that Aloysius is used to seeing: "All the white women he had seen in the streets had puffy bellies that jiggled when they walked, mounds of flesh that bounced off their arms and chests. The bodies of the old ones looked spongy, watery; the young ones were ungainly, bony – like new-born calves" (p. 41). (Elsewhere, in the figure of Charlene in *The Great Yacht Race,* Winkler has depicted the "puffy", "spongy" white woman most memorably.)

On reading the above, one can hardly be surprised that many readers assume that the author is black. Winkler's general depiction of white people in this novel is no more enlightening in this regard: the principal characters – Busha, Sarah, Mr Saarem – are all bumpkinish (Busha does not under-stand poetry, does not like music or art) and, more damningly, racist. "My God not black!" insists Busha. One's impression of Sarah's innocuousness is disturbed by her reaction to the cohabitation of the lunatic and the mad white woman: despite being told that Inga "bite a piece outta de tree" just like Busha gnaws on a chicken leg, her focus is clear: "Every time I think of a white woman in de bush wid dat nasty mad negar man, I lose my appetite" (p. 107).

Mr Saarem's characterization is particularly interesting because Saarem is "of Syrian descent" (p. 166), as is the maternal side of Winkler's family, and indeed, as suggested in *Going Home to Teach,* the author's real-life close con-nections to the Saarem type of individual are much more likely than any such connections to the white plantocrat type represented by Busha and his wife. Yet (or possibly as a result – again suggested by *Going Home to Teach*) Saarem's description is the least flattering of the three: "[H]is breath smell[ed] like soup. He was renowned as a glutton . . . in the years of the socialist government he had lived in Miami. . . . When he returned to

Jamaica he quickly saw that the island needed a new kind of graveyard" (p. 167). One's overall impression is of a greasy, palm-rubbing, money-grubbing parasite feeding on death.

Winkler's negative portrayal of white people extends to those who are socially if not physically white – those who are exploiters, like the Indian fisherman: "This man was the white man – the Backra, the Busha, the Boss – whatever name you gave him, he was not the one who threw his body into the sea and went after the coins. It was the other one who did the diving – for half the money" (p. 310).

In this "parody of power relations between local and expatriate, black and white, rich and poor, male and female",[41] Lalla suggests that *The Lunatic* "exposes stupidity, greed, brutality at all social levels and in a variety of ethnic possibilities without romanticizing ignorance among the poor".[42] Ignorance may not be romanticized, but Aloysius certainly is; Winkler's portrayal of black people, "used to hard life and wicked treatment" (p. 145), seems, as is customary with his books, ultimately sympathetic in contrast to his portrayal of whites.

Busha is placed in opposition to Aloysius in terms of privilege versus want: Busha was born into wealth, whereas Aloysius could have been a barrister (p. 147) if poverty and deprivation had not crushed all hope. Busha is an integral part of the community, and of the land – "a man of the soil; his brain was of the earth" (p. 58), his face "resembled a rich and arable mountain land suitable for planting coffee" (p. 59) – while Aloysius is excluded from the former and in a constant struggle for survival with the latter. Furthermore, Busha is racist and unforgiving, while Aloysius is loving and charitable. Busha, in his own eccentric way, is as obsessed with death as Service is, whereas the lunatic, despite all his "hard life and wicked treatment", embraces life.

And so the wily Barrister Linstrom's summary of what he suggests are the real issues behind the court case, although theatrical and manipulative on one level, seems also to summarize Winkler's views of at least some of the real issues behind the farce and fun of *The Lunatic*:

> "My client is a poor black man who had been in and out of the madhouse all his life. He is what we call in Jamaica a 'sufferer' – one of the many among us carrying the heaviest load. The man whose house he is accused of breaking . . . is a

white man. The wicked woman . . . who used sex and money to inveigle this poor black man to become a thief, is white. . . . Color has everything to do with this case, sah. Color and money." (p. 197)

Jamaica may, as the barrister suggests, be much more advanced in its thinking about colour than, say, America where "Dey don't call a brown horse black. For a man dey have only two color: white or black", versus Jamaica where "we have our brown man, our dark brown man . . . God make man in at least thirty forty color, and here in Jamaica we see dem all" (p. 210). Nevertheless colour and money still, regrettably, have much to do with one's level of existence in Jamaica today.

No person in *The Lunatic* is able to transcend such limitations – although, ironically, it is Inga who makes a possible gesture of transcendence by her rejection of the label "white": "Don't call me a white woman, you bitch!" she hisses (p. 145). However, this is more likely to be, at least in part, a result of her guilt over what white represents in her radical worldview – that is, exploitation and oppression. Transcendence is left to the flame heart tree and bushes:

> "One thing 'bout tree," the tree cut in [to the discussion between the lunatic and the butcher where Aloysius has just declared that he is "only half" negar].
> "Tree no white, tree no black, tree no Chiney, tree no Coolie. Tree is pure tree."
> "Same wid bush," a bush mumbled. "We is all one wid God family."
> "Praise de Lord!" another bush cried. (p. 145)

Yet the inability of the human characters in *The Lunatic* to transcend these limitations is not the bottom line. A clue to the location of the bottom line may be found in the fondness and affection permeating Winkler's portrayal of Busha as (yet another) wacky eccentric rather than reprehensible bigot. Winkler's affection is transmitted to the reader: as Brown says, "This Busha is one of the novel's engaging characters. Winkler's attitude to him . . . is one of amused tolerance, even of paradoxical fondness; and so Busha, ignorant, foulmouthed and as racist as they come, nonetheless comes across as a sympathetic character."[43] Brown uses, as an example, Busha's declaration to Mr Saarem that "when I dead de one thing I don't want sitting on me head is negar angel" (p. 169). Such outrageous racism is trivialized to absurdity, and the reader, rather than being repulsed, chuckles along with Mr

Saarem. Chuckles only cease later when Busha refuses to accept Aloysius's love, refuses to forgive – at which point he slips from being an amusing figure to being a pathetic one.

Critically, when Busha exclaims in court,

> My grand-daddy built that house, not me! My great-great-great-grand-daddy buy dat land . . . I didn't buy it . . . I was born into it. Did I ask to be born into it? . . . I don't take nothing from anybody. I never trouble anybody! Dese damn people break me house and nearly kill me . . . and why? Because it's my fault to be born! Dat's reason enough to kill a man? (p. 201)

it is a painful moment, reminding one of a similar moment in Pauline Melville's short story "McGregor's Journey", when a disapproving black crowd cuts short a rare, meaningful and totally innocent connection between the white McGregor and a black woman: "Later that night, the police arrested a man. . . . He was smashing shop windows. . . . As the glass exploded in each one, he yelled: 'I want you to know that I never owned a fucking slave in my life. Never.' "[44]

There is no simplistic black and white of innocence and guilt in the question of blacks versus whites. Life is unfair. Life is hard. "De times hard on every man" (p. 28). As Shacochis says, "The overriding madness is that everybody in Jamaica pays dearly for the crimes of the past and, in so doing, suffocates the present with the same pathetically familiar mistakes."[45]

So that while the novel is on one level a story of the triumph of good over evil, its more powerful message is one of life's ambiguities, and of the necessity for compassion, compromise and conciliation in the face of such ambiguities: "We all owe life and love to one anodder" (p. 224).

Winkler's refusal to condemn Busha totally to the role of villain in this novel is a gesture of such compassion, a small echo of the compassion which Aloysius shows in his own refusal to condemn Busha, his own refusal to embrace hatred, greed and death over love, charity and life. Aloysius may be unable to transcend the limitations of his madness, of his poverty, of his imagined or real inadequacies, but by embracing the cause of compassion, he, alone in this novel, succeeds in transcending the suffocating limitations of his history-warped, lunatic society with its moral ignorance. This is the novel's bottom line.

Brown rightly observes,

There are things that comedy cannot do, and there are things it can do uniquely well. . . . Consider how gracefully in the end . . . *The Lunatic* deals with and dispels (as unworthy of more serious treatment) subjects filling the letters' pages of our newspapers with such self-righteousness, bad temper and spleen![46]

Thus *The Lunatic* – entertaining, hilarious, a quick write and a quick read; slack, vulgar and out of order; containing, in other words, all the components of popular as opposed to serious fiction – nevertheless transcends its own possibly self-imposed limitations as popular fiction. It may be full of pumpum, hood, wee-wee and doo-doo, but it proves Inga's outrageous assertion: Shit, in this case, does indeed have deep meaning.

Winkler's black protagonist provides upliftment and cause for hope in a lunatic Jamaican society. And, notwithstanding any puzzlement on the part of the author, *The Lunatic* may be not only Winkler's most popular book, but his best work of fiction to date, on course to becoming a West Indian classic.

6

Carnival Meets
Dancehall

✤

"Dat is blasphemy!"
. . . "Some people call it that," I said gloomily.
– *The Duppy*

THE DUPPY IS an outrageous representation of heaven. The transition from
this life to the afterlife takes place not in a fiery chariot but in an over-
crowded minibus; instead of sailing through a tunnel towards heavenly lights
one must squeeze through a culvert; instead of sheep, angels and manna
there are mangy dogs, thieving gardener boys and tinned bully beef; instead
of celibacy there is celebratory sex; and, most outrageous of all, God as
Source of Light is actualized as a peenywally.

"What you going do next, grind de universe?" (*The Duppy*, 130). The
question asked by an indignant moral voice in the text may justifiably be
redirected to Winkler, whose novels have increasingly displayed an eagerness
to attack normally taboo subjects such as race, sexuality and religion with
raucous irreverence. Indeed, the assertion of the narrator Baps on the first
page of the book – "I welcome this opposition" – could easily be taken for
Winkler's motto.

Such outrageousness, presented in a package of off-the-wall humour, has largely been responsible for the popularity of Winkler's other novels – most notably *The Lunatic. The Duppy* proceeds at a similarly jaunty pace. Unlike *The Lunatic,* however, *The Duppy* cannot conveniently be enjoyed as mere farce: not even the most cursory reading can ignore the religious irreverence which may be seen by some to be blasphemous. Winkler pushes outrageousness to a new extreme.

Winkler's heaven parallels the world as we know it in geographical terms: there is Jamaican heaven, American heaven, French heaven, and presumably the whole gamut of heavenly nations. But it is Jamaican heaven which seems most outrageous, resembling earthly Jamaica in its topography and populace – in nearly every way, in fact, except that first, like other heavenly nations, Jamaican heaven allows no pain, due to God's universal law, "Thou shalt feel good no matter what" (p. 92); and second, unlike other heavenly nations, Jamaican heaven has replaced sexual inhibitions and restraint with freeness and female sexual aggressiveness, resulting in abundant joyous mingling of hood and pumpum.

Hood and pumpum are recognizable, to anyone who has read *The Lunatic,* as subjects of which the author is fond. We recall that novel's eagerness to focus on body parts, especially those related to sexual activity, and on bodily functions, from the doo-dooing and wee-weeing of cows and goats, referred to by Busha as "too much damn slackness" (*The Lunatic,* 61), to the running stomach of Sarah or the loud farting of Widow Dawkins. It may have been such evident eagerness, combined with the novel's satirical humour, that led one American reviewer of *The Lunatic,* Bob Shacochis, to refer to Winkler as "Jamaica's Rabelais".[1]

Indeed, given Winkler's evident fondness for blatant discussion of body parts and bodily functions, the comparison to Rabelais is inevitable, and ultimately the connection to Bakhtin's notions of the carnivalesque, albeit unintended (Winkler says he has never heard of Bakhtin)[2] is as inescapable. Bakhtin celebrates a Rabelaisian "flowering of a gay, affirmative, and militantly anti-authoritarian attitude to life, founded upon a joyful acceptance of the materiality of the body".[3] For Bakhtin, carnival laughter "builds its own world versus the official world, its own church versus the official church, its own state versus the official state", with the basic goal of "destroy[ing] the official picture of events".[4]

In *The Duppy*, Winkler seems determined to destroy the official picture of heaven. The narrator Baps, a conservative, middle-aged black countryside shopkeeper with very firm ideas about what is decent and appropriate, is at first not altogether comfortable with the Jamaican heaven that he encounters, which is a departure from all that he has been taught by established religion. This is an out-of-order heaven, with no hell, no sheep ("heaven without sheep was clearly out of order" [p. 39]), no tunnel with sweet music, and most annoyingly, with "decent people chuck-up with criminal" (p. 13). However, he soon begins to feel at home when he realizes that, in accordance with the heavenly principle of "what you want you get" (p. 20), he can continue to keep shop, drastically marking up goods and imposing artificial shortages like any respectable Jamaican entrepreneur, thereby being able to pursue his favourite pastime of imposing "discipline and fiscal restraint" on nasty, unruly, freeness-seeking socialist ole negar (p. 18). And although he is at first resistant to the corpulent matrons who are quick to offer him a welcoming grind ("Angel not supposed to be so meaty" [p. 46]), he soon recognizes the advantages of a land in which "hood thrives and prospers" (p. 31), "every wish or whim is granted" (p. 60) and there is "no harm, hurt, sorrow or regret. All is joyful and fun" (p. 61). God's peenywally appearance is a surprise – "my upbringing had led me to expect a big and powerful Somebody with meat on the bone and plenty muscle" (p. 76) – but such surprise is quickly superseded by his awe in coming face to face with the Almighty: "Baps, you lucky son of a gun! Imagine, you, a humble, dirty-minded, lowdown shopkeeper, and here God is flying beside your earhole and chatting with you as if the two of you were best friend" (p. 77).

There is only one heavenly principle to which Baps cannot become reconciled: the preposterous notion that "there may be good in the heart of all" (p. 133), even the *butu* rabble known as ole negar.[5] The issue of the black Jamaican's distancing of himself from other black Jamaicans resurfaces in all of Winkler's books, and here Baps is no different from Winkler's other black protagonists. Despite all indications and lessons from God to the contrary, he stubbornly clings to his prejudices. Such prejudices amount to schizophrenic self-hatred, as Winkler illustrates when Baps, having just died, sees his own body lying on the floor and indignantly wonders if "some ole negar come and dead in my drawing room . . . without asking permission" (p. 4). Baps heatedly points out to God that "it is an act of colonialism to venture onto our shores and try to gainsay what we Jamaicans know to be unshakeable truths about the most degenerate members of our population" (p. 14). Such a delicious example of pompous colonialist posturing aside, the institution of self-hatred is in itself, of course, one of the vilest acts of colonialism.

When God and Baps decide to visit American heaven (Baps seeking, like many Jamaicans, "the broadening of knowledge that comes with foreign travel" [p. 151]), God decides to travel in disguise as the ole negar Egbert, much to Baps's distress and embarrassment. Egbert's subsequent out-of-order behaviour, demonstrating his worship of "the idols of rum, dancehall and canepiece pumpum" (p. 134), actualizes Baps's prejudiced predictions, but Baps rejects God's claim that Egbert has been constructed out of Baps's mind. When Baps reluctantly agrees to be changed into Egbert so that he can "dwell inside the flesh and bone of [his] own creation" (p. 134), Egbert eventually transcends his supposed ole negar limitations by nobly sacrificing his own safety in the interest of God's. Although the stubborn Baps refuses to acknowledge this, the significance of the merging of Baps and Egbert is clear: Baps is Egbert, and Egbert is Baps, and there is good in all men. By attacking the identity crisis of black self-hatred, Winkler succeeds in subverting one of the more destructive relics of colonialist distortion. (And by such subversion, of course, Winkler subverts his own whiteness, as he has done in nearly all his novels.)

Baps eventually accepts the other terms of Jamaican heaven, but his indoor parson, that is, the inner voice that played the role of his conscience on earth, certainly does not: "Dis peenywally is God? Where the golden throne? Where de cherub? Where de hosts bawling hosanna?" (p. 77). Or as the parson scathingly notes elsewhere, "Dis heaven is a land of pumpum and dumpling. I wonder if we in hell?" (p. 57).

The indoor parson is much more comfortable with American heaven, which satisfies more of the conventions of established Judaeo-Christian (and certainly American fundamentalist) teachings: angels float on clouds plunking harps and tending sheep, everyone eats manna fallen from the sky instead of bully beef or sardines, all residents have compulsorily had their hoods sheared or pumpums caulked (so that "woe unto fornicators" [p. 47] is an expression of patriotism), and all residents are white. In fact, any visitors to heavenly America staying longer than two weeks must have their skin

bleached. Not all the conventions of established religion are satisfied, however: the indoor parson agrees with the disgruntled Americans that "without
a hell, there [is] no point in heaven" (p. 119), that without pain and suffering heaven is "a demented and unholy land" (p. 89), that "taking away pain
and suffering ruin dere American way of life" (p. 124), that "this universe is
not up to American standards" (p. 146). The deprived Americans try to
compensate by celebrating Hell Day, complete with a grand parade with
"float after float show[ing] similar scenes of wicked torture and cruelty that
the sponsoring civic group thought belonged in hell". "Yes, sah! Now you
talking!" bawls the indoor parson (p. 121). "Maybe God isn't moral, but
America is!" snaps an irritated Republican (p. 120). Not surprisingly, the
soft-spoken, humble, peace-loving God prefers to reside in Jamaican heaven
– which may be just as well, since the Americans have put a federal bounty
on him because of his un-American anti-hell position.

It soon becomes apparent that Winkler has set up a clear dichotomy:
Jamaican heaven (read: Jamaica) is paradise; American heaven (read:
America) is a madhouse. Jamaican heaven is full of innocent joy – with
Baps's pleasure at romping with God at cricket matches over the Jamaican
countryside being no more or less than his pleasure at going for the quarter-
century in a bed romp.

The American madhouse, on the other hand, full of hell-bent fanatics,
harp-plunking shepherds and baaing sheep, becomes more and more ridiculous: "Kiss me neck! It drizzling bread crumb again" (p. 114). Small wonder
that the ole negar Egbert is driven after a few short hours in this land to wail,
"Dis place weird!" (p. 109), and to croak, "Baps! . . . I need a white rum
bad!" (p. 108).

Egbert soon gets fed up with all the infernal eternal baaing, and eventually loses control: "Hush you rass mouth, ole sheep!" (p. 112). As a result,

> A robed shepherd stopped his harp-plunking and peered down at us over the edge
> of his cloud. "Foreigner," he cried, "wouldst thou like to sit on my cloud with me
> and my sheep?"
>
> "Not a backside!" Egbert bawled. ". . . I am a Jamaican duppy! We don't walk
> wid sheep, we curry them!" (p. 112)

Winkler ridicules not only America, but also those Americans visiting
Jamaican heaven, all of whom are represented as being fanatical in one way

or another: from the group of university students who want to stone God because He made the dinosaurs extinct ("Dinosaurs!" Baps explodes. "You stone God because he clean de earth of a few nasty lizard?" [p. 72]) to the American philosopher who refuses to acknowledge that God or heaven exists except in his head, and who is viewed, like his country of origin, as being "stark, raving mad" (p. 79). The figure of foreign interloper/destructive force brings to mind the doctor in *The Painted Canoe* and Inga in *The Lunatic*; both of these, however, wreak much more havoc than the philosopher, whose greatest offence is to become an increasing irritant to everyone (including, it appears, the author, who bumps him off unceremoniously by letting him be suddenly reborn).

By ridiculing America and Americans, and by establishing, in contrast, Jamaica as God's choice of heavenly location, Winkler makes transparent at least one part of his agenda, one with which readers of *Going Home to Teach* will be especially familiar: despite having spent most of his life in America, Winkler has rejected the heartbeat of that country, and regards nowhere but Jamaica as home.

Intertwined with this is another subversive strand, as suggested earlier: Winkler's ridiculing of established Eurocentric constructions of the afterlife, and of morality. It was a nun, it is revealed, who first told Baps the lie about "shearing [as opposed to sharing] of hood at heavenly gate" (p. 32). When Baps asks God how He can be so relaxed about pumpum after everything He wrote about it, God declares firmly, "I never wrote a word about it."

> "Den who wrote all dose harsh words 'gainst pumpum?"
>
> God thought for a brief moment or so and said that He didn't really know but that a long time ago there was a bearded chap who had been bucked off a horse someplace in the Middle East. . . .
>
> "You talking 'bout St Paul on de road to Damascus!" my parson bellowed with outrage. "Dat is blasphemy!"
>
> He remembered now, God recalled dreamily. The fellow who dropped off the horse and hit his head got up screeching against women.
>
> "Some people call it dat," I said gloomily. (p. 80)

Roman Catholicism's anti-woman distortions are touched on elsewhere: when, for example, Baps marvels that "when a Christian repent, de first thing him give up is woman! Even if woman have nothing at all to do with him criminality", and God responds that it is "plain to him that [Baps] had never attended Catholic school" (p. 106).

When God says, "A man is not just flesh and bone, Baps. A man is also an idea. And the idea behind a man is what makes him what he is, good or evil" (p. 133), the comment seems to reflect the Platonic philosophy of dualism, which separates matter from ideas and posits that the world of ideas is superior to the material world; however, Winkler's God resists any Roman Catholic distortion of this philosophy[6] which has determined that libidinous desires are evil, and that the body is bad. At the end, when Baps has been granted a return stay on earth in order to rescue his shops from disorderly stacking of goods and thiefing maid and gardener boy, he asks God if He has any deep message that He wants Baps to put in his forthcoming book about his life as a duppy.

> God said, yes. We should stop all the fool-fool preaching against tom-tom. . . .
> "Is 'pumpum', not 'tom-tom'!"
> Whatever. Stop all the fretting about it and be kind and loving to one another.
> (p. 178)

Such distortions are the principal, but by no means the only, ones: some of the lesser, miscellaneous distortions of established religion, *The Duppy* suggests, include inaccuracies in the Bible – for example, God reveals that His first creation was not light but stick, and after stick came scratching with the stick (p. 84). We learn that the reason God talks funny, "thying" and "thouing" and "theeing" up the whole place, is because of all the years of listening to Baptists and Holy Rollers (p. 93). More critically, Baps learns that violence supposedly perpetrated in God's name was in fact done without proper authorization. "Out of order", then, takes on new and deeper meaning.

The distortions of established religion are, of course, a legacy of colonialism, and are firmly ascribed hereto by Baps's lover, Miss B. When he agrees to "an inspirational feel-up during the service when the spirit moved her, but not while she clutched the hymnal", she hisses that "this [is] a ridiculous colonial regulation" (p. 55). And when Baps is firm that it is "either hood or hymnal, not both", he is fiercely rebuked "for fostering a backward colonial mentality" (p. 56). Such jabs at colonialism by Winkler may seem partly tongue-in-cheek, but they echo the anticolonialist views expressed explicitly in *Going Home to Teach.* And, given America's assumption of the role of evangelical leadership in the Caribbean in recent decades, not to mention its overpowering of all other aspects of Caribbean life, Winkler's entire anti-American position can be interpreted as anti-neocolonialist.

In this regard Baps's pro-American indoor parson becomes more than merely the voice of convention. The conflict between Baps and his parson represents another equally insidious aspect of Baps's schizophrenia, and of the inner conflict of the colonized: the embracing of foreign values, the rejecting of self for other. So that when Baps admits to God that "a parson dwelled inside me" and God recommends that he "try exorcism" (p. 78), the implication of evil to be exorcized takes on special significance.

By injecting a defiantly rootsy, black Jamaican consciousness into the traditional Judaeo-Christian, white representation of heaven, by subverting established religion, by constructing a no-nonsense, unpretentious alternative to traditional heavenly conceptions, Winkler overturns one of the most resilient bastions of colonialist and neocolonialist dominance in the Caribbean. Thus Winkler's challenge to the Eurocentric religious construct is the ultimate subversion.

The theology expressed in *The Duppy* shows certain similarities to dialectical incarnationalism, a theology recently developed by the former Jesuit Martin Schade, an American turned Jamaican citizen and a casual acquaintance of Winkler's.[7] The philosopher-theologian Schade describes dialectical incarnationalism as "a total unity between God, creation and humanity". Creation becomes God's "total otherness, a dialectical otherness . . . creation is distinct from God but not separate from God", like the "total unity of a mother and child".[8] We are reminded of God's disclosure to Baps in *The Duppy:* "He had used Himself as raw material to create the universe . . . everything of Himself had gone into His handiwork of creation" (p. 133). According to Schade, God is to be found, as the Jesuits teach, "in all things",[9] while in *The Duppy* God says, "all things are me and I am all things" (p. 165). For Schade, "God is unconditionally forgiving, therefore there is no hell. God hurts by us."[10] Winkler's God explains to Baps why there is no hell: "If thou burnest a sinner to suffer real pain thou burnest me. I hateth the pain of fire, Baps" (p. 165).

According to Schade, "Original sin is the starting point of Western theological anthropology for nearly the entire history of Christianity."[11] The doctrine of Original Sin, introduced by St Augustine, holds that God gave mankind free will but that Adam, the first man, abused it and thus committed the original sin, causing the loss of God's grace and resulting in mankind's inability to refrain from sin. In Schade's theology, however, God became flesh not because of sin but in spite of sin, and mankind began in a state of Original Grace, not Original Sin. Schade refers to this new perspective as "revelation from below"[12] – a term that aptly describes Winkler's theology in *The Duppy* as a whole, and, specifically, at least one of the revelations of Winkler's God: "God said light came later [after stick, leaf and assorted other creations], that He didn't create the universe from the bottom up, no matter what you read. Stick was first. Light was last" (p. 85).

In Winkler's heaven, "free will always prevails" (p. 149), which disrupts Baps's efforts to maintain order. However, when God allows him to try to create a better heaven, God teaches him that the alternative of mankind without free will produces "nasty batty-kissing brutes" who "come just like robots" (p. 162). Baps asks God to re-institute free will, which produces a "kingdom of random where all manner of wickedness and viciousness spread among [his] people" (p. 165). Eventually Baps asks God how people will ever get better, especially without hell and with everyone going to heaven.

> God said, They must get better on their own, Baps.
>
> "Hah! Without fire and brimstone?"
>
> Yea, Baps. And better that springs from the heart is always better than better that comes from fear of fire.
>
> . . . [A]t that moment I gave up my creation, for I saw that God's brain was filled with wisdom while mine own had been ruined over the years of coping with pettifogging earthly woe. (p. 170)

Winkler's novel teaches one to love God because one wants to, not because one should – it is "shouldisms" which are a "poison" (p. 132). One is reminded of the Jesuit teaching (embraced by Schade) that the highest motivation to do good is for its own sake.[13] God is not punishing us, Winkler suggests: "God don't have nothin' to do wid dis" (p. 59).

Similarities in theological viewpoint might suggest the possibility of a direct sharing of ideas between Winkler and Schade; however, neither of the two recalls any specific discussions on theology during their encounters.[14] The fact that Winkler was raised as a Roman Catholic (and schooled in his formative years in the "shouldist" environment of Mount Alvernia Preparatory School) raises another possibility: that Winkler and Schade may be demonstrating a similar response to certain aspects of conservative Roman Catholicism, a response which, though unique in its individual manifestations, echoes in many respects the positions of the reformist or "radical" element within the Roman Catholic Church.[15] The current debates within the Roman Catholic Church between its conservative and radical elements over issues such as celibacy, birth control, the role of women in the church, sin and punishment, Catholicism as the only means to salvation, and the absolute authority of the pope have been widely publicized. Winkler's theology could be seen as expounding and at times exaggerating the radical Catholic view,[16] explicitly with regard to sex and women, and more implicitly with regard to issues of sin and punishment:[17] the idea of God being a part of rather than apart from His creation, and the concept of universal love and an ever-loving God equally accessible to all men of all races and creeds. The absence of the pope from Winkler's vision of heaven in *The Duppy* may be seen by some Roman Catholics as a most significant omission[18] – one which conservative Catholics might find as problematic as his most outrageous inclusions of pumpum in the heavenly picture, and as offensive as Missus Grandison's dismissal of the pope in *The Great Yacht Race* (who, she observes, "mad up [Father Huck's] brain wid foolishness" [p. 265]). Indeed, Winkler's heavenly schema in *The Duppy* is an expansion and exaggeration of the brief, unorthodox sketch presented, safely, as the Catholic Father Huck's dream in *Yacht Race:* an unruly Jamaican resident of heaven objects to the arrival of a murderer, a "gallows bird", a common "Montegonian quashie" with whom she will be obliged to "rub up at the dinner table" (p. 347); Backra Angel becomes fed up with the behaviour of all the out-of-order Jamaicans disrupting heavenly peace, and threatens that when he catches "de blinking priest responsible, all glory goin' pop!" (p. 348). Father Huck, the blinking priest responsible in the novel for mildly subversive gestures such as trying to save a madman from the gallows, and breaking his vow of celibacy by happily succumbing to Missus Grandison's overtures, is a gentle and inoffensive Catholic rebel whose cause Winkler will take on with great vigour in *The Duppy.*

So although Winkler's vision of heaven in *The Duppy* is not Roman Catholic in any direct way, nevertheless it may be indirectly revealing strong

Catholic influences: there is a congruence with current trends in radical Catholic thinking which are in reaction to a conservative, "shouldist" Catholic upbringing. In fact, in its very ability to be subversive of orthodox religion and orthodox morality while affirming the existence of an ever-loving God, Winkler's *Duppy* reflects qualities which are themselves very catholic (in the sense of all-embracing or universal) as well as Catholic: Catholicism, particularly in the New World, has proven itself historically capable of embracing subcultures, of enabling subversion and appropriation, double meanings and expressions of sexuality.

Winkler's subversion of the orthodox Roman Catholic belief in the sinfulness of sexuality resists an othering of the body which was reinforced in Western European Renaissance culture, as explored by Bakhtin:

> The ever unfinished nature of the body was hidden, kept secret. . . . The individual body was presented apart from its relation to the ancestral body of the people. . . . It did not fit the framework of the "aesthetics of the beautiful" as conceived by the Renaissance.[19]

Bakhtin's condemnation of the privileging of "the aesthetics of the beautiful", high culture, over the grotesque body of popular culture during the Renaissance translates to his articulation of "an aesthetic which celebrates the anarchic, body-based and grotesque elements of popular culture, and seeks to mobilise them against the humourless seriousness of official culture".[20] Jamaican popular culture, especially dancehall culture, can readily be described as anarchic, body-based and grotesque, and its subversiveness has been explored by Carolyn Cooper in her book *Noises in the Blood*. Cooper refers to the "vulgar body of Jamaican popular culture" as "a subversive discourse of marginality and vulgarity"[21] or as "a profoundly malicious cry to upset the existing social order", converting "a form of subordination into an affirmation". As she says, "hierarchy inversion is an important project of these low-culture texts".[22]

One is reminded here of *The Lunatic*. To quote Barbara Lalla, "Flaunting its disregard for taboos, flouting maxims of appropriateness to literary discourse, screaming obscenities, *The Lunatic*'s initial shock value lies in its flagrant unorthodoxy and irreverence." Such flagrant flouting of verbal taboos, suggesting Winkler's "targetting [of] Jamaican conventions specifically by [a] highlighting [of] local obscenities",[23] is part of that novel's overall out-of-order outrageousness.

A significant part of the hierarchy inversion of *The Lunatic* is Winkler's questioning of the power attached to words, or at least its excesses – especially a tendency within the society for verbosity and pomposity. By highlighting the absurdity of Aloysius's prized but meaningless names, Winkler draws our attention to other verbal absurdities also. Inga's dislike of the label "white" (p. 158) may at first seem silly, but Barrister Linstrom's courtroom speech on race not only fulfils his intention of ridiculing simplistic American racial categorizations, but inadvertently makes us question *all* labelling, even the "thirty forty color differentiation in Jamaica" that he upholds (p. 210). Inga's fondness for yelling "O-Isopropoxyphenyl", which happens to mean cockroach poison (p. 53), when she is in the throes of ecstasy may be a little eccentric, but how much more so than the aversion of Jamaicans to the supremely filthy word "bumbo", which many Jamaicans, including Aloysius, don't know the meaning of? And the possibly coincidental juxtaposition of four lines of Aloysius's names ("Aloysius Gossamer Longshoreman Technocracy Predominate", and so forth) and three lines of Inga's stress-relief language ("shit shit shit shit piss piss", and so forth) on adjacent pages (pp. 42–43) demands the question: which set is more absurd (and who is madder)? On the other hand, Winkler's usage of vulgar colloquial terms such as hood, pumpum, wee-wee and doo-doo is so frequent that it ceases to shock after the first few chapters, gradually succeeding in modifying the reader's views of decency and indecency so that these words eventually read as natural and unpretentious. Such is Winkler's success that if one were to substitute, say, "vagina/pudenda/female genitalia" for "pumpum", it is the former that would seem awkward, prudish and even silly, just as the Widow Dawkins's censoring of Inga's letter seems awkward, prudish and silly. As Lalla observes, "rule flouting occurs at so dangerous a level that it assists in . . . a deconditioning of the reader".[24] In just such a way Winkler parodies notions of "slackness" – a word which has been used frequently by Jamaicans in criticizing dancehall culture, and which he seems to delight in playing with in this book. Not only are the unruly wee-weeing and doo-dooing of cows and goats condemned as slackness, but also assorted other, apparently arbitrarily selected, activities. Such outrageousness is a principal component of the novel's humour, inviting such reviewer descriptions of it as "vulgar", "bawdy", "raucous", "lusty",[25] "ribald"[26] or "off-the-wall", and (of the fiction) as "offbeat".[27]

Offbeat it may be in terms of the pulse of conventional Eurocentric literature, but it may well be perfectly in beat with Jamaican popular culture, which is infamous for its embracing of slackness, its privileging of sex. *The Lunatic,* then, is popular not only in terms of its commercial success, but also in that its characteristics conform in many ways to popular culture. In fact, the book's popularity with Jamaicans may well be connected to its culturally popular nature. *The Lunatic,* more so than any of Winkler's other novels, is certainly full of slackness. "Too much damn slackness", some of its readers might say – of this book, and certainly of *The Duppy.*

Bakhtin focuses on the grotesque body in popular culture. In striking contrast to the classical body with its "perfect" physical proportions, the grotesque body, full of protrusions and orifices, with exaggerated genital organs and bowel functions, celebrates its imperfections. Winkler has also consistently depicted grotesque exaggerations of the human body in his works: from the hideously deformed Zachariah and his ugly wife Carina in *The Painted Canoe* to the short, thick, stubby Inga in *The Lunatic,* to the excessively corpulent Father Huck and his equally capacious lover Missus Grandison in *The Great Yacht Race* and, in *The Duppy,* to a plethora of generously apportioned elderly church sisters and respectably hospitable matrons like Miss B, who, when asked by Baps "why she continues to resemble a breeding Red Poll cow when she could just as easily look like better", growls in response that "she happened to love herself black and fat, which was why she hadn't availed herself of government bleaching and thinning. She boastfully declared that she liked being beefy, loved her jelly belly, and was perfectly content to perch on her stool and float on a tube of batty fat" (p. 53). She then challenges Baps to say that "a fatty woman wasn't a comfortable smooth ride and better by far than any bony woman" (p. 53), which Baps is hard pressed to deny, given the fact that she brought him to the point of ecstasy fifty-five times the previous night. " 'I practise fatty power!' she cockadoodledooe[s]" (p. 54).

Such fatty power is hard to miss in Jamaican dancehalls, whose generously apportioned, gold-bedecked queens emphasize and exaggerate their protrud-

ing stomachs, jelly bellies, breasts and buttocks by adorning them in lumi-
nescent spandex, while dancehall divas like Lady Saw proclaim their superior
sexual prowess in a way that reminds one very much of Miss B:

> Mi waan wuk wid you
> Mi ave di fatness inna mi clothes
> An it waan you too . . .
> Gi mi di wuk, boy, try no complain
> Mek yuh groan an groan again an again. . . .
> Mi ave di grease to grease yuh waistline
> When yuh done yuh come time after time.[28]

Pumpum does indeed rule: these powerful, aggressive women of the
dancehalls attest to the reality that they are the ones who hold the true
power, not the men. They are the ones who have supported their families,
raised their children, and, as dramatically exemplified by the higglers of the
1980s, kept the Jamaican economy afloat. In all his novels, Winkler's black
women, who constantly call and call for the shots, consistently reflect this
reality of the *precise* location of power in Jamaican culture. Aloysius,
although initially intimidated by the out-of-order foreign female (Inga),
reminds himself that

> [m]ore than once he had had to cope with strong women, violent women.
> Jamaican country women were strong from a hard life of laboring beside their
> men in the fields, violent from a love of hood and rum. . . . So they were made by
> the Almighty. . . . It made no difference that these women carried a soft wet spot
> between their legs. . . . They broke heads and smashed bones and bit off noses and
> ears in fights. . . . Some of them were strong enough to squeeze a hood so tight
> during lovemaking as to make any man bawl for mercy. (pp. 40–41)

The Widow Dawkins, who at the end of *The Lunatic* undertakes to manage
Aloysius, knows that "management was what man needed – management by
a strong woman. In God's plan, man was a shop and woman the shopkeeper"
(p. 217). God's plan in Aloysius's (and seemingly Winkler's) world, then, is
for a rule of pumpum perpetuated by warrior-shopkeeper women in control
of men in need of management – not an unrealistic view of real-world, out-
of-order Jamaica. As discussed by Carolyn Cooper, Louise Bennett's poems
have long proclaimed this fact:

> Look how long Jamaica oman
> – Modder, sister, wife, sweetheart –
> Outa road an eena yard deh pon
> A dominate her part!
>
> . . .
>
> Neck an neck an foot an foot wid man
> She buckle hole her own;
> While man a call her "so-so rib"
> Oman a tun backbone![29]

Cooper notes that "[t]he speaker's disdainful allusion to the biblical narrative of origins, conveys her contempt for a sanctimonious patriarchal prejudice that dehumanises women in the name of religion",[30] reminding one of the Judaeo-Christian distortions attacked by Winkler in *The Duppy*.

Again, the church sisters who eagerly offer their services (before, during and after service) to Baps in *The Duppy*, like Missus Grandison in *The Great Yacht Race* who eventually succeeds in seducing the hapless Father Huck, are not merely a satirical comment on societal/religious hypocrisy or a tool of satirical subversion for Winkler. They are a reflection of real Jamaica, where sex and religion are not, have never been, incompatible. The sexual involvement of fundamentalist church sisters with their male church leaders (who often sound like Baps's indoor parson) has of course long been accepted as a common, albeit scandalous, practice in Jamaica and elsewhere. But sex need not undermine religious integrity; in many non-Western religions it has always been an integral part of religious ritual, and even in the case of Catholicism, as Robert Antoni has suggested both directly (in a seminar)[31] and indirectly (in his novel *Blessed Is the Fruit*), religious excitement and sexual excitement become indistinguishable, so that "the agony and the ecstasy" takes on new meaning. Jamaican popular culture has been recognizing this compatibility in recent years, with figures like Lady Saw and, for a time, Capleton espousing carnality and spirituality with equal enthusiasm, and without public censure. As Joe Pereira notes,

> Lady Saw, . . . top female DJ who continues to be undisputed queen of sex lyrics, can sing a highly successful song of praise and thanks to God ("Glory be to God") for her material advancement resulting from those same "slackness" songs. In the midst of his album of sex lyrics, "Gold", of 1991 Capleton sings a song "Bible fi dem", proclaiming his religious righteousness. It is neither that these singers are

being inconsistent nor that they are being opportunist. Indeed, their reconciliation of sex with spirituality is consistent with a value system that does not dichotomize carnality and spirituality.[32]

We recall God's denial to Baps, mentioned earlier, that He ever wrote a word about pumpum, and His perplexity at mankind's preoccupation with it. The sexual eagerness of Miss B and others is conveyed as healthy and innocent. Carolyn Cooper refers to a "vulgar Port Royal ditty" named "Me Know No Law, Me Know No Sin", and points out that "we can trace its genealogy in that vibrant tradition of contemporary Jamaican dancehall music in which women, in the spirit of the *persona* of that song, vigorously celebrate their freedom from the constraints of law and sin: echoes in the native bone".[33]

For Bakhtin, the grotesque body is "a body in the act of becoming": "it represents either the fertile depths or the convexities of procreation and conception".[34] From a carnivalesque perspective, the prominence given to sex and the tools for sex in Winkler's novels then becomes a signifier for Winkler's affirmation of the cycle of life, as opposed to merely an affirmation of the joys of shedding one's misguided inhibitions. As Baps points out, if all grinding ceased then "de whole population [would] perish" (p. 84). Certainly all Winkler's works have displayed what Wayne Brown, in his discussion of *The Lunatic,* has called a "scandalous joie de vivre".[35] And as we recall the scene in *The Lunatic* where Aloysius attempts to grind the ground, this seemingly absurd act may then transcend its limitations, becoming replete with the symbolism of a desperate yearning for renewal and regeneration as Aloysius seeks to plant his seed in the womb of the fertile Mother Earth.

For Bakhtin, "the essential principle of grotesque realism is degradation",[36] but this degradation is not merely negative, but rather ambivalent, linked to regeneration and renewal. In Jamaican dancehall culture, too, some of the more blatantly degrading lyrics are often ambivalent: for example,

> Hol up yu han, cause yu arm smell good. . . .
> Dem de gyal, dem no bathe, dem wipe up
> An come a dancehall, an dem a jump up
> An dem a wain up, and dem sweat up
> An den di frowsy scent it start come up.[37]

Once one gets past any initial revulsion, the listener can regard these lyrics simply as an exhortation for good hygiene. Winkler, however, often seems unambivalent in his use of such tools of degradation. Alongside an abundance of hood, pumpum and "roly-poly batty flesh" (p. 45) are numerous, less fond references to batty, batty hole and gaseous emissions. For example, "New York on earth is a sinkhole of human wastes, with . . . air so dirty that it curdles in the crowded streets like a fart at a tea party" (p. 108). Given Winkler's seemingly unambivalent position with regard to America, such negativity is not surprising.

When Baps gets an opportunity to play God his first plan is to create a fart-free woman: "I don't care what anybody say, a farting woman is a hardship on creation" (p. 155). He institutes a ritual where he subjects his followers to the ultimate degradation: batty-kissing during worship. To his disgust, they comply, "no matter what trouble and woe I visited upon them, for they had no free will" (p. 162). This ritual remains in place until Baps, "weary of the nasty batty-kissing brutes" (p. 162), institutes free will – and batty-kissing occasionally turns into subversive batty-biting. Indeed, in such instances of references to body parts and bodily functions, subversive batty-biting seems to be Winkler's main motive – in other words, such a discourse of vulgarity reads simply as Winkler's desire to shock, to interrogate established values, to proclaim in his "politics of noise" a carnival of clashing world views – high/refined versus low/vulgar.

So when Baps flies innocently naked through heaven, the indoor parson's indignant screeching that he is "exposing de purity of starlight to nasty batty hole" (p. 130) could speak for a conservative reader's view of *The Duppy,* yet this is surely an act of supreme liberation and connection with the cosmos for Baps. Moreover, Baps's guess that the leaves of *The Duppy* may be used "to wipe batty" (p. 141) extends way beyond Baps's assumption of the reader's adverse reaction to a positive portrayal of ole negar, to Winkler's presumed anticipation of an outraged public reaction to his entire out-of-order, but celestially down-to-earth, representation of the afterlife. And, at another level, we recall Inga's declaration in *The Lunatic:* "Shit has deep meaning" (p. 101).

However negative Winkler's references to batty in *The Duppy* may be, those to hood and pumpum are unadulteratedly delighted, and delightful – unlike *The Lunatic,* where Winkler displays some ambivalence in his depiction of the role of pumpum (as suggested in chapter 5). So in *The Duppy*, hood and pumpum are the pivotal tropes around which the novel ultimately revolves. God's message to mortals – "stop fretting about pumpum and be kind and loving" (p. 178) – may be deeper than Baps first realizes, because pumpum and all that it represents, that is, the positive forces of regeneration described by Bakhtin, have been marginalized and suppressed by modern culture since the Renaissance. In the suppression of the carnival-grotesque spirit – with its function of "liberat[ing] from the prevailing point of view of the world, from conventions and established truths, from cliches, from all that is humdrum and universally accepted", offering instead "the chance to have a new outlook on the world, to realize the relative nature of all that exists, and to enter a completely new order of things"[38] – natural joy and spontaneity have been replaced by a "uniform, fixed, hierarchical world view".[39] What is real has been distorted by elite regulation; hypocrisy abounds. God's plea is for the "shouldisms" that have been distorted by mankind to be rejected, for "a lot of *should* leads to principle and principle leads to murder" (p. 131). Rather, God calls for tolerance and recognition that there is "good in the heart of all" (p. 133) – because, as we recall, God says, "all things are me, and I am all things" (p. 165).

Long before we have reached the end of *The Duppy*, Baps's, and seemingly Winkler's, affection and respect for the simplicity and goodness of the humble, self-effacing Almighty have been imparted to us as readers. So that *The Duppy*'s final message, found in its last line, is but confirmation of what we already know: mankind has "more to fear from man than from God" (p. 183).

Bakhtin asserts,

> True ambivalent and universal laughter does not deny seriousness but purifies and completes it. Laughter purifies from dogmatism, from the intolerant and the petrified; it liberates from fanaticism and pedantry, from fear and intimidation, from didacticism, naivete and illusion, from the single meaning, the single level, from sentimentality. Laughter does not permit seriousness to atrophy and to be torn away from the one being, forever incomplete. It restores this ambivalent wholeness. Such is the function of laughter in the historical development of culture and literature.[40]

Finally, then, *The Duppy* satisfies the essential criterion of carnivalized writing by "[taking] life for a joke" (p. 93); by projecting the "positive regenerating power" of carnival laughter; by representing, as Bakhtin says, "the culture of folk humour . . . that reflect[s] the struggle against cosmic terror and create[s] the image of the gay, material bodily cosmos, ever-growing and self-renewing"; by creating a world in which "terror is conquered by laughter".[41]

Carnival meets dancehall: in its representation of "the vulgar body of Jamaican popular culture", the culture of folk humour, and in its subversion of authority, be it the overturning of conservative Eurocentric religious teachings or of American culture or of colonial distortions of identity, *The Duppy* is undoubtedly successful. But its most enduring success lies in its affirmation not only of God, but of life itself.

Searching for
the Centre

It was the smell of naseberries . . . that had brought him back. Everywhere he went
in America it haunted him.
   – *Going Home to Teach*

GOING HOME TO TEACH is described in *Contemporary Authors* as "a work of
social and cultural biography".[1] This description was provided by the author
himself: "The description is mine, but I wouldn't add too much importance
to it. I said that because it would seem presumptuous if I'd simply said 'autobiography'. The question that then popped into my head was, Who are you
to write an autobiography?"[2]

   The question may have been valid. When Winkler completed the first
draft of *Going Home,* he had just published his second novel, *The Lunatic.*
Although this book had made his name well known in Jamaica, and brought
him to the attention of the US market since it was copublished there (hence
his listing in *Contemporary Authors*), nevertheless his Jamaican publishers felt
that it was unlikely that many readers would be interested in an autobiographical work by a relatively unknown writer, even one masked as a work of
social and cultural biography – hence their decision to hold the publication
until after his third novel had been published.

Winkler's reluctance to use the word "autobiography" may not be unusual, at least within the West Indian canon: as Sandra Pouchet Paquet points out in her essay "West Indian Autobiography", autobiographical works by such celebrated writers as George Lamming, C.L.R. James, Derek Walcott and V.S. Naipaul, in one way or another, contain the disclaimer, "This is not an autobiography" – and in fact, in all the cases examined in that essay, the works both were and were not autobiography.[3] In the case of *Going Home to Teach,* Winkler's description is not inaccurate: the book offers a detailed commentary on various aspects of Jamaica's society and culture.

Yet *Going Home* is of course very much autobiography. It is an autobiographical account not only of a year spent in Jamaica, but also of the author's family background and his own past. As a personal statement, it is an explanation of his migration to America at the age of twenty, his repatriation to his homeland at the age of thirty-three, and his abrupt return to America one year later. And it is an assertion of the author's Jamaicanness – of his right to call himself a Jamaican and be regarded as such, despite his white skin and despite his decision to reside abroad.

The spine of the narrative is a chronological account of a year in the author's life (1975–76): his decision to return home to Jamaica after thirteen years of living in America; his preliminary job-seeking trip to the island in which he is offered the position of lecturer in English at a rural teacher-training college, and in which he meets his future wife Cathy, an American holidaying in Jamaica; and his move to the island a month or so later, accompanied by Cathy, to take up the post at Longstreet College (a thinly disguised version of Moneague Teacher Training College). There he spends close to a complete academic year before an abrupt and "rash" (p. 260) departure back to the United States, due to his fury at a seemingly malicious act by the school principal.

Branching off from this spine are numerous observations of Jamaican society, particularly concerning the Jamaican identity and personality; racial and class interactions and reactions (including reactions to the political changes being introduced by the prime minister at the time, Michael Manley); the country's educational system; and the role of history in the evolution of all of these. And equally numerous are anecdotes about his family background.

Framing this account, as signalled by what may be regarded as an informal foreword and afterword to the book, is Winkler's evocation of his paternal grandfather as a defining point of reference. Grandfather Winkler loved Jamaica and insisted on returning home with his American wife to live there, but his wife hated Jamaica. He turned to writing in his sixties, and wrote a novel which was regarded as having great potential by an English publisher, but he died before completing it. His unhappy and homesick wife burnt the manuscript shortly after his death. Given the fact that throughout the book Winkler has gradually established Cathy's growing unhappiness in Jamaica, the parallels are clear, the probable influences equally clear – providing the reader, therefore, with an understanding of some of the unstated forces behind the author's sudden decision at the end of the book to return to America.

Whether his grandfather's efforts to write a novel directly influenced Winkler to become a writer is never openly addressed in *Going Home to Teach* – all we are told is that "it was a dream that Grandfather and I shared except that his had blossomed late in life while mine began haunting me on the day I first stepped out of the mists of childhood" (p. 5). Nevertheless, the continual and deliberate drawing of parallels suggests this as a distinct possibility – bringing to mind the influence of V.S. Naipaul's father on his son's career, as explored in Naipaul's "Prologue to an Autobiography" in *Finding the Centre*. Like Winkler's grandfather, Naipaul's father was a creative writer – modestly successful, much more so than Grandfather Winkler, but unacclaimed. Like Winkler, Naipaul states that his decision to become a writer came at an early age. For Naipaul, the centre of his creativity is his father, and finding the centre means discovering the facts and the essence of his father's life – a discovery which necessitates a mental as well as physical return to Trinidad. "To become a writer," Naipaul says, "I had thought it necessary to leave. Actually to write, it was necessary to go back. It was the beginning of self-knowledge."[4]

Winkler, too, had thought it necessary to leave Jamaica that first time, at the age of twenty, in order to write: "I had come to America because I wanted to be a writer. . . . [S]hortly after my twentieth birthday it was plain to me that to develop as a writer I needed to be better educated and to taste life in a big country" (p. 5). Elsewhere he recalls an interview with Vic Reid which took place when Winkler was eighteen, in which Reid was asked if anyone could develop as a writer in Jamaica. "He said no, one had to leave to gain distance to write about Jamaica. These words meant a lot to me and confirmed what I had always suspected which was that I was too close to my subject."[5]

Indeed, in America Winkler succeeded in educating himself in a way that would not have been possible in Jamaica: having left school at the age of fourteen (expelled, as he likes to relate, for example in *Going Home* [p. 6] or in his interview in the *Caribbean Review of Books*), with grades having fallen from A to F, he would never have been able to make up for lost opportunities within the rigid, British-based Jamaican educational system in the way that he did in California, where he worked his way through an associate degree, a bachelor's, and then finally a master's in English at an accredited university (California State).[6]

On the other hand, despite his academic successes, and his financial success in establishing himself as a writer of English-language college textbooks, Winkler found that in America he was having no success with his creative writing. He had written over two dozen plays, some poetry and a novel, but, "All I was getting were rejection slips! You see, I was trying to write about Americans, and I don't think I knew enough about Americans to write about them."[7]

His first novel, *The Mary Anne Papers,* written in his early twenties, was, by his own admission, "a very vulgar book. . . . [T]he readership committee at Harper's . . . said it was the most vulgar book they had ever read!"[8] Elsewhere he says, "What I did was this. I took all the attitudes Americans have . . . the pomposity of Americans in their country, and carnalised it, carnalised it. I got outraged reviews. Readers were mortified by it."[9] Whether Winkler was hitting the nail too hard on the head or missing it altogether is unclear; whatever the reasons, his American-focused creative writing efforts were failures.

Naipaul found it necessary to "go back" to Trinidad in order to write, and first he went back creatively rather than physically. In "Prologue to an Autobiography" he relates how, in a British Broadcasting Corporation room in London at the age of twenty-two, five years after leaving Trinidad, "after two failed attempts at novels" (p. 19), and "without having any idea where I was going, and not perhaps intending to type to the end of the page" (p. 16), he wrote what would become the first line of his first written (and third published) Trinidadian novel, *Miguel Street.* In that line appeared the character

Bogart, based on Naipaul's childhood memory of a man by that name who lived on his street, who unexpectedly entered the head of the young writer. Similarly Winkler recalls how, in 1972 or thereabouts, ten years after leaving Jamaica, after one failed attempt at writing a novel and numerous failed attempts at writing plays and poetry, he was attempting to write a textbook piece when the fisherman Baba, whom Winkler remembered from his early adolescent years in Montego Bay, suddenly "leapt onto the page".[10] The story, "The Man Who Knew the Price of All Fish", was Winkler's first Jamaican story; Baba "ended up being the prototype for Zachariah Pelsie"[11] – the fisherman in *The Painted Canoe,* Winkler's first published (and second written) novel. Like Naipaul, then, Winkler began to find his centre when his creativity turned to his country and culture of origin. As it was for Naipaul, this was for Winkler "the beginning of self-knowledge".

And *Going Home to Teach* suggests that the year that Winkler spent in Jamaica provided him with more fuel to advance towards that state of self-knowledge. In observing the society and culture in which he had spent his formative years, with the benefit of the distance and increased objectivity afforded one who has spent many years away from that society and culture, Winkler appears to have gained insights not only into the environment in which he had been raised, but also into his own family background, and ultimately, into himself.

Sandra Pouchet Paquet observes of Naipaul's "Prologue to an Autobiography" that "the autobiographical act unfolds as a quest for the familial and ethnic roots of his creativity". And of this work as well as a number of others she suggests that "issues of self-identity merge with issues of West Indian identity. The individual predicament of the writer as autobiographical subject illuminates the collective predicament of the island community. The autobiographical act emerges as a means to an end rather than an end in itself."[12]

Such an approach may differ from, say, American autobiography where writers may have tended to ground their work in the context of the American Dream: as Robert Sayre suggests in his essay, "Autobiography and the Making of America", "American autobiographers have generally connected their own lives to the national life or to national ideas. . . . America has been an idea, or many ideas."[13] Most classic American autobiographies, Sayre suggests, seem to have assumed that the life being described is an emulation of the idea of America, and that there is consequently a desire for emulation of the individual life on the part of the reader.[14] Sayre finds this to be the case not only in mainstream autobiographical works such as those by John Adams, Benjamin Franklin or Walt Whitman, but also in such vastly different ones as those by Frederick Douglass, Richard Wright or Malcolm X, where a quest for and successful or failed attainment of freedom/equality/self-expression become a comment on the idea of America: "The person who can write his own story can rise from the status of the unknown and inarticulate. . . . [I]n writing his or her story, the autobiographer becomes the known individual that most Americans would like to be . . . the autobiographical hero enters the House of America."[15]

Where the American Dream represents freedom, individuality and opportunity, the history of the West Indies has meant violence, oppression and exploitation, each island still struggling with independence, nationhood and a crisis of identity exaggerated by the slow-healing wounds of colonialism. The idea of the West Indies, then, is not yet one for emulation. Rather, West Indian autobiographers, it seems, seek to grasp and to come to terms with both the West Indian identity and self-identity. For the writers examined by Pouchet Paquet, "self-inquiry is self-imaging and self-evaluation, but it is also cultural assessment" and "intellectual history".[16] Pouchet Paquet observes

> a clearly defined tension between the autobiographical self as a singular personality with psychological integrity and the self as a way into the social and political complexities of the region. . . . Self-revelation becomes a way of laying claim to a landscape that is at once geographical, historical, and cultural. . . . [A]utobiography emerges as a compelling way to embody the collective West Indian experience. . . . [A]utobiographical modes create an exemplary space for the reconstruction of self and community that accompanies the withdrawal of the British Empire, a totalitarian institution, from the region.[17]

Pouchet Paquet suggests a sequence wherein each of the texts that she examines "can be read as a successive attempt to create a new narrative space for the representation of self as West Indian".[18] Winkler's *Going Home,* as social and cultural biography as well as autobiography, as self-revelation as well as a claiming of the Jamaican landscape, becomes another link in the chain of West Indian autobiography.

Pouchet Paquet rightly suggests that Derek Walcott's endeavour in *Another Life* is to write "the spiritual history of this region", and that he "characterizes his childhood in terms of the antithetical values of the colonial Caribbean, then traces the painful process of recovery and restoration of self beyond the disillusionments of post-colonial politics".[19] Winkler's endeavour seems much more modest, but in his own way he too evokes a spiritual history of his country, or in particular a history of the evolution of the Jamaican identity. His analysis is grounded in his views of the country's anti-thetical colonial values, just as his hopes for individual as well as collective self-recovery are seemingly tempered by the disillusionments of postcolonial politics – specifically, Michael Manley's democratic socialism.

Winkler's account of the period 1975–76 in Jamaica's history could in some perverse way be regarded as the sequel to Rachel Manley's account of the period 1951–69 in her autobiographical *Drumblair: Memories of a Jamaican Childhood*[20] – although, of course, Winkler's book was published two years before *Drumblair*. Written by another Jamaican who has spent most of her adult life outside of Jamaica, *Drumblair* relates the birth of a nation and the role played by Norman Manley, Rachel's grandfather, as father of that nation, with his wife, Edna, as cultural mother, at his side. *Going Home* continues this story by providing a brief glimpse of that nation six years later, with Norman dead but with his younger son Michael at the helm – both in his father's place as leader of the People's National Party, and in a place never attained by his father, as prime minister of the country. Moreover, Michael is steering the country not necessarily to certain death, but certainly along a treacherous, perilous course – one which the helms-man, Winkler suggests repeatedly, could have avoided while still heading for the same destination, a destination which in fact might have been reached had a different course been chosen.

Drumblair is, of course, a very different book from *Going Home,* in style, content and purpose. While *Drumblair* is lyrical, obviously the work of a poet, *Going Home* is fiery, outspoken, often combative. *Drumblair* romanti-cizes the life of the author's grandparents; *Going Home* reveals harsh realities in its author's family history, and exaggerates absurdities. In *Drumblair* the author's own autobiography is secondary to painting the portrait of her grandparents; in *Going Home* autobiographical details are as important as family biographical details in painting the portrait of the author, and both are as important as historical details in painting the portrait of the Jamaican identity.

Drumblair, told from the point of view of an adoring granddaughter, "is not history. It is memory" (p. xiv), thus allowing for historical inaccuracy (such as the author's claim that her grandmother designed the federal flag [p. 159]), even as it seems to attempt to redress historical wrongs. *Going Home,* told from the point of view of an angry young man, also seems to seek to redress historical wrongs – but those wrongs inflicted on a people's identity by three hundred years of colonialism, not the wrongs inflicted on one man who spearheaded the country's independence yet did not greet independence as the country's leader. *Drumblair,* then, is deliberately narrow in focus, essentially a very private recollection of Norman Manley and his wife, Edna, with few references to the larger world outside of the gates of Drumblair. *Going Home,* in consistent and insistent social commentary, embraces the larger world of Jamaica as essential to an understanding of the author's family, the author's marriage, the author's history, the author himself. As private as the recollection in *Drumblair* may be, nevertheless one has the impression that the author may be attempting to convert into legend even the couple's most private moments; for example, private conversations to which the author could not possibly have been privy are presented as factual, although they read as artificial, stylized, romanticized, so that fact is mythologized. In *Going Home* Winkler obviously exaggerates fact, and conceals the identities of people and places by using fictional names and details, yet in so doing reveals essential truth.

Drumblair, as a biography of two people who did immense good to the lot of the common Jamaican, contains few depictions of the common Jamaican – and those which do exist, generally sketches of servants, are two-dimensional. So that *Drumblair,* written by someone who proclaims herself to be one-quarter black (p. 397) and who tries to establish her own social consciousness (for example, by recording her participation in the Rodney march), reveals the author as what she is: three-quarters white, and solidly middle-class, with all the attendant privileges and protections that stereotypically accompany that package in the Jamaican environment. *Going Home,* in contrast, teems with lively depictions of common Jamaicans, and refers to middle-class Jamaicans with some impatience – again predictably for the reader who is familiar with Winkler's other books, but still surprising to some, given Winkler's whiteness, which in the context of Jamaican social stereotypes automatically projects him into the elite category, despite all indications to the contrary.

Pouchet Paquet refers to the "spiritual reconnection with the poor and oppressed as the definitive posture of the West Indian writer in relation to the regional community".[21] Not surprisingly, since this is not the nature of the work, and yet at the same time ironically, given the life's work and achievements of Norman Manley and to some extent his wife, Edna, *Drumblair* shows no such spiritual reconnection. *Going Home* does.

Winkler's spiritual connection with Jamaica, as an integral component of his construction of community and his construction of self, is manifold in *Going Home to Teach*. From the beginning of the book, Winkler establishes himself as a Jamaican who has never regarded anywhere but Jamaica as home, and as a reluctant migrant to America. In fact, his decision to migrate was not really his decision at all, but rather that of his mother, who "was determined to transplant her loved ones to a richer land" and so "hustled him onto the plane" (p. 7). However, Winkler acquiesced because "it seemed to [him] that [he] had reached the end of the line" in Jamaica (p. 6), and America was, after all, the land of opportunity.

But Winkler's dislike of America never wavered, even after he "had accumulated three degrees in English" (p. 7), one divorce, "money in the bank, furniture in the apartment, and a paid-for car in the garage" (p. 8), US citizenship and gainful employment. "I still felt no love for this land, America," he says. "It was nothing more than a place where I worked. My home was Jamaica and my heart longed to return there" (p. 8). Earlier he states,

> I had always wanted to go home. I did not wish to spend the rest of my days in the company of Americans, for as a whole I did not understand them and was certain that I never would. . . . It was like walking into a movie that was half over and picking up the storyline in the middle. Some things you got from the context; others escaped you. . . .
>
> I felt no love for the land. It did not smell right. Even after thirteen years it still had the alien, unrecognizable spoor of a foreign place. . . .
>
> It did not sound right. (p. 3)

Winkler's dislike of America is focused on southern California, where he accumulated his three degrees. Southern California is a sterile, empty place: "Where the land lays down no laws and traditions, there is vacuum; and where there is vacuum there is always an inrush of tormented ideology into people's minds. Southern California is a vast desert dominated by the ethics of 'should' " (p. 20) (reminding one of the "shouldist" American philosopher later unflatteringly presented by Winkler in *The Duppy*). So an apt image for southern California is "[g]uts and intestines and entrails held in check by a freshly applied gauze of Mao, Janov, Freud, Steinem . . . Macrobiotics, and whichever Indian guru had lately crossed the ocean in search of a Rolls Royce" (p. 21). Like a typical immigrant, Winkler keeps on deferring a return to his homeland until such time as he can arrive there "in glory and triumph" (p. 16), but meanwhile he has "a recurring nightmare . . . of being buried in Southern California" (p. 21). So, once he persuades himself that his three degrees and three textbooks do, after all, represent a reasonably respectable achievement, his final decision to leave is easy: "One does not mourn leaving a motel, no matter how opulent and beguiling its décor" (p. 21).

His arrival in Jamaica occurs despite the incredulity of middle-class family and friends who, frightened by socialism, have either fled the country or are trying their best to do so – an incredulity which presumably contributes to first-night jitters, in which even the landscape reads as desolate and threatening:

> The road . . . plunges down a flat spit of land where the wind and surf bleat endlessly.
>
> My brother points to a spot off the side of the road as the place where a man and a woman were murdered a month ago. . . .
>
> [O]ut of the night an enormous mountain looms, its massive flanks brooding over the city. . . . [E]ven in the darkness you can see the excavated wound, and during the daylight you can see tractors and earthmovers gnawing ceaselessly at its ragged edges.
>
> We drive past the rotting hulks of freighters that lost their way through the shoals and impaled themselves on the windward claw of the peninsula. During the daytime, you can see the ocean licking at their open ribs. . . .
>
> Then we are on the Windward Road. . . . We drive through quickly . . . not looking at the rows of dirty shops, the ramshackle hovels, the throngs of people who slouch and lean and sag and eye us as we pass. (p. 36)

But the jitters are transitory: "I was home again, laughing among my own people. There was joy in my heart" (p. 74). Seeing a woman "cut her eyes" or another "kiss her teeth" (p. 34) are familiar gestures that he was unable to use in America. These are nuances that he understands, like the phrase "see yah now" (p. 74), which is untranslatable into American; at last he can speak patois, the language of his childhood, which was "what [he] missed the most" while he lived abroad (p. 72). "Now I could say what was in my heart in the most natural and instinctive way without filtering my speech. . . . I wallowed in my childhood tongue for the first month I was back in Jamaica like a mute who had miraculously regained his tongue" (pp. 72–73). Ultimately, he has returned to his own culture: "Jamaicans do not see the world the way Americans do. Culture is in the person, and the person is an embodiment of the culture and the lessons it teaches" (p. 118).

Culture is inextricably linked to history, and Winkler's view of the influence of history on the national psyche pervades *Going Home:*

> [W]hen I went home to teach I soon saw that history, like pollen, is constantly in the air. We breathe it in and out . . . it affects the way we live and think. . . . [W]e foolishly think that what we do we do because of personal preference or individual temperament, when the truth is that we are practising an ancient, invisible, and inherited pattern. (pp. 103–4)

Winkler's focus is, inevitably, on colonialism and slavery:

> Three hundred years of colonialism: a people who were brought here as slaves or came as plunderers, who grew into nationhood simultaneously clinging to the passive resistance mentality of the enslaved while unconsciously admiring and aping the ways of the English master; who resent and despise authority of all kinds and make a national sport of constantly haggling with it; a people mixed and hybridized in every conceivable way – racially, culturally, linguistically, spiritually – and to whom life has been so capricious and unfair that they have come over the centuries to see it as the stuff of makeshift drama. (p. 35)

Winkler is particularly concerned about the damage wreaked by colonialism and slavery on the Jamaican sense of self. His indictment of colonialism, and of its English perpetrators, is strident and relentless (and, at times, overemphasized). "The upper-class colonial Englishman," Winkler suggests, "often seemed to be squinting at the world dimly through the clutter of superstition and protocol inherited by his membership in a privileged group. He seemed perpetually blundering about in a fog of rigidly correct English, etiquette, and a doltish worldview" (p. 209). Such a blundering existence is not restricted to those of the upper classes: no matter how uncouth in his homeland (p. 80), the colonial once transplanted onto Jamaican soil was obliged to put on a pose of superior breeding "as a defence against being engulfed by the preponderant black races. . . . [T]his effort made [him] a figure so clotted with distinctive mannerisms, ceremonies, and pretensions as to be ludicrously theatrical" (pp. 80–81) (and here one is reminded of the depiction of the colonials in Earl Lovelace's *Salt* when "they begin to discover how hard it was to be gods").[22] "The slaves," Winkler continues, "witnessed this white man daily enacting his theatre of what it was like to be English and thought to themselves: so that's what it means to be white" (p. 81). So the pseudo-Englishman was created, the native mind having been overcome by "an endless succession of stupid rules about grammar, pronunciation, ceremony, politeness and manners" (p. 71). And, "the pernicious influence of the Englishman and his excessive emphasis on rightness in ceremony and grammar is a feature so typical of Jamaicans as a whole as to be almost a national characteristic" (p. 70).

Winkler perceives this characteristic in the school principal, Dr Levy, during his initial interview, as a result of that gentleman's response (or lack thereof) to a lizard on his desk, which Winkler suggests was about to bite his finger. Although Winkler seems to be the one who was overreacting – such extreme action by an innocent lizard seems highly unlikely – nevertheless, overall, Winkler's initial reading may be not inaccurate.

Winkler is particularly scathing about the "witless association between class and profession" of the English (p. 207), which he contrasts with the American respect for achievement – a contrast which explains why "the American is today riding space shuttles while the Englishman is wondering how he happened to fall off his high horse" (p. 209).

The confusion of "manners, accents, and glibness with competence" (p. 205) has sinister implications with regard to the British-based colonial educational system: the importance of knowing one's place in the society was critical within a "hierarchical and rigid society where advancement and preferment were based as much on accident of birth as on talent and industry" (p. 62). Knowing one's place meant not knowing. So, for example,

Henry, the illiterate handyman at the Chest Hospital who knows how to whack an oxygen tank to make it work, but not why, is best left in his ignorance, otherwise: "The next thing you know, you have educated Henry to the point that he begins to wonder what the devil you're doing in his country and who the dickens is this bloody Queen you expect him to bow down to morning, noon, and night" (p. 65).

This emphasis on knowing one's place rather than knowing has carried over, Winkler suggests, into our present-day educational system. This is a particularly sore point for the author given, first, his own unhappy experience both within it (memories such as meaningless memorizing [p. 62] and vicious canings [p. 210] predominate) and – reading between the lines – without it (as stated earlier, its exclusivity prevented him from making up for past mistakes – in order to do that he had to go to America); second, the fact that his chief endeavour for the year was teaching – and teaching students how to teach. Rote learning has "wreaked a terrible destruction" on the minds of Winkler's generation, and many of his colleagues, he says, "could only pass on in parrot fashion what they themselves had been force-fed as students" (p. 209). "That was what was wrong with our schools. We had learnt the wrong lessons and now taught the wrong lessons. We were not realistic in what we taught" (p. 205). Winkler's frustration with this misdirected system reaches a climax towards the end of the school year when he visits elementary schools to test his students' performances as teachers. These pages, full of understated anguish (in contrast to his rantings on the British colonialists), are moving, and they confirm the author's tremendous love for his country and his countrymen.

The problems evident in the country's educational system, Winkler indicates, are part of the vacuum in which Jamaicans have been left since our colonial masters departed, one in which we are still floating, searching for our identity in various ways, uncertain to what extent we should discard our pseudo-Englishness (with its absurd superficial vestiges, such as woollen suits worn in the tropical climate):

> We did not know who we were. We had been reared by a grand ancestor who had suddenly died leaving a rich legacy but no will. Now that he was gone we did not know how to dress. We did not know how to talk. We did not know how we should live. We did not know what we should believe. All we had to guide us was

the memory of his example and the chequered history he had left behind, the epitaph scrawled on his tomb. We did not know who we were. (p. 92)

The legacy may be rich, but such riches are obscured by all manner of distortions, and the probating of the will is fraught with confusion and pain.

Winkler's analysis is occasionally cliché, for example when he discusses the "ravaging of the nuclear family" brought about by slavery (p. 104), or at least unoriginal – as when he professes agreement with Michael Manley's suggestion that a prime contributor to the increasing indiscipline and cruelty in the society is the "overly harsh grandmother, who bears a disproportionate burden of the island's child rearing" (p. 106). Yet his interpretation of such truisms or oft-quoted theories often remains fresh, as does his pain. In relation to the above example of the grandmother, his account of hearing a child beaten is disturbing, and lingers in the mind:

> For half an hour, the desperate wailing and sobbing echoed off the hills to the merciless gnawing of leather against flesh. . . . Twenty years from now with a gun in his hand and a victim impaled in its sights, what mercy would he show when his own pitiful pleas and grovelling had provoked only insensate anger and further blows? (p. 106)

Some of the behavioural manifestations of Jamaican history observed by Winkler are as amusing as they are disturbing. Customs officials "wearing the hardened look of the bored – the trademark expression of West Indian civil servants" (p. 33), or the surly low-level government official who wants her bottom smooched (p. 119), represent a type of service disposition commonly encountered in Jamaica, which may, Winkler suggests, be due to "our experience with slavery when we waged an endless war of passive resistance against the slavemaster's desires and struggled hard to repudiate what he wanted us to become" (p. 117). Another type of behaviour is represented by such figures as the school bursar who resents being asked why paycheques are three days late (p. 121), or the glowering Ministry of Education employee who keeps the author waiting for hours before telling him that his file cannot be found (p. 236), or, damningly, the school principal who on the morning of the A-level exam decides that the two students who have been preparing for it all year cannot sit it (p. 259), or, most disturbing of all, the headmistress who lets a little boy go hungry every day in order to teach him a lesson (p. 166). These seem to be illustrations of "the most poisonous axiom in our national theorems: Jamaicans would rather hinder than help their own kind" (p. 189). But Winkler suggests that this axiom too is a relic of slavery: the struggle for a few "cushy" job places in the manor house as a relief from back-breaking work in the fields "pitted slave against slave in a bloody rivalry whose outcome immeasurably improved life" (p. 189).

Yearning for a job in the manor house has other effects:

> Plainly put, the Jamaican on his home soil dislikes physical labour . . . not because he shirks hard work . . . but because over the centuries physical labour has come to be associated with blackness and lowly field-hand status. This idea was exported wholesale from the days of slavery . . . and is now practically etched in the genes of the nation. (p. 87)

The desire to escape from any association with slavery, Winkler says, inevitably extends to a desire to disassociate from blackness, since the blackest Jamaicans have traditionally occupied the "base of the pyramid", with "the white men occupying the apex" (p. 86). The abovementioned axiom that Jamaicans would rather hinder than help their own kind therefore has an especially disturbing implication: hindering one's own kind means hindering one's self, hating oneself. The theme of black self-hatred which recurs so consistently in Winkler's novels is again explored in *Going Home*. Blacks do not refer to themselves as black: a dark brown man calls himself white (p. 28), a blue-black woman refuses to stay in a club because of the presence of "a lot of ole negar . . . Too much! Too much!" (p. 78).

The expression "ole negar" refers to the lowest of the low on that pyramid, and a disassociation from ole negar is essential. The opinion of ole negar expressed by one middle-class Miami exile explains the need for such distancing:

> You know what the poor Jamaican wants? . . . First he wants a woman he can breed. . . . Second, he wants rum to drink on a Saturday night. . . . Come Monday morning and you call him over and say, "Hubert, I got a little job to do. If you do it for me, it might mean a little extra money." . . . "Lawd, God, sah," he bawls, "hard work nearly kill me already, sah. . . ." You can't get him to do the extra work for you. . . . That is how the typical poor Jamaican is. . . . He's poor because as long as he can flash his dick around and drink a little rum on Saturday . . . he is a happy man, content with his life. (pp. 31–32)

Such a description could easily have come out of the mouth of Baps in *The Duppy*; such a sentiment, common enough in middle-class Jamaica, explains to a great extent Winkler's inspiration to create the figures of Zachariah (in *The Painted Canoe*) and Aloysius (in *The Lunatic*), and even Egbert (in *The Duppy*) as subversions of this destructive (albeit convenient) cliché. Ole negar is vilified, ole negar is othered – and at the same time ole negar is the skeleton in one's own closet.

Blackness is associated with poverty; colour is associated with class. Winkler himself, as a young migrant to the United States, thinks of a brown man as white because of his class and profession (he is a law student, his father is a prominent barrister [p. 79]) and is shaken when an American defines him as a "nigger". Nigger . . . nayga . . . the son of a barrister is certainly no ole negar.

Winkler is of course greatly disturbed by American racism and racial categorization. "Growing up," he says elsewhere, "all my best friends were black. My doctor, teachers, minister, girlfriends were black. I never saw them as anything but people. It was when I got to America that I got a glimpse through the telescope America uses to look at these people. It scared the hell out of me."[23] His anger at the racism of some motel owners encountered in his journey with Cathy through the southern United States en route to Jamaica confirms his decision to leave that country. It is "the trait I had come to most passionately despise: the endless preaching about freedom and equality, the constant yapping about land of the free and home of the brave, accompanied by the hypocritically nasty practice" (p. 27). On racial matters, Winkler suggests,

> Americans are the world's most consummate casuists. . . . Americans see colour strictly as a consanguineous and physical quality: it is to them so much a matter of blood that a pint inherited from a great-great-great black ancestor is enough to classify anyone as black no matter how white he may look. (p. 80)

But the Jamaican method of racial categorization, Winkler implies, may be equally warped: "When it comes to colour, nothing in Jamaica is simple" (p. 79). We recall his observation that Jamaicans "regard colour as inseparable from manners, behaviour, background, education, and culture" (p. 80). The vilification of ole negar in the Jamaican culture is therefore an expression of both class and colour prejudice, disproving, Winkler implies, "the fairy tale often repeated that the island suffers only from class, but not from colour, prejudice" (p. 79). He says also, "Jamaicans persisted in denying that racism had anything to do with either social advancement or the way they treated one another. Class was always touted as the determining factor, apparently on the belief that discrimination based on class was morally superior to that based on colour" (p. 86).

Winkler acknowledges the role played by Michael Manley in the 1970s in exposing this fallacy, and "speaking out against racial discrimination" (p. 86). He notes, "it was . . . plain to me that his influence in instilling a feeling of pride and self-worth in Jamaicans had taken hold and with good effect" (p. 91). Winkler has, from early in *Going Home,* established where his sympathies lie in terms of socialism – after all, he did come home when the fearful Jamaican middle and upper classes were scuttling to sell property, usually at a loss, salvage what they could and then take one of those five flights a day to Miami (or, in the case of Jameson the landowner, to Canada [p. 264]). As Winkler says, "Jamaicans are notorious for their callousness towards the poor. Foreigners. . . . are struck . . . by the obscene and gaping difference between the destitute and the conspicuously rich. . . . So if Manley was trying to right this long-standing wrong . . . I wanted to be there when he did it" (pp. 13–14).

Winkler understands some of this callousness. The streak of it that "ran in our people," he suggests,

> sprang from the capriciousness of our history, from the wearying and brutalizing poverty whose stench was constantly in the wind. . . . Want was everywhere. . . . You could not avoid the sights and sounds of suffering. . . . So a rind of insensibility hardened over your heart. You looked on misery and grief and found humour. . . . As part of your tropical seasoning, you became almost religiously serene in your horror. (pp. 220–21)

Winkler's use of the second person in this passage encourages a reading of this as a personal confession. But he does not forgive it.

Similarly, he understands the very thin line on which someone who is privileged must walk in a society characterized by want:

> In a third world country like Jamaica you must be prepared to pay reparations to bands of scavenging sufferers. It is more than alms-giving: it is a kind of unofficial

exacting of tribute. There are vastly more of them than of you, and they could rise up at any minute and drown you and yours in an unrelenting tide of class retribution. (p. 225)

The thin line becomes dangerously frayed on occasions such as the one in which Winkler is approached by a beggar who offers to "kill anybody you want kill" (p. 226), because "Boss man! We love you, you know, sah! We would kill for you!" (p. 223). Reality approaches nightmare; the frayed line may be the last link to civilization.

As a result, the questions "implicitly raised by Manley in his attempts to restructure our national life" – "who was our brother, and what did we owe him? Where were we going as a people?" – are ones which Winkler and his colleagues debate "incessantly" (p. 100), and it is clear that Winkler is again commending Manley for forcing such debates, for opening up minds, for engendering an awareness of self and black self-worth in a way that had never been experienced before in Jamaica (and probably has not been experienced since).

But such commendation is heavily qualified. Winkler repeatedly suggests that Manley, as well meaning as he was, blundered in his methods. One critical mistake, in his view, concerns the very animal that Manley worked so hard to erase from the national identity: the demeaning concept of ole negar. Winkler points out that for the managerial and middle classes, ole negar or blackness connoted "not merely colour, but also a certain manner of thinking and behaviour linked in the popular mind with indiscipline, uncultured-ness and general ill-mannerliness" (p. 89).

> Indiscipline is the one word that most Jamaicans . . . would equate with blackness. Jamaicans of all walks of life seem to spend a lifetime bemoaning indiscipline. . . . And it was here . . . that Manley stumbled. His administration, he declared often, was for the common man. . . . But to be for the black man, in the Jamaican mind, is to be for . . . that *bête noire,* indiscipline, and as his term dragged on, Manley seemed to give tacit support to the middle-class criticism that he had sided with the beast. (pp. 89–90)

Winkler recalls a speech in which Manley seems to excuse indiscipline as being caused by societal injustice. "I remember thinking at the time," Winkler says, that if I had been Manley's speechwriter, I could have stopped at least fifty middle-class managers . . . from migrating. . . . America's Satan is communism, Jamaica's is indiscipline. Even the Ayatollah of Iran . . . could not afford to speak equivocally about America, the national Satan of his own people. (pp. 90–91)

As a result of his alienation and frightening away of the middle class, there is a shortage not only of goods but of services and expertise: "Manley's fiery sermonizing . . . had sent specialists, fixers and technicians fleeing in droves to foreign lands" (p. 179). Winkler suggests that a deficiency of local expertise may have been a longstanding relic of the colonial system of deliberate semi-education, as noted earlier, but he emphasizes that Manley exaggerated the problem, resulting in absurd situations which Winkler gleefully illustrates with a number of anecdotes: for example, the so-called car mechanic from the village who reduces a neighbour's Fiat to a pile of parts which he cannot reassemble; the Kingston garage which eighteen months later has still failed to reassemble the same Fiat because it continually bungles the importation of the necessary car part; or – surely one of the best anecdotes in the book – a simple attempt to get a car horn (or indeed anything) fixed, which inevitably sends one "down de road" (p. 180) from one person to the next, from one place to the next: "[I]n Jamaica, nothing technical is ever that simple. There is a labyrinthine complexity to virtually every chore. You start up here and end up there, and wonder how you got there when all you set out to do was get your radio fixed" (p. 179).

Winkler refers to Manley's tendency to get carried away by his own rhetoric in extended speeches as "government by jawbone" (p. 203) (and one is reminded of the eight-hour speeches mentioned in *The Painted Canoe* and *The Lunatic* – one of which, in the latter case, is suggested by Busha to have been the reason that Aloysius went mad).

> It went like this: Mr. Manley would wake up one morning with an urge and decide to give a speech about it. Everyone would sit up and take note and wonder what the speech meant and what the devil the government was up to now. And more people would become sufficiently agitated to spark anew another rush for visas. (p. 203)

Winkler eventually feels that "democratic socialism was too Sundayschoolish and well-meaning, too filled with dogmatic rectitude. . . . [Manley] didn't have to be so insufferably righteous just because he was right" (pp. 203–4). And in all of this Winkler hardly ever questions Manley's moral rightness. Only at the end of *Going Home* does he wonder tentatively whether the reason that socialism failed in Jamaica, that "Manley's well-meaning and humane government was so bungled and futile", was because "his socialism lacked the attraction of betterment" (p. 265).

Manley's blundering in his method of discouraging black self-hatred may have directly or indirectly encouraged another type of evil: hatred of whites. Although applauding the fact that "[u]nder the Manley regime, Jamaica had taken a definite turn against the white and fair-skinned people who had enjoyed favoured status up to then" (p. 86), Winkler seems somewhat ambivalent about another change that has taken place "in the scant thirteen years . . . since our Independence" (p. 99): as signalled when a colleague assures him that she would never marry or have a baby for a white man, no matter who he is, because "this is 1975. Me want children of my own colour. My mother and father want grandchildren of their own colour. So Jamaica go today" (p. 99). The pendulum has swung, and Winkler's disturbance at such reverse discrimination can be seen behind his intellectual rationalization of it as being nationalistic and thereby unavoidable (p. 99). Similarly, he pushes aside his hurt at the prejudice and bitterness vented at him by his colleague Raymond: "Part of his attitude no doubt was due to Manley's rhetoric with its constant harping on the sins of a colonial past" (a tendency of which Winkler surely has some understanding). "But much of it was in the bloodstream of the West Indian people and the inescapable consequence of our history" (p. 103). Winkler is impatient with Manley's attempt to stem this flow of reverse discrimination by suggesting that this is "not the way of democratic socialism":

> It was then, after I had listened to this dimwitted speech, that I finally grasped what was idiotically flawed about Manley and his programme: it was all too doltishly theatrical. . . . No doubt every hothead and firebrand on the street corner, every illiterate, pauperized and aggrieved Jamaican who had reason enough – personal or historical – to resent white people, would be struck dead in his tracks by this tepid blast of ministerial logic. (p. 162)

That Winkler is very much aware of the personal or historical reasons for a hatred of white Jamaicans by black Jamaicans is very clear. And his sketch of Jameson the white landowner, like his depictions of most of the white characters in his novels, attests to this: Jameson (like Busha in *The Lunatic*) owns all the land "as far as the eye could see" (p. 40) and his family has done so for generations: "we've been here forever, before any of them," he boasts (p. 47), referring to the black community surrounding him. He and his wife do not socialize with "them": "We get so lonely up here for a white face, it's terrible!" as Mrs Jameson says (p. 47). Jameson and his wife, like stereotypical plantocrats, have sent their children to school in England. They treat their staff as children and refer to their headman, who is approaching forty, as "a good boy" (p. 48). This good boy had to be trained to become dependable: "They all have to be taught. Discipline does not come naturally to them the way it does to us" (p. 48). So the ole negar-equals-indiscipline equation is here presented in its original form, with the "ole" missing. The similarity to the opinions expressed by middle-class Miami exiles is readily apparent, as is Winkler's unstated but unequivocal disgust.

Winkler does not deny the advantages of being white – especially in the 1950s, as he recalls, when "it gained you access to places to which you could not otherwise go. . . . It stereotyped you as a member of the ruling class, even if you were poor and utterly without influence. . . . [I]f you were male, it made you an object of sexual attraction to poor black women." Even with such advantages, however, to be white is "a mixed blessing" (p. 93). Inevitably, to be white is also to be "a pariah, an ambiguous entity. It is to be simultaneously respected and despised, to arouse suspicion and curiosity, to evoke defiance, rudeness, envy, and condescension" (p. 75). And for Winkler in *Going Home,* the advantages seem greatly obscured by the disadvantages of being a representative of an oppressive ruling elite.

One of the most moving aspects of *Going Home* is the author's awareness of the logic and inevitability of a black hatred of whites, counterpointed by his anguish at being the recipient of such hatred. "It was a knife in my heart, this hatred I felt from my own people" (p. 162). As a child, abused by street urchins, he feels the abuse is justified: "Personal hatred was a relief, a blessing, compared to this. . . . But this widespread resentment was too collective, too deeply symbolic, to be placated by any personal word or gesture" (p. 159). Much as it pains him, he excuses the use of "pork" as an insult: "in

Jamaica with its miasmic colonial past, with its lingering ill-will of racial and class prejudice . . . the urchin who screams 'pork' at a passing white man or woman is crudely about the business of redressing old sins" (p. 158). A few lines down, Winkler relates the explanation of a colleague about the origin of the term: the fat lying beneath the rind of roast pork is "ghastly and rheumy like congealed egg white" (p. 159).

Ghastly and rheumy: earlier in the book, we recall, Winkler says that as a white Jamaican schoolboy, he was "painfully aware of being clothed in a loathsome skin" (p. 111). So this ghastly and rheumy, loathsome skin becomes a source of great pain, possibly an index of white self-hatred. Indeed, white self-hatred may contribute towards Winkler's eagerness – reading occasionally as obsessiveness – to blame colonialism for Jamaica's societal wrongs in *Going Home:* in so doing he, as an unwilling representative of the white oppressor, may be blaming his own kind.

In a piece entitled "The Looks That Blind Us", Winkler opens with a description of his parental family: "None of us look Jamaican. We're all ghastly white with lanky hair and Caucasian features."[24] Winkler obviously uses the word "ghastly" to be provocative (and the word may have been in his mind since he may well have been proofreading *Going Home* when he wrote this piece). Nevertheless it is interesting that he chooses here to repeat the word used by his colleague in her memorable explanation of "pork".

Both in Atlanta and in Jamaica, then, Winkler seemingly has to prove that he is not a "bogus Jamaican" (p. 162), that he "born and grow nowhere else but here in Jamaica!" (p. 173). But in Jamaica the rejection by his countrymen is much more painful: "The hardest thing about growing up white in a black country is the nagging feeling of not belonging" (p. 76).

> "You not a Jamaican" [says a young boy who has observed Winkler looking at his old family home in Montego Bay and been told that he used to live there].
>
> "I was born in Kingston Public Hospital," I said angrily. "I went to Cornwall College, right here in Montego Bay. I lived in that house for seven years."
>
> "You not a Jamaican," he repeated stubbornly. "You a white man."
>
> This was too much to bear in front of the very house in which I had spent so much of my childhood.
>
> "I'm a rass claat Jamaican!" I snapped. . . .
>
> The boy was unmoved. "Any white man can learn bad word from book," he said scornfully. (p. 76)

Given, on the one hand, Winkler's rejection of America and Americans, clearly established in *Going Home,* and, on the other hand, his rejection by Jamaicans (or at least those Jamaicans by whom he wants to be accepted – the black majority), his dilemma of unbelonging becomes all the more poignant. Yet he is buoyed by his love of his country. "[I]t was the land itself that I loved, and even if my own people despised me on sight, nothing they said or did could lessen this raw blood love, this passion I felt for my homeland" (p. 163). These words, taken in isolation, could allow for a misreading, whereby Winkler is categorized as a typical alienated white West Indian, conforming to the stereotype implied by Kenneth Ramchand in his interpretation of Rhys, Allfrey and others: where the attachment is to the land, not the people.[25] However, throughout *Going Home,* as well as in his novels, Winkler has clearly established his love not only for the land but also for the people.

"[I]n Jamaica, black is not always black, nor is white always white" (p. 78). When Winkler makes this statement, his main focus seems to be the type of black Jamaican who identifies with the white English cultural model and distances himself from his fellow black man. On the same page he suggests that blackness in Jamaica is more a way of being than a colour. However, on the next page he says, "I, who had been born white, had internalized a black [identity]" (p. 79). As a result, his earlier statements take on greater significance.

Undoubtedly, growing up as part of a visible and hated white minority in a black country had a lot to do with Winkler's internalization of a black identity, as did the author's obvious artistic sensitivities, moral conscience, and socio-historical awareness. *Going Home* makes this clear. What it also makes clear, however, is that Winkler's own family background played a large role.

White as his family was, they were also poor. Winkler's great-grandfather had established a very successful music import business with "the only music store on the island" on King Street in downtown Kingston (p. 11), but his son, Winkler's grandfather the aspiring novelist, was a careless businessman and "lost [the business] to a junior clerk who plundered the books while [he] was globetrotting on an extravagant spending spree" (p. 1). Bankruptcy followed, and Grandfather Winkler ended his days in a small rented wooden house on Jacques Road.

Grandfather's children, Winkler's father and aunt, were nevertheless on a much higher social scale than that of Winkler's mother, whose family was merely of Lebanese trader stock and therefore excluded from the mainstream of planter-class genteel respectability – into which Winkler's great-grandfather had gained acceptance two generations earlier, resulting in his offspring being "smugly encased in the prejudices and airs of the landed gentry" although "in fact they owned little land" (p. 11).

> My father's family regarded my mother's as vulgar shopkeepers. It was one thing to be an importer of pianos from Europe and to sell these refined instruments to the best households in Jamaica and another to go jiggling through town hawking cloth to the poor from the back of a donkey. (pp. 12–13)

Although Winkler's mother's three brothers eventually became successful businessmen with stores of their own (albeit "dirty shops on the side of town where the poor congregated" [p. 13]), this wealth was never extended to the women in the family, who were expected to marry "well" – meaning, ideally, to marry someone handpicked from among the Jamaican-Lebanese population, but if not, hopefully someone rich, and definitely someone white.

Winkler's mother satisfied only the last criterion in marrying Winkler's father, who presumably made up for his other shortcomings by being of high social standing, with the consequent potential to make good use of the business opportunities that Grandfather Winkler had squandered. But, in fact, Winkler's father was an even worse businessman than Grandfather. Winkler, born at Victoria Jubilee Hospital (a part of Kingston Public Hospital) on 25 February 1942, grew up in poverty. The family would eventually contain eight children; Winkler was the second. For most of Winkler's childhood his father could barely support them on his low salary as a car tyre salesman, working for John Crook.[26] Winkler's mother supplemented the household income by growing and selling callaloo.[27] Winkler spent his early years in a rented house on Mountain View Avenue which was owned by Marcus Garvey's wife, Amy Jacques Garvey (in retrospect, a symbolic and fitting arrangement, given Winkler's political, social and racial sensitivities).[28] The house was just down the road (literally, this time) from his grandfather's. He attended a primary school run by a Mrs Simpson, and then Excelsior Primary School for a year.[29]

Then fortune smiled on the family. Winkler's father was promoted to the position of regional manager for the western parishes, and sent to Montego Bay to head the branch there. The family moved to Montego Bay in 1950, and for seven years they enjoyed a lifestyle of privilege and wealth: "My father owned a sailboat, belonged to the yacht club, and we lived in a big house overlooking the ocean. We were white, upper-crust, and seemingly well off" (p. 214). Memories of that period would form the basis for Winkler's first-written Jamaican-based novel, *The Great Yacht Race*; in fact, the memory of Baba, the prototype for the hero of his first published novel, *The Painted Canoe,* also came from that period.

In an interview, Winkler relates his memories of Baba:

> [W]hen we moved to Montego Bay I was eight years old and there was a cave behind our house and we discovered that . . . this fisherman . . . was keeping his nets there and his fishing equipment. . . . [H]e came hat in hand to my father and said you know, I use this cave as a storage area sir, do you mind? and my father said no man, go ahead – his name was Baba and as a child I always . . . used to ask him, "Baba, take me fishing with you nuh man", and . . . he'd always say "You too young to go fishing with me, you too young." . . . He looks exactly the way Zachariah is described. Now, he died when I was about ten, he had a heart attack and all of a sudden he disappeared from our lives, from *my* life, and the week after he died somebody came . . . and cleaned out the cave . . . took his canoe and that was the end of that. I was just aghast that this man could just disappear off the face of the earth as if he had never existed. No marker, no memorial. . . . Even at that age I was just stunned. . . . So I like to think that even though Baba didn't take me fishing I took him fishing when I became a man and wrote *The Painted Canoe.*[30]

(It should be noted that Baba may not have disappeared *completely* off the face of the earth, as his ghost apparently made itself heard on the property for some nights after his death – see *Going Home,* 43.)

Winkler has other memories of that period in Montego Bay, ones which for the most part have not appeared – at least as directly – on the pages of his books to date: "I have many unpleasant memories of a drunken father roaring in the drawing room, and a terrified mother shrieking from a doorway."[31] Such memories are only hinted at in *Going Home:*

I had seen [my father] injured many times, usually because of something rash that he did while he was drunk, and I had even seen him in a wheelchair nursing a broken leg he suffered after kicking a solid mahogany door behind which my mother was hiding to escape his drunken rage. (p. 195)

And, earlier, he mentions a car accident in which his father, "in a drunken stupor", "rammed [a] telephone pole because he thought [his passenger] had been having an affair with [his] mother" (p. 23). Not mentioned in *Going Home* is Winkler's recollection of walking home from Cornwall College and being taunted by prostitutes who would shout, "Winkler, boy, I pick up you poopa last night."[32] (So Winkler's father may have been at least in part, then, the prototype for the drunken, prostitute-friendly Fritzie in *The Great Yacht Race*.) For a sensitive young adolescent, such taunts were unbearable. Winkler decided that he was not going back to school; forced to by his mother, he stopped working. His grades dropped from A to F; he became a rebel.

It was around this time, he relates, that he "started taking racial pricks personally"[33] – as referred to in *Going Home* when he recalls being attacked by street urchins because he was white, and not fighting back because he felt he deserved their abuse (p. 16). He hated his English schoolmasters for "riding roughshod over Jamaicans", and once cursed an Englishman in the street – who turned out to be a teacher at his school.[34] Winkler was eventually expelled from school at the age of fourteen, as noted earlier, for refusing a caning – and although the headmaster eventually retracted his position, Winkler refused to go back. (Given this history of rebelliousness on his part, and explosive impulsiveness on his father's part, it is easy to understand the troublemaker side of Winkler that reveals itself from time to time in *Going Home to Teach*, for example in his altercations with the vice principal over student representatives [p. 51] and the giving of a sermon at assembly [p. 100], or in his goading of the older teachers [pp. 209–10], and the rashness of his action in resigning from the college in a burst of fury over the principal's apparent maliciousness.)

Meanwhile, following his father's example, the young Winkler befriended the whores on the street and started drinking too. At this time his father had started a business on the side, wherein he would travel from one rural district to the next with a movie projector and mount film shows on weekends.

Winkler would travel with him, and recalls that his father increased his drinking, took on local women, and fought their boyfriends. He remembers people stoning them on occasion, and remembers also frequent, vicious fights between the cultivators and their women. He comments, "A lot of my material is from these memories."[35]

The movie business was doing well, but Winkler's father began to spend more than he had. "He bought a Doozleburg, a glass-bottom boat", as well as the boat on which the description of *She Two* in *The Great Yacht Race* is based, and "money from the cinema got mixed up with money from the job".[36] The anecdote related in *Going Home* about the uncle who was saved from a charge of embezzlement by the happy circumstance of a burglary which concealed the uncle's misdeeds was actually closer to home, and Winkler's father's employers eventually caught on, and fired him. (In fact, charges were not pressed only because an American priest drove to Kingston to the head office of John Crook and pleaded for leniency[37] – another fore-shadowing of *The Great Yacht Race*.)

Winkler's father got a low-paying job in Kingston selling tractors, and died suddenly of a heart attack one year later, in 1958, at the age of forty-four. The family – with baby number eight on the way – was plummeted into poverty:

> We had been living hand to mouth ever since he'd lost his last job, were lodged in a rented house in Kingston, and owned nothing except the clothes on our backs and a few worn sticks of furniture. . . . [F]ather . . . left us so poor that we could not even afford to bury him. (*Going Home*, 197)

Two days after his death the rent came due (p. 197), and there was no money to pay it. But fortunately Winkler's maternal grandfather had left a provision in his will that the family home on Kensington Crescent "should always be available to unmarried or widowed daughters in need" (p. 95) – so on the same day that the rent was due, Winkler's family moved from Dillon Avenue to share the family home with Winkler's maiden aunt (represented as mad Aunt Petulia in *Going Home*). There Winkler remained, working along with his older brother to support his mother and siblings, until his migration to the United States in 1962.

Winkler's formative years in Jamaica, then, were an on-the-edge exis-tence, with financial security being an alien thing, family stability nearly as alien – in short, a life bereft of all the luxuries and sheltering commonly assumed to be a part of the Jamaican white or middle-class lifestyle. Except for those in that seven-year period in Montego Bay, most of his neighbours were black and lower middle class or poor. Even in those prosperous years, although his family socialized with the Fritzie/Angwin/O'Hara types, he himself not only continued to have his many black friends ("dear Mando, and dear Errol, and dear George, and dear Tom, Dick and Harry", not to mention dear Doris or dear Josephine [p. 103], as he recalls when accused by his radical socialist colleague Raymond of basing his boyhood friendships on a congenital desire to lord it over nonwhites), but also socialized with street urchins and street whores. And from all of this, as well as from following his father from rural district to rural district with his movie projector, he formed an impression of the common Jamaican folk – sometimes unruly and violent, usually hardworking but very poor, full of real life – that would take root in all his future creative endeavours.

Winkler's Jamaican reality, then, coincided with that of the black and poor. His family ties on his father's and mother's sides did not affect this. As *Going Home* shows, his paternal grandfather lived a hand-to-mouth existence, raised chickens, and chased black women. His father's relatives distanced themselves from his father, with his Lebanese wife and his brood of eight children, because they considered him to have married beneath their status.

Meanwhile Winkler himself was clearly, as we see in *Going Home,* unimpressed by his mother's family, especially his maternal grandfather and his uncles, whom he regarded as vulgar ("mammon and racehorse ruled supreme over music and books" [p. 13]), backward, narrow-minded, racist and hypocritical ("The idea of their ugly sister sleeping with a black man would have driven her protective brothers berserk even though most of them kept black mistresses on the side" [p. 94]). Their distancing of themselves from the land of their birth irritated him considerably:

> As I came to know them these uncles seemed to me to be the most dreamless creatures men could become. Haggling with poor Jamaicans over pennies had made them stingy, avaricious and incapable of understanding anything that was not visible or had no price. They owned racehorses and gambled wantonly on weekends, but they were tight-fisted and mean with their riches. They lived in wonderful houses, sent their children to the best schools abroad, and no one persecuted them

for their Christian beliefs. Yet they despised the country that had made all this possible and were openly contemptuous of the poor black people from whom they earned their daily bread. . . . [T]hey would rather a child of theirs had been stillborn than grow up to marry into a family that was not white. (p. 11)

These uncles, remaining on the periphery of the closed Anglo-Saxon/Jewish elite Jamaican society no matter how successful their businesses, yet denying any connections with the larger society, thus encasing themselves in a claustrophobic little world of their own, seem to have been the antithesis of a role model for the young Winkler. It is telling that none of his novels feature any character resembling them – except for the briefly appearing Mr Saarem, the Syrian graveyard proprietor in *The Lunatic*.[38] With the exception of his beloved, eccentric paternal grandfather, and possibly the "cultured uncle-in-law" (p. 266) who had encouraged his writing (p. 5), Winkler's role models were not to be found in his family, or in the world of white Jamaica with which he had had a seven-year encounter.

In *Going Home* one of the tutors at the college suggests that for a white man he is "certainly peculiar", and the others jump to his defence: "There isn't a white bone in Tony's body"; "Him only look white. But him definitely not white"; "I know lots of families in Kingston much whiter than Tony" (p. 170). As ludicrous as this is on one level, on another level, given his background, it makes sense. It reminds us of Honor Ford-Smith's childhood revelation: White is not a colour. And it confirms Winkler's own statement: "I had internalized a black identity."

On the other hand, *Going Home* also suggests the influence of Winkler's Lebanese relatives in another direction. Madness, as has been observed elsewhere in this book, is a recurrent theme in Winkler's works, with a madman featuring, obviously, in *The Lunatic,* but with others making cameo appearances in *The Painted Canoe,* in *The Great Yacht Race,* and again in *Going Home.* There is also the picture of societal madness, drawn most vividly in *The Lunatic,* but also in *The Duppy* (this time looking at American society), with occasional sketches of mad societal quirks in the other novels (like the prime minister's eight-hour speeches). In *Going Home* Jamaica is referred to by the author's brother as "dis damn madhouse" (p. 46) (reminding one of that line in the courtroom scene of *The Lunatic:* "Lemme out of dis damn madhouse!"), and incidents such as Winkler's visit to the Ministry of Education in an attempt to sort out his back pay certainly support this view. Nothing does this more, however, than Winkler's vivid and distressingly accurate portrayal of the elementary schools visited by tutors and students as part of the college's final-year assessment of student-teacher performances: where a cacophony of sounds, all competing for dominance in one large space which has been divided into seven or eight classes without any interior walls, renders all learning impossible. (Clearly Winkler's description of the village school in *The Lunatic* is taken directly from such memories.)

> Instead of arming our students with practical schemes . . . that would permit at least a modicum of teaching to take place in these overcrowded and blaring class-rooms, we had spent a whole year bandying about the sophistries of grammar and punctuation. . . . We had been playing tutors but hadn't taught a single lesson that was applicable (p. 246). . . . I'd wasted a whole year . . . on trivialities when I might have been devising guerrilla tactics that would allow lessons to be taught even in the madhouse. (p. 247)

As often as it is directly stated, madness is indirectly implied in Winkler's descriptions of societal conditions in *Going Home.* The dependency of the Chest Hospital on one handyman to fix essential life-saving equipment by giving it "a stout whack" with a stone (p. 65) may have been intellectualized by the author, as stated earlier, as being a consequence of British colonialist semi-education, but it is certainly madness (and so this memory makes a fitting contribution to Winkler's depiction of societal lunacy in *The Lunatic,* translated to Busha's experience in St Ann's Bay Hospital). And surely one of the most memorable, yet unstated, suggestions of societal madness is to be found in that delightful "down de road" anecdote (pp. 179–86), in which a simple attempt to get something fixed takes one along a labyrinthine trail all over the countryside, in search of "one indispensable little man planted by a mischievous providence in a far-flung place" (p. 179); halfway through which the reader, chuckling by now, is told, "You laugh, but this is no joke" (p. 183); and in the last part of which Winkler, as past victim of down-de-road mischief and current victim of post-down-de-road paranoia, is now himself behaving rather strangely (read madly) at the car rental counter.

Culture shock can indeed, as Winkler says, "affect those suffering from it in the oddest ways" (p. 186) – suggesting that the author, having been sent "down de road", may also have been driven "round de bend".

The prevalence of madness and madhouse motifs takes on added significance when we realize from reading *Going Home* that madness in fact runs in Winkler's family. Two of his mother's sisters are portrayed as being mad: the repressed, sex-starved, frustrated Aunt Petulia whose life is a cycle consisting of "a torpor of listlessness" (p. 95) broken by occasional sexual dalliances with any passing man off the street, followed by shock treatments at St Joseph's Hospital, followed by more listlessness; and the physically abused Aunt Sophia, who becomes "hopelessly mad" (p. 10) as a result of her husband's "brutal mistreatment", and whose firstborn son, also abused, "went berserk in his teens, was committed to the insane asylum and eventually died there" (p. 9). In his accounting of the fates of the "slurry of aunts and uncles inherited from my mother's side", he states that after he left Jamaica "[m]adness struck at least three of them and for years they stumbled over the land in occasional dementia" (pp. 265–66). Not revealed in *Going Home* is the fact that two of Winkler's siblings are also mentally ill: his youngest sister is retarded and schizophrenic, and his youngest brother is also schizophrenic.

Madness and the madhouse, then, have featured so integrally in Winkler's life as to be almost common and everyday. Thus, on one level Winkler's frequent usage of such references may have no greater significance than that they are for him just that: common and everyday. Yet on another level the motifs of madness and the madhouse must inevitably take on deep personal significance – causing us, for example, to look again at the issue of madness versus sanity, of who madder than who, raised by Winkler in *The Lunatic*.

The portrayal of American society as mad in *The Duppy* is an echo – albeit amplified – of a similar portrayal in *Going Home*. Southern California is certainly portrayed as being at the very least "slightly demented" (p. 20). America is seen as a landlady, and Winkler's experiences of bizarre American landladies include one who spoke in a gibberish; one, seemingly schizophrenic, who was fussy and exacting by day but "every Friday night would come hammering drunkenly at my door demanding violent lovemaking"; and one who "went mad at nights, practising fellatio on her youthful lodgers while . . . she tried, vainly, to simultaneously mouth favourite biblical passages, but who in the daylight hours was an inspector of mental hospitals in Southern California" (pp. 25–26). In other forums Winkler is more blunt: Southern California, he tells Donal Black, is "a madhouse".[39] And in a radio interview: "When you migrate you feel like you are in a madhouse."[40] As someone wisely observes in *Going Home,* "foreign living madden up de brain of Jamaica man, you know" (p. 185).

No wonder, then, that Winkler chooses to follow the example of the previous three generations of his family – *not* on his mother's side – who have demonstrated "an honourable impulse of love for country" (p. 13) by deciding to live in Jamaica.

By leaving America to go back home to Jamaica, and by taking his new-found love Cathy with him, he also more directly follows the example of his grandfather, who was so homesick for Jamaica that "he couldn't get [the smell of naseberries] out of his nose. Everywhere he went . . . it haunted him", and so he "chose to go home and end his days in the place where his life had begun" (p. 8), taking his American wife with him.

But Grandfather's wife never adjusted to Jamaica. She grew steadily more miserable over the years, "flew into tantrums and raged with discontent at the drop of a pin" (p. 8). She "suffered homesickness all her life" (p. 84), "[u]nhappily transplanted for life to Jamaica" (p. 199). While her husband was alive he could not afford to send her home for a visit (p. 84), and when he died she was unable to return home and so "lingered unhappily for some fifteen years after Grandfather's death. She became impossible to live with, a chronic complainer who moaned endlessly about her loneliness and troubles." Buried in a cemetery at Matilda's Corner, beside "Grandfather where he belonged, Grandmother [was] webbed forever in a land she hated" (p. 267).

Yet Winkler's grandmother was initially excited at the prospect of going to Jamaica. In photos "on the deck of a ship bound for Jamaica" her "eyes are shining with excitement at the adventure of life abroad that lies ahead of her" (p. 81). Cathy, too, initially transported by the intoxication of new love, insists on following Winkler home despite his warnings: "She vowed that she would adjust. It didn't take too much argument to win me over" (p. 24). Her apprehensions grow when she hears all the dire warnings from Jamaicans in Miami; Winkler's perspective of the Jamaican landscape on the first night of their arrival, referred to earlier (clawing/gnawing/thundering/plunging/rotting [pp. 35–36]), is surely coloured by her nervousness. But when they are house-hunting in Moneague/Longstreet and find a house that Winkler fears may be too isolated,

> "I love it," Cathy whispered at my side.
> "It's very lonely," I said.
> "I love it," she repeated. (p. 40)

But she does find the house lonely, and she does not adjust. In contrast to her husband's joy at being home,

> there was no joy in Cathy. . . . The house was too small to occupy her days and when I was away at school she sat alone and idle on the hilltop surrounded by the beauty and stillness of a land that was foreign to her. There was no telephone. . . .
>
> But mainly she was suffering from the lonely isolation of the stranger. She did not understand the people she lived among. . . . She had only a dim grasp of patois. . . .
>
> But what she found especially difficult was the obvious attention her white skin provoked wherever she went. . . . Often the stares were resentful and hostile, but mainly they were inquisitive or probing. . . . To be white in a black country . . . is to be separated from that inalienable birthright every white American enjoys in his country: the expectation of being treated with indifference in a public place. . . .
>
> Bewildered and hurt, Cathy began to slowly withdraw inside herself. (pp. 74–75)

Finding a job eases the loneliness to some extent, but Cathy is disturbed by the fact that it was obviously offered to her because she is white (p. 86). She is unhappy that she and Winkler are not married (p. 146); so they – with some difficulty – get married, which makes her happier. However: "She was troubled by the poverty around us . . . by the nicks and dents of scarcity and inconvenience" (p. 158). Then there are "the mosquitoes, the cow ticks, the sandflies, and the fleas" (p. 144) – and the sandflies are "Cathy's nemesis" (p. 145), biting her so badly one day at the beach that they have to go to a doctor in Kingston the next day. Rats seem to thrive on American rat poison, and when a rat is accidentally roasted in the oven, Cathy seems to be near breaking point (p. 228).

Winkler's attitude is never openly unsupportive or impatient, although he has warned her from the beginning that "even raw Kingstonians who had lived in Jamaica all their lives found the countryside harsh and depriving" (p. 24); that their cottage would be lonely; that sandflies may be neither seen nor heard but still present: " 'This used to be a swamp,' I told her uneasily" (p. 145). She is "troubled by the occasional racial insult in the streets" (p. 158), but he uses the word "occasional" and notes elsewhere, as quoted above, that although she "often" encountered hostility, "mainly" the stares were inquisitive or probing (p. 75).

Yet he loves her deeply; he understands her sense of alienation in Jamaica because this is exactly how he has felt in America, and because he remembers the fate of his grandmother. So that when he says, "It must have been hard for Grandmother to spend her life in a land she did not love, among people she only dimly understood. It must have been harder still to age, grow feeble, and die in that faraway and foreign place among a race of strangers" (p. 84), it is clear that he is not only speaking with compassion about his grand-mother, he is speaking about Cathy, and an understanding of either one feeds the other. It is clear, too, that his repeated references to his grand-mother's burning of her husband's unfinished manuscript indicate that such an act of vengeance, such a display of bitterness, as a consequence of years of deep unhappiness, is etched deeply in his mind.

So when Winkler decides – impulsively, rashly, some might say unjustifi-ably – to quit his job abruptly and return to America, it is again clear that the reason presented by the author (the principal's act of treachery) is not the only reason. Nor are the frustrating occurrences of the preceding weeks: the visits to the schools, the visit to the Ministry of Education. And Winkler's careful framing of this book, with references to his grandfather and grand-mother at the beginning, at the end, and with frequent insertions in between, seems to be Winkler's conscious or subconscious means of convey-ing the message that he gave up the happiness of being in the country he loved in order to ensure the happiness of the woman he loved – that ulti-mately he did it for Cathy.

On the very last page of the book Winkler discusses his grandfather's writ-ing of his novel, his dithering over the ending and his final supposed selection of a happy one in which the two lovers are reconciled, an ending which Winkler believes he must have selected because "[h]e would have chosen love. He would have chosen life" (p. 268). These are Winkler's last words on the matter. But the last thoughts in the reader's mind may be the following: Grandfather chose love of country. Life for him meant life in his beloved country. But life became miserable because of his unhappy wife, and so on his deathbed he cursed God; and after his death his wife destroyed the novel he had written. Winkler chooses love of his woman. Life for him means life with a happy partner, even in a country he dislikes. Winkler decides that the misery of living away from the land and people he loves cannot compare to the misery of living with a wife whose unhappiness he has caused. And he goes back to America.

In a letter dated six years after his return to America, Winkler wrote: "Jamaica is a bone in my throat; I pine for her like a lover with an unfaithful mistress."[41] Compromise for Winkler, in making his wife happy, has meant frequent visits to this unfaithful mistress: "Odd things always seem to be popping about me in the United States, and I must periodically run home to Jamaica for a taste of normalcy."[42] Visits to his homeland take place by plane, as well as via his imagination. Since his year in Jamaica in 1975–76, Winkler has written many novels (and short stories), all Jamaican. Included are two novels, *Dog War* and *The Crocodile,* which at the time of writing are scheduled for imminent publication.

The Crocodile, written after *The Duppy,* follows the trend of that novel in that it laughs at some of the absurdities of organized religion while affirming God's love. According to the author it tells the story of "a woman at her wits' end":[44] Josephine, angry at God for the suffering she has had to endure, and for the failure of her attempt to end her misery by inviting the local crocodile to devour her, decides to take her revenge on Him. *Dog War,* written earlier, is a somewhat bizarre story set in Miami, where the Jamaican protagonist, Precious, has come to work as a housekeeper, having migrated after her husband's death. She finds America very strange, especially when she realizes that her real job is to be maid to the pampered house dog. According to the author, the theme of the novel is "a parody of the goofy tendency of the

American animal rights movement to anthropomorphize animals".[45] Precious fights the strangeness of America by battling with the house pet (while in Winkler's short story "The Annihilation of Fish", the lonely, and slightly demented, Jamaican migrant Fish battles with the devil himself).[46]

For Winkler, then, America is bizarre, and Jamaica is a bone in the throat, an unfaithful mistress. The lot of an immigrant is not a happy one; one is a victim of the "neither-fish-nor-fowl syndrome that immigrants inevitably suffer in both their host and native countries" (p. 102). In America he will always be subjected to the quizzical observation, "Funny, you don't look Jamaican" (as he notes in his piece "The Looks That Blind Us"); meanwhile in Jamaica he will always be subjected to such rejection as that of the little boy in Montego Bay who declares, "You not a Jamaican. . . . You a white man" (p. 76). However, as he says in a 1990 interview, "My essence is Jamaican, and I will never be anything else but Jamaican. And anywhere else I live other than Jamaica, I will automatically be an expatriate, because my home is Jamaica."[47] In another interview, in 1993, Winkler sounds more resigned than comfortable about his choice of country of residence:

> I do love Jamaica . . . when you're an expatriate you become so enmeshed in the society you're living in . . . economically . . . emotionally . . . in terms of the duty you have as a citizen . . . basically financially and it becomes very hard to go back where you came from . . . until your life has reached a certain plateau. Because the economic consequences of my moving back to Jamaica are incalculable. . . . How would I make a living? . . . It's very hard to make a living as a writer if you're living in Jamaica.[48]

Nevertheless, a recent article by Winkler about Atlanta suggests that he is beginning to come to terms with living in America – or at least in Atlanta. "I am not an Atlantan. I am a Jamaican", the piece begins, yet Winkler acknowledges that Atlanta is "as lovely and livable a city as exists anywhere on the face of the earth".[49] Winkler says that "for all its gruff skyscrapers, Atlanta remains surprisingly personal, almost tender in its dealings with its citizens", and suggests that such tenderness may have originated after Atlanta, previously "arrogant, overweening . . . utterly callous to the misery it had inflicted on another race", was humbled in the Civil War, after which, "the city rose painfully from the rubble. . . . Atlantans remind me of a reformed bully who had learned such a bitter lesson behind the woodshed that forever after he feels compelled to put on his best Sunday manners for the world" (p. 66).

Winkler is quick to say that Atlanta, with its fair share of contemptible racists, is no paradise. Yet he seems to suggest that somehow this city (unlike, say, New York – "hell is New York," he says [p. 66], reminding one immediately of *The Duppy*) has somehow transcended its Americanness. "Jamaica is my mother," Winkler says, "but Atlanta is now my home. When I move from here I'll either go to heaven or back to Mummy" (p. 66).

So Winkler's compromise, then, may have worked. Thirty years after his return to America, he remains happily married to Cathy, and resident in a city that he likes. And he is comfortable there: "In America, no one gives you a second glance."[50] He makes enough money as a writer of textbooks – something he could never have done in Jamaica – to be able to visit home at least once a year, where his novels have achieved immense popularity, and his work is gaining literary respect. He may not have remained in the physical environment where the language of his heart is spoken, but over the course of his eight books he has located the creative environment which enables him to write from the heart.

For the sensitive immigrant, "the penalty of dislocation from his native culture" is a perpetual "sense of disorientation, a gnawing sense of things not being quite right", we recall that Winkler said (p. 115). So Winkler's compromise in one sense will always remain just that. Yet in another sense it may eventually turn out to be not a compromise, but a way of achieving the best of both worlds – as his grandfather might have done.

The information that this book would be looking at Winkler as a white West Indian writer was greeted with some impatience by that author: "I don't consider myself as a white writer," we recall that he said, somewhat testily. "I consider myself as a writer."[51]

A similar sort of impatience was encountered with a number of other writers interviewed for this study: Robert Antoni, Michelle Cliff and Pauline Melville, all of whom, in one way or another, emphasized that they too reject such superficial labelling, preferring instead to embrace notions of hybridity – notions which, in the case of Antoni and Melville, may possibly be romanticized.[52]

"My heart is not black but not white either," Winkler has said,[53] a view which seemingly supports the position of hybridity; we are reminded of Antonio Benítez-Rojo's earlier quoted statement that in the Caribbean, skin colour pertains to no fixed race. This lack of fixed definition allows for a dissolving of barriers, a process which is undoubtedly necessary as well as ideal for all West Indians of all colours in the Caribbean of the new millennium. Perhaps for many white West Indian writers, however, such dissolving also counters the sense of marginalization, enables an escape from collective guilt, and allows one access to the best of both worlds.

Yet Winkler stands apart from these other writers of white/near-white/hybrid identity. For, to return to the point raised at the beginning of this study, unlike these other writers, Winkler is often taken by his readers to be black. This is because Winkler, unlike the others, writes not white, near-white or hybrid, but black. Winkler departs from the stereotype of the white or near-white West Indian voice in its different generational manifestations, from the terrified consciousness and anguish of the earlier writers to the now seemingly fashionable embracing of hybridity shown by some of Winkler's contemporaries. Unlike these other writers, Winkler does not retain a white or near-white voice. Winkler not only transcends but subverts the planter legacy that is an inevitable part of his Jamaican whiteness by choosing not to invest in this whiteness, by instead immersing himself creatively in a black identity. And, as has been shown in earlier chapters, Winkler succeeds: he sounds black.

The above statement must immediately be qualified, because it is not an all-encompassing blackness *per se* that Winkler embraces. In fact, in his view the prevalence of black protagonists in his works is incidental: "Someone asked me how I always write about black people. I don't do this. I am writing about Jamaicans." He relates that early in his career he realized that he "should write about matters that [he] know[s] about". In order to write successfully, he maintains, "[y]ou have to live it. If it's not in the bone you can't write it." Winkler writes about black people because they are the people that he knows. "The people I grew up with were black."[54]

The people that Winkler grew up with, at least those whose personalities etched themselves most forcefully on his mind in his formative years, were not only black but poor black. Nor were they only family servants, unlike the few blacks depicted in the works of the other white West Indian writers surveyed in this study; they were his friends. In writing about poor black Jamaicans, those who make up the majority of the country's population, and in doing so with familiarity rather than distance, Winkler transmits the pulse of his country. And in so doing, as has been suggested in an earlier chapter, more so than any other white/near-white/hybrid West Indian writer, Winkler approaches the possibility of a creole authenticity spoken of thirty years ago by Edward Kamau Brathwaite. As Winkler has said, "If you are not true to yourself, language is going to trip you up. . . . Be truthful to yourself. If you have any talent, it will come out on the page."[55]

❧

Notes

Introduction

1. Anthony C. Winkler, *The Painted Canoe* (Kingston: Kingston Publishers, 1983). Subsequent references appear parenthetically in the text.
2. Winkler, *The Lunatic* (Kingston: Kingston Publishers; Secaucus, N.J.: Lyle Stuart, 1987). Subsequent references appear parenthetically in the text.
3. *Concise Oxford Dictionary*, tenth edition.
4. Winkler, *The Great Yacht Race* (Kingston: Kingston Publishers, 1992). Subsequent references appear parenthetically in the text.
5. Winkler, *The Duppy* (Kingston: Kingston Publishers, 1997). Subsequent references appear parenthetically in the text.
6. *Concise Oxford Dictionary*, tenth edition.
7. Winkler, *Going Home to Teach* (Kingston: Kingston Publishers, 1995). Subsequent references appear parenthetically in the text.
8. The copublisher was Lyle Stuart Inc.
9. Winkler, *The Annihilation of Fish and Other Stories* (Oxford: Macmillan, 2004). Subsequent references appear parenthetically in the text.

Chapter 1

1. Winkler, interview by author, Atlanta, Georgia, 14 July 1996.
2. An intriguing demonstration of this over-zestful categorization is shown by Mary Louise Pratt in *Imperial Eyes: Travel Writing and Transculturation* (London and New York: Routledge, 1992), 24–37.
3. George Lipsitz, *The Possessive Investment in Whiteness: How White People Profit from Identity Politics* (Philadelphia: Temple University Press, 1998), 2.
4. Sidney W. Mintz, "Ethnic Difference, Plantation Sameness", in *Ethnicity in the Caribbean,* ed. Gert Oostindie, Warwick University Caribbean Studies (London: Macmillan Caribbean, 1996), 41.

5. H. Hoetink, " 'Race' and Color in the Caribbean", in *Caribbean Contours,* ed. Sidney W. Mintz and Sally Price (Baltimore and London: Johns Hopkins University Press, 1985), 82.

6. Pauline Melville, "Beyond the Pale", in *Daughters of Africa: An International Anthology of Words and Writings by Women of African Descent from the Ancient Egyptian to the Present,* ed. Margaret Busby (London: Cape; New York: Pantheon Books, 1992), 740.

7. In his groundbreaking work on race and ethnicity in the Caribbean, Hoetink, according to Gert Oostindie, "emphasized time and again the socially construed psychological dimension to perceptions and definitions of 'race' " (Oostindie, "Introduction: Ethnicity, as Ever?", in *Ethnicity in the Caribbean,* 4).

8. Antonio Benítez-Rojo, "Three Words Toward Creolization", in *Caribbean Creolization: Reflections on the Cultural Dynamics of Language, Literature and Identity,* ed. Kathleen M. Balutansky and Marie-Agnes Sourieau (Gainesville: University Press of Florida; Kingston: The Press, University of the West Indies, 1998), 58.

9. Benítez-Rojo, "Three Words Toward Creolization", 61.

10. Glyne Griffith, *Deconstruction, Imperialism and the West Indian Novel* (Kingston: The Press, University of the West Indies, 1996), 25.

11. Michael Omi and Howard Winant, *Racial Formation in the United States: From the 1960s to the 1990s* (London and New York: Routledge, 1994), 24. It should be noted that the term "race", historically used in some contexts to refer simply to ancestry, or to compare the attributes of, say, the English versus the Irish races (David R. Roediger, *The Wages of Whiteness: Race and the Making of the American Working Class* [London and New York: Verso, 1991], 133), has also long had class dimensions: "British upper classes also regarded their own working class as almost a race apart, and claimed that they had darker skin and hair than themselves" (Jan Nederveen Pieterse, *White on Black: Images of Africa and Blacks in Western Popular Culture* [New Haven and London: Yale University Press, 1992], 215). Pieterse argues that not only were " 'race' and 'nation'. . . synonymous until fairly recently" (p. 214) but also, perhaps more fundamentally, "class distinctions were biologized" (p. 219).

12. Lipsitz, *Possessive Investment,* 2.

13. Philip D. Curtin, *Two Jamaicas: The Role of Ideas in a Tropical Colony, 1830–1865* (Cambridge, Mass.: Harvard University Press, 1955).

14. M.G. Smith, "Ethnic and Cultural Pluralism in the British Caribbean", in *The Plural Society in the British West Indies* (1965; reprint, Kingston: Sangster's Book Stores; Berkeley and Los Angeles: University of California Press, 1974), 10–17.

15. See, for example, Charles Mills, "Race and Class: Conflicting or Reconcilable Paradigms?", *Social and Economic Studies* 36, no. 2 (1987): 69–108.

16. See, for example, Carol S. Holzberg, *Minorities and Power in a Black Society: The Jewish Community of Jamaica* (Lanham, Md.: North-South Publishing, 1987); or R.T. Smith, "Race and Class in the Post-Emancipation Caribbean", in *Racism and Colonialism: Essays on Ideology and Social Structure,* ed. Robert Ross (The Hague: Martinus Nijhoff, Publications of the Leiden Centre for the History of European Expansion, 1982), 93–119. In a study focusing on Jamaica, Smith observes that "even when . . . barriers to occupational mobility have been weakened or broken down, racial identification continues to cut across class and to distort incipient class solidarities" (p. 114).

17. Frantz Fanon, *The Wretched of the Earth* (1961; reprint, New York: Grove, 1968), 40.

18. Roediger, *Wages of Whiteness,* 8.

19. W.E.B. Du Bois, *Black Reconstruction in America* (1935; reprint, New York: Atheneum; Toronto: Maxwell Macmillan Canada; New York: Maxwell Macmillan International, 1992).

20. Roediger, *Wages of Whiteness,* 13.

21. Mills, "Race and Class", 100.

22. Kenneth Ramchand derives the phrase "terrified consciousness" from the following quote from Frantz Fanon's *Wretched of the Earth*: "[B]ut the possibility of [a change in the social order resulting from decolonization] is equally experienced in the form of a terrifying future in the consciousness of another 'species' of men and women: the colonisers" (p. 36). Ramchand uses the term to describe what he suggests may be a characteristic of the white West Indian experience, expressed in a number of works written by white West Indians. See Ramchand, *The West Indian Novel and Its Background* (London: Faber and Faber, 1970), 224–25.

23. Anthony P. Maingot, "Haiti and the Terrified Consciousness of the Caribbean", in *Ethnicity in the Caribbean,* ed. Gert Oostindie, Warwick University Caribbean Studies (London: Macmillan Caribbean, 1996), 53.

24. Ibid., 56.

25. See Griffith, *Deconstruction,* 36.

26. Ron Muschette, on IRIE FM, 21 February 2005.

27. Lisa Douglass, *The Power of Sentiment: Love, Hierarchy, and the Jamaican Family Elite* (Boulder: Westview, 1992), 106.

28. Ibid., 123.

29. Mintz, "Ethnic Difference", 47.

30. *Population Census 2001, Jamaica,* vol. 1, *Country Report* (Kingston: Statistical Institute of Jamaica, 2003), xli, xlii. Interestingly, this report states, "With changing social and political climates, race has come to be defined in social rather than biological terms. In many countries, including Jamaica, the responses from the censuses are thought to reflect more of people's perception of themselves rather

than ascription to a particular racial group on the basis of physical appearance.
. . . The question asked of respondents in 2001 was *'To which race or ethnic group
would you say you belong?'* The interviewers were instructed to read the response
categories as listed on the questionnaire and to *'Accept the respondent's reply'* "
(pp. xl–xli).

31. Morris Cargill, interview by author, Kingston, Jamaica, 5 March 1995.

32. Mordechai Arbell's book, *The Portuguese Jews of Jamaica* (Kingston: Canoe Press,
2000), emphasizes this marginalization by the ruling white elite as well as by free
coloureds and blacks up to emancipation; he also strenuously asserts that, contrary to the views of the plantocracy at the time, the Jews aligned themselves not
with the slaves but with the white elite (pp. 50–54). The marginalization may
have extended beyond the early part of the twentieth century: John Hearne, in a
1963 description of Jamaica's different racial groups, could state only that the
Jews at that time had been "nearly completely identified with the Europeans"; see
John Hearne and Rex Nettleford, *Our Heritage* (Kingston: University of the West
Indies, Department of Extra-Mural Studies, 1963), 33. And Hoetink finds it
"curious" that in a 1982 article, the social anthropologist R.T. Smith describes the
Jamaican upper class as consisting of "Creole Whites" and "Jews", "as if the latter
were neither white nor Creole" (Hoetink, " 'Race' and Color in the Caribbean",
73).

33. Holzberg, *Minorities and Power,* 172. See also, as an illustration of Holzberg's
point, Suzanne Issa's book about her father: *Mr. Jamaica Abe Issa: A Pictorial
Biography,* ed. Jackie Ranston (Kingston: Suzanne Issa, 1994). Suzanne Issa rightly
suggests that her father's entrepreneurial achievements, especially in tourism, were
extraordinary; the Issas are now one of Jamaica's most wealthy and influential
families.

34. Lipsitz, *Possessive Investment,* viii.

35. Hoetink, " 'Race' and Color in the Caribbean", 69. Such distancing, as Hoetink
reminds us, would not of course preclude sexual interaction with nonwhites, but
"marriages of this type that recognise the children as legitimate heirs have always
been exceedingly rare" (p. 70).

36. Lipsitz, *Possessive Investment,* vii.

37. *Population Census 2001, Jamaica,* vol. 1, *Country Report,* xlii.

38. USA QuickFacts from the United States Census Bureau. http://quickfacts.census
.gov/qfd/states/00000.html.

39. Rex M. Nettleford, *Mirror Mirror: Identity, Race and Protest in Jamaica* (1970;
reprint, Kingston: Kingston Publishers, 1998), xxxiv.

40. This interpretation of the term is, I believe, more common in colloquial Jamaican
usage. See also Douglass, *Power of Sentiment,* 112.

41. Nettleford, *Mirror Mirror,* xxxiv.

42. Ramchand, *West Indian Novel,* 97.

43. Rhonda Cobham, "Herbert George de Lisser (1878–1944)", in *Fifty Caribbean Writers: A Bio-Bibliographical Sourcebook,* ed. Daryl Cumber Dance (Westport, Conn.: Greenwood, 1986), 172.

44. Hearne's maternal grandfather was a cousin of H.G. de Lisser (Hearne's mother was Doris de Lisser).

45. Michelle Cliff, *Claiming an Identity They Taught Me to Despise* (Watertown, Mass.: Persephone, 1980), 43–48. Subsequent references appear parenthetically in the text.

46. See, for example, Veronica Marie Gregg's exploration of Rhys's creole identity in *Jean Rhys's Historical Imagination: Reading and Writing the Creole* (Chapel Hill: University of North Carolina Press, 1995).

47. Rhys herself, according to Judith Raiskin, used the label "white Creole" in reference to her own identity; see *Snow on the Cane Fields: Women's Writing and Creole Subjectivity* (Minneapolis: University of Minnesota Press, 1996), 2. Raiskin refers to both Rhys and Michelle Cliff as "Creoles" (p. 7). H.G. de Lisser, as mentioned in the text, has been called "White Creole". Meanwhile a publisher's blurb on the author Lawrence Scott refers to him as "Caribbean Creole"; see Lawrence Scott, *Witchbroom* (1992; reprint, Oxford: Heinemann-Caribbean Writers Series, 1993), i. The Antoni brothers would undoubtedly be called "French Creoles" in Trinidad, a categorization which distinguishes them from other, non-Catholic, white Creoles and, of course, from (black) creoles (see note 52). (The word creole usually appears with a capital "c" in the name "French Creole", so I have retained the capitalization here. Otherwise, for consistency I use the lower case, except where quoting from a source which uses the capital "c".)

48. Raiskin, *Snow,* 1.

49. Ibid., 3.

50. Ibid., 4.

51. Jean Rhys's use of the word "Creole" in referring to both the presumably white Bronte character Bertha Rochester (*Jean Rhys: Letters 1931–1966* [1984; reprint, London: Penguin, 1985], 156–57) and her own creation, the mulatto Selina in her story "Let Them Call It Jazz" (*Letters,* 186), illustrates this plasticity.

52. In Trinidad, for example, the word "creole" when it stands alone is used in reference to black or mixed-race people (as shown in Robert Antoni's *Divina Trace*), but in that country the name "French Creoles" refers to the (white) descendants of the eighteenth-century French and other Roman Catholic European immigrants to that island, while the name "white Creoles" refers to white Trinidadians generally, including the French Creoles. See Bridget Brereton, "The White Elite of Trinidad, 1838–1950", in *The White Minority in the Caribbean,* ed. Howard Johnson and Karl Watson (Kingston: Ian Randle; London: James Currey, 1998),

32–70. Brereton defines the French Creoles as being "families of mostly French descent, but the term was (and is) generally understood to include those of English, Irish, Spanish, Corsican and German origins, born in the island and almost invariably Roman Catholic. . . . [T]he 'English Creoles' came to constitute a distinct enclave. These were people of English or Scottish origins, born in the island, Protestant (mostly Anglican or Presbyterian) in religion" (p. 33).

53. Indeed, Richard Allsopp's *Dictionary of Caribbean English Usage* (Oxford: Oxford University Press, 1996) defines "creole white" as "a Caribbean person of strongly marked European stock, with no obvious signs of African mixture", and quotes Edgar Mittelholzer's use of the term in support of this definition; see Mittelholzer, *The Life and Death of Sylvia* (1953; reprint, London: Four Square, 1963).

54. Raiskin, *Snow,* 3.

55. Cargill, "Returning to the Battle", *Daily Gleaner,* 15 January 1998, A4.

56. Cliff, *The Land of Look Behind* (Ithaca: Firebrand Books, 1985), 14. Subsequent references appear parenthetically in the text.

57. R.T. Smith notes that "after the British departed, the emphasis of the independ-ent [Commonwealth Caribbean] states on the equality of all racial groups in the building of the new nation soon came to be seen as a device to ensure the contin-uing hegemony of the Anglicised elite, and the economically privileged position of the local capitalist classes formed out of the light-coloured or white minorities" (Smith, "Race and Class", 119).

58. Balutansky and Sourieau, *Caribbean Creolization,* 6.

59. Lipsitz, *Possessive Investment,* viii.

Chapter 2

1. Phyllis Shand Allfrey, *The Orchid House* (1953; reprint, Oxford: Clio Press, 1992). Subsequent references are to this edition and appear parenthetically in the text.

2. Jean Rhys, *Wide Sargasso Sea* (1966; reprint, London: Penguin, 1997). Subsequent references are to this edition and appear parenthetically in the text.

3. Geoffrey Drayton, *Christopher* (1959; reprint, London: Heinemann Educational Books, 1972). Subsequent references are to this edition and appear parenthetically in the text.

4. J.B. Emtage, *Brown Sugar* (London: Collins, 1966). Subsequent references appear parenthetically in the text.

5. Ramchand, *West Indian Novel,* 223.

6. Edward Long, *The History of Jamaica, or General Survey of the Antient and Modern state of that Island: With Reflections on its Situations, Settlements, Inhabitants,*

Climate, Products, Commerce, Laws and Government (1774; reprint, London: Frank Cass, 1970).

7.   W.P. Livingstone, *Black Jamaica: A Study in Evolution* (1899; reprint, London: Sampson Low, Marston, and Co., 1900).

8.   Ramchand, *West Indian Novel,* 224.

9.   Cargill, born in 1914, died in 2000.

10. Cargill, *Jamaica Farewell* (1978; reprint, New York: Barricade Books, 1995). Subsequent references are to this edition and appear parenthetically in the text.

11. Cobham, "Herbert George de Lisser", 168.

12. Augusta Zelia Fraser, a white Englishwoman resident in Jamaica who wrote under the pseudonym "Alice Spinner", could in a sense be regarded as a predecessor of de Lisser. *A Study in Colour* (London: T. Fisher Unwin, 1894) relates the histories of a number of black servants as seen through the eyes of their sometimes bemused, often amused, white Missus. Spinner's second novel, *Lucilla: An Experiment* (London: Kegan Paul, Trench, Trubner and Co., 1896), is less blatantly condescending, but even more satirical. However, as pointed out by Patrick Bryan, "it is true that Spinner satirises almost every aspect of Jamaican society. No racial element was saved from her biting barbs. It is essentially the work of an observant expatriate who is unfavourably impressed by the artificiality, hypocrisy and pretentious nature of San José (Jamaican) society." See Patrick Bryan, unpublished paper on Alice Spinner, *c.*1995, 26.

13. Ramchand, *West Indian Novel,* 224–25.

14. Ibid., 225.

15. M.J. Steel, "A Philosophy of Fear: The World View of the Jamaican Plantocracy in a Comparative Perspective", *Journal of West Indian History* 27, no. 1 (1993): 4–5.

16. Las Casas was sensitive to the plight of the Indians, Rochefort demonstrated sympathies to both Indians and blacks, and du Tertre, according to Gordon K. Lewis, regarded slaves as "human beings placed in a miserable predicament rather than an inferior sort of humankind". See Gordon K. Lewis, *Main Currents in Caribbean Thought: The Historical Evolution of Caribbean Society in Its Ideological Aspects, 1492–1900* (Kingston: Heinemann Educational Books [Caribbean], 1983), 65.

17. In the account of the Maroon Wars by the Jamaican settler-historian Dallas, according to Lewis, the "theme of the white settler battling against a hostile internal enemy reached its fullest expansion" (Ibid., 105).

18. The scientifically inclined Edward Long (see note 6), writing before Ste Domingue, after denying the "invidious claim that the cruel usage inflicted on negro slaves in Jamaica by their masters is the reason why insurrections there are more frequent than in the French or other sugar islands" (Long, *History of*

Jamaica, 2:441), then goes to some trouble to identify the troublemakers among the negro population as being "imported Africans" as opposed to creoles, thereby establishing some sense of control, albeit limited, over the situation. Writing some twenty years later, the more humane Bryan Edwards, in his *History, Civil and Commercial, of the British West Indies: With a Continuation to the Present Time* (1793; reprint, New York: AMS Press, 1966), although morally revolted by slavery and the slave trade, "on which no good mind can reflect but with sentiments of disgust, commiseration and sorrow" (2:40), seems much more revolted by the "atrocities shameful to humanity" reported in Ste Domingue, atrocities at times seemingly almost unspeakable – "how shall I relate it!" (3:99) – almost, but not enough to stop him from devoting many pages to these atrocities. Edwards is clearly shaken by the evidence that, contrary to the somewhat consoling notion voiced by Long and clung to by planters up to this time, "in St Domingo, a very considerable part of the insurgents were – not Africans but – creoles, or natives" (3:xix).

19. Lady Maria Skinner Nugent, *Lady Nugent's Journal of Her Residence in Jamaica from 1801 to 1805* (1907; reprint, edited by P. Wright, Kingston: Institute of Jamaica, 1966). Subsequent references are to this edition and appear parenthetically in the text.

20. M.G. Lewis, *Journal of a West India Proprietor, 1815–17* (1834; reprint, London: George Routledge and Sons, 1929), 145.

21. Michael Scott, *Tom Cringle's Log* (1838; reprint, London: J.M. Dent and Sons, 1915), 247. Subsequent references are to this edition and appear parenthetically in the text.

22. De Lisser, *The White Witch of Rosehall* (1929; reprint, London and Basingstoke: Macmillan Caribbean, 1982), 81. Subsequent references are to this edition and appear parenthetically in the text.

23. Rhys, *Smile Please* (1979; reprint, London: Penguin, 1981), 48–49. Subsequent references are to this edition and appear parenthetically in the text.

24. Douglas Hall, *In Miserable Slavery: Thomas Thistlewood in Jamaica, 1750–86,* Warwick University Caribbean Studies (London: Macmillan Caribbean, 1989).

25. An example is Edward Long's indignation at the unfortunate practice of the creole ladies who "[disdain] to suckle their own offspring! They give them up to a Negroe or Mulatto wet nurse, without reflecting that her blood may be corrupted, or considering the influence which the milk may have with respect to the disposition; as well as the health, of their little ones" (Long, *History of Jamaica,* 2:276).

26. The white Jamaican Clarine Stephenson's *Undine: An Experience* (New York: Broadway Publishing, 1911), interestingly, features no black characters at all, relegating them without exception to a shadowy and only briefly encountered background.

27. Mrs Carmichael, *Domestic Manners and Social Condition of the White, Coloured, and Negro Population of the West Indies* (1833; reprint, New York: Negro Universities Press, 1969), 2:31. Subsequent references are to this edition and appear parenthetically in the text.

28. Lawrence Scott, *Witchbroom* (1992; reprint, Oxford: Heinemann Educational Books, 1993). Subsequent references are to this edition and appear parenthetically in the text.

29. Robert Antoni, *Divina Trace* (New York: The Overlook Press, 1992). Subsequent references appear parenthetically in the text.

30. Brian Antoni, *Paradise Overdose* (New York: Simon and Schuster, 1994). Subsequent references appear parenthetically in the text.

31. Robert Antoni, *Blessed Is the Fruit* (New York: Henry Holt, 1997). Subsequent references appear parenthetically in the text.

32. This pattern can also be seen in the work of the English resident in Jamaica, Alice Spinner. In her first novel, *A Study in Colour,* Spinner focuses, with a combination of curiosity – about "a life so strange and fantastic, that at first I could hardly realize its existence" (p. 8) – and detachment, on the life of the black servant Justina, while her second novel, *Lucilla: An Experiment,* reverts to a white protagonist.

33. Tom Redcam, *Becka's Buckra Baby* (Kingston: Times Printery, 1907).

34. Redcam, *One Brown Girl and –* (Kingston: Jamaica Times Printery, 1909).

35. De Lisser, *Jane's Career* (1913; reprint, New York: Africana Publishing, 1971). Subsequent references are to this edition and appear parenthetically in the text.

36. Ramchand, introduction to de Lisser, *Jane's Career,* ix. A similar observation is made by Ramchand in *The West Indian Novel and Its Background* – see p. 57.

37. De Lisser, *Susan Proudleigh* (London: Methuen, 1915).

38. Alice Durie, *One Jamaica Gal* (Kingston: The Jamaica Times, 1939), 80.

39. Spinner's Justina in *A Study in Colour,* like de Lisser's Jane, also achieves material success and societal advancement, but with a compromise to her integrity. Having found out that the no-good man to whom she has remained faithful for years, awaiting his release from prison, has been dead for a long time, Justina decides to accept the offer of the old Irish shop owner who had long before invited her to be his "housekeeper", so that she can raise her child properly. Spinner's ending to this tale practically drips with irony and condescension: "She is a good deal looked up to by her neighbours, and indeed, from their point of view and her own, is a most respectable and prosperous woman. Even the rigid Josiah is proud of his sister's success in life, and admits that, though at one time he had doubts about her, she is now a credit to the family. For my part, I do not presume to offer an opinion on such a delicate question" (p. 204).

40. Alfred Mendes, *Black Fauns* (1935; reprint, London and Port of Spain: New Beacon Books, 1984).

41. Mendes, *Pitch Lake* (1934; reprint, London and Port of Spain: New Beacon Books, 1980).

42. Mendes, quoted by Michèle Levy in her introduction to Mendes's collection of short stories, *Pablo's Fandango* (Harlow: Longman, 1997), vi.

43. John Hearne, "Roger Mais: Part of a Life" (incomplete manuscript, n.d., accessed courtesy of the Hearne family).

44. Hearne, "Roger Mais: A Personal Memoir", *Bim* 6, no. 23 (1955): 147–48.

45. Hearne, "Roger Mais: Part of a Life", 8.

46. In fact, this romanticization of the underprivileged was part of an international movement and, as Petrine Archer-Straw notes, Edna Manley herself may well have been influenced by the British art theorist Roger Fry. See Archer-Straw, "Vision and Design: Where Nationalism Meets Art and Crafts", in *Fifty Years – Fifty Artists,* ed. Petrine Archer-Straw (Kingston: Edna Manley College of the Visual and Performing Arts and Ian Randle, 2000).

47. Roger Mais, *The Hills Were Joyful Together* (London: Cape, 1953).

48. Mais, *Brother Man* (London: Cape, 1954).

49. Mais, *Black Lightning* (London: Cape, 1955).

50. Sylvia Wynter, "Strangers at the Gate: Caribbean Novelists in Search of Identity", *Sunday Gleaner,* 18 January 1959, 14.

51. Winkler, letter to author, 26 January 1984.

52. Ramchand, *West Indian Novel,* 40.

53. Hoetink, " 'Race' and Color in the Caribbean", 70–71.

54. One of the ugliest portrayals of a coloured character is Da Costa in Spinner's *Lucilla: An Experiment.* Da Costa, by means of his wealth, lures the English teacher Lucilla into a disastrous marriage, despite the best efforts of white Jamaican society to warn her of the inevitable tragic consequences. It is a very short time before Lucilla realizes that beneath the superficial veneer of sophistication lurks a primitive, uncouth animal of a man. Probably the most interesting aspect of this novel is that Spinner clearly finds her protagonist Lucilla quite irritatingly self-absorbed, but not even this creature, she seems to suggest, deserves such a fate.

55. Rhys, *Tigers Are Better-Looking: With a Selection from* The Left Bank (1968; reprint, London: Penguin, 1972). Stories from *The Left Bank* were first published by Jonathan Cape in 1927.

56. Ibid.

57. The attractiveness of brown women occurs also in a number of early works by visiting white writers. For example, "Monk" Lewis and Michael Scott clearly find coloured women exceptionally alluring – Lewis waxes especially lyrical about the young Mary Wiggins (M.G. Lewis, *Journal,* 66), although he does complain about the lack of bosoms to be found generally in this type (p. 95); and Michael Scott's Tom Cringle is equally impressed: "I had never seen more beautiful crea-

tures than there were amongst the brown sets" (Scott, *Tom Cringle's Log*, 245).

58. De Lisser, *Psyche* (1942–43; reprint, London and Basingstoke: Macmillan Caribbean, 1980).

59. De Lisser, *Morgan's Daughter* (1930–31; reprint, London and Basingstoke: Macmillan Caribbean, 1980).

60. Cobham, "Herbert George de Lisser", 172.

61. De Lisser, *Myrtle and Money*, published in *Planter's Punch* 4, no. 4 (1941–42).

62. Long, *History of Jamaica*, 2:329–30.

63. Gordon Lewis, *Main Currents in Caribbean Thought*, 233.

64. Ibid.

65. Esther Chapman, *Study in Bronze: A Novel of Jamaica* (1928; reprint, London: Chantry Publications, 1952). Subsequent references are to this edition and appear parenthetically in the text.

66. Chapman's Lucea reminds one of the coloured beauty Liris in Spinner's *Lucilla: An Experiment*. Liris is similarly accomplished, has been similarly exposed to European culture, and similarly spoilt by it; unlike Lucea, however, Liris deals with her frustrations by immersing herself in charity work.

67. Gordon Lewis, *Main Currents in Caribbean Thought*, 236; emphasis added.

68. Ibid.

69. Ramchand, *West Indian Novel*, 41.

70. Evan Jones, *Stone Haven* (Kingston: Institute of Jamaica Publications, 1993). Subsequent references appear parenthetically in the text.

71. Laura Tanna, "Evan Jones: A Man of Two Worlds", *Jamaica Journal* 18, no. 4 (November 1985–January 1986): 38–45.

72. Cobham, "Herbert George de Lisser", 173.

73. Hearne, *Voices Under the Window* (London: Faber and Faber, 1955), 36–37. Subsequent references appear parenthetically in the text.

74. Hearne, *The Faces of Love* (London: Faber and Faber, 1957).

75. Ramchand, *West Indian Novel*, 47.

76. Michelle Cliff, *Abeng* (1984; reprint, London; Penguin, 1991). Subsequent references are to this edition and appear parenthetically in the text.

77. Cliff, *No Telephone to Heaven* (1987; reprint, New York: Random House, 1989). Subsequent references are to this edition and appear parenthetically in the text.

78. Honor Ford-Smith, *My Mother's Last Dance* (Toronto: Sister Vision, 1997). Subsequent references appear parenthetically in the text.

79. Wilson Harris, *The Palace of the Peacock* (1960; reprint, London: Faber and Faber, 1998), 39.

80. Margaret Busby, ed., *Daughters of Africa: An International Anthology of Words and Writings by Women of African Descent from the Ancient Egyptian to the Present* (New York: Pantheon Books, 1992).

81. Jean Rhys, *Voyage in the Dark* (1934; reprint, London: Penguin, 1969), 27.

82. Lizabeth Paravisini-Gebert, in her biography of Phyllis Shand Allfrey, states that Allfrey was "fond of describing herself as 'a West Indian of over 300 years standing despite my pale face' ". See *Phyllis Shand Allfrey: A Caribbean Life* (New Brunswick: Rutgers University Press, 1996), 6.

83. Philip Curtin, writing of the post-emancipation period, suggests that "a feeling of exile [was] a key to the white Jamaican" (Curtin, *Two Jamaicas,* 55), that the white Jamaican traditionally considered himself a transient, in Jamaica only temporarily (p. 52), while regarding England or Europe as home. Hoetink suggests that "the white group's intrinsic insecurity" may explain "the insistence of the white Creoles [in Jamaica and the lesser Antilles] on maintaining as close an identification as possible, culturally as well as politically, with its only secure (if remote) ally – the metropolitan country" (Hoetink, " 'Race' and Color in the Caribbean", 71).

84. Anthony Trollope, *The West Indies and the Spanish Main* (1859; reprint, London: Dawsons of Pall Mall, 1968), 24.

85. Mona Macmillan, *The Land of Look Behind: A Study of Jamaica* (London: Faber and Faber, 1957), 194. Subsequent references appear parenthetically in the text.

86. Hoetink suggests that white creoles in Jamaica and the Lesser Antilles traditionally "preferred to see themselves as representing English, French or Dutch civilization and their own institutions as extensions or copies of those in the mother country. Only the recent development of easier and more frequent communications has taught them that this was not so, that in the course of generations they had acquired different inflections, manners, and beliefs – in brief, that they too had been subject to a process of creolization. . . . [T]he native white's ambivalence is one between 'here' and 'there', between the urge to stay in their native country and the preparedness to withdraw in the face of decreasing power and influence, aggravated at times by the clear message that one's group is no longer perceived as native by the majority of the population, or that it is being isolated by some moral distinction" (Hoetink, " 'Race' and Color in the Caribbean", 71).

87. J.A. Froude, *The English in the West Indies, or The Bow of Ulysses* (London: Longman, Green, and Co., 1888).

88. John Henderson, *Jamaica* (London: A. and C. Black, 1906), 36.

89. De Lisser, *Under the Sun: A Jamaica Comedy* (London: Ernest Benn, 1937). Subsequent references appear parenthetically in the text.

90. Cargill, interview.

91. Ian McDonald, *The Hummingbird Tree* (1969; reprint, Oxford: Heinemann, 1992), 161. Subsequent references are to this edition and appear parenthetically in the text. It should be noted that Ian McDonald has stated that he has never experienced a feeling of marginalization as a white West Indian: "I have never felt

the white colour of my skin or my European ancestry might preclude me from complete status as a West Indian. More remarkably, I have never felt in the new dispensation of political independence . . . any pressure of rejection or even resentment from the huge majority of West Indians with different skin colour and different ancestries now in a position to dictate complete marginalisation for people like myself." See McDonald, "No Other Home", in *Enterprise of the Indies,* ed. George Lamming (Port of Spain: Trinidad and Tobago Institute of the West Indies, 1999), 29. Similarly, Lawrence Scott, interviewed by James Ferguson for *Caribbean Beat* (May–June 2000), says he never encountered any hostility as a white person in Trinidad: "Trinidad society is incredibly tolerant and inclusive when it comes to race and colour" (p. 51).

92. Cargill, "It's All a Bit Dotty", *Daily Gleaner,* 24 October 1996.
93. As noted by Wayne Brown in a piece entitled "The Child of Nature", third of a three-part review of *The Lunatic,* in his column "In Our Time", *Trinidad Express,* 27 April 1989.

Chapter 3

1. Cargill co-authored three novels with John Hearne under the pseudonym "John Morris": *Fever Grass* (1969), *The Candywine Development* (1970) and *The Checkerboard Caper* (1971). While these novels, especially the first one, did well commercially, they had a short shelf life and are unremarkable as works of literature.
2. Cargill's first wife was Jewish, a fact which upset his family; less so, however, than his second wife, who was working-class black.
3. Cargill, interview.
4. W. Adolphe Roberts, "Herbert George de Lisser", in *Six Great Jamaicans: Biographical Sketches* (Kingston: Pioneer Press, 1952), 100.
5. Cobham, "Herbert George de Lisser", 167.
6. Ibid.
7. Tanna, "Evan Jones".
8. Ibid., 38.
9. Most of the biographical information on Winkler presented in this chapter was obtained during a personal interview, Kingston, Jamaica, 12 April 1996.
10. Douglass, *Power of Sentiment,* 106.
11. Ibid., 107.
12. Ibid., 112.
13. Ibid., 115.
14. Ibid., 90.

15. Ibid., 92.

16. In her interview, "Evan Jones: A Man of Two Worlds", Laura Tanna quotes Jones as saying that " 'Song of the Banana Man'. . . came about as a result of a discussion with Neville Dawes about what West Indian poetry should be. I remember arguing that it should not be just like English poetry, or dialect verse but should be comprehensive, and incorporate the rhythms and language of both. And Neville challenged me to prove it. So I wrote 'Song of the Banana Man' " (p. 40).

17. Evan Jones, "The Song of the Banana Man", in *Caribbean Voices,* ed. John Figueroa (Washington and New York: Robert B. Luce, 1971), 4.

18. Ramchand, introduction to de Lisser's *Jane's Career,* xiii.

19. Roberts, "Herbert George de Lisser", 102.

20. Ramchand, introduction to de Lisser's *Jane's Career,* xiii.

21. Evan Jones, "The Lament of the Banana Man", in *Caribbean Voices,* 86.

22. Cobham, "Herbert George de Lisser", 169.

Chapter 4

1. The People's National Party's (PNP) 1997 election campaign highlighted the issue of race by comparing the relative ability of the black PNP and white JLP (Jamaica Labour Party) leaders to merge in terms of physical appearance with the people whom they were supposed to be representing. This is referred to by Peter Espeut in his election-eve column, "Telling Believable Lies", in which he says, "What we are getting is what Trinidadians call 'picong' bantering about colour and race" (*Daily Gleaner,* 17 December 1997, A4+); and it is commented on by Morris Cargill in his post-election column "Returning to the Battle" (*Daily Gleaner,* 15 January 1998, A4): "It is clearly and understandably against the wishes of a large number of people that whites should be in a dominant public position. . . . It should be obvious that we cannot any longer have a major political party led by a member of a small and fast disappearing minority."

2. Don Robotham, *Vision and Voluntarism: Reviving Voluntarism in Jamaica,* Grace, Kennedy Foundation Lecture 1998 (Kingston: Grace, Kennedy Foundation, 1998), 57–59.

3. Diana McCaulay's column, "DB's New Girlfriend" (*Sunday Gleaner,* 18 January 1998, 9A), was about her Dearly Beloved's newly acquired Jeep Cherokee. This, as well as Christine Nunes's piece of the previous week, "The Best Things in Life" (*Sunday Gleaner,* 11 January 1998, 9A), resulted in an aggrieved letter to the editor ("Gleaner Columnists", *Daily Gleaner,* 31 January 1998, A5) in which the writer, E.H.Y., said, "Every once in a while, Ms. McCaulay and Mrs. [*sic*] Nunes seem to go off on a tangent and endeavour to educate us about the finer things in

life such as sipping tea from real China teacups, skiing or DB's new 'girlfriend' . . . I'd buy a Jeep Cherokee tomorrow if I was earning the money they obviously are, but I wouldn't feel the need to write and tell you all about it." In response, Dawn Ritch felt compelled to defend McCaulay and Nunes in her column "Taking Life Too Seriously" (*Sunday Gleaner,* 8 February 1998, 9A) which opened, "From time to time a silly little letter turns up in this newspaper from some reader who is offended by a columnist's choice of subject, or way of expressing it. Some of them take great exception to humour, because white people in particular mustn't tease them. This of course affects three of our columnists directly. Morris Cargill, Christine Nunes and Diana McCaulay. They regularly run the risk of offending many readers simply because their accompanying pictures show that they are white. The hackles on this kind of reader rise rapidly when the subject matter has to do with public manners, indolence, foolishness and things like real China, skiing trips, chilled vodka and brand new Cherokee Jeeps." Certainly, from time to time, Cargill had to defend himself against charges of racism: for example, in his *Sunday Gleaner* column of 1 February 1998 ("Baffling Dilemma for Investors", 9A): "It's amazing how people who carry large chips on their shoulders, especially on the matter of colour, can invent slights when none exist . . . . I recently wrote a piece on obesity . . . in Jamaica . . . I got a most angry and rather insulting letter [in response] . . . . In my column I never mentioned black women. Indeed, the most obese people I've ever met have been white." And in the *Sunday Gleaner,* 17 May 1998 ("Discipline the Brats", 9A): "a letter to *The Gleaner* . . . claims that I was guilty of colour or class prejudice or both, when I said that I didn't much care for the look of some of our law school graduates. I was not referring to either class or colour. Why did [the writer] assume that I was?"

4. In his column "On Obesity, Dogs and Party Problems" (*Sunday Gleaner,* 14 December 1997, 9A), Morris Cargill said of his dog Peanuts, "He is highly intelligent and I often think of getting him into politics but he is white, and as we all know, few people seem to think that whites can be rated as true Jamaicans. Indeed, as I have noted before in this column, Jamaican whites, like coneys and green parrots, are a fast disappearing species. By the middle of next century I don't think any will be left. But then, if things keep on going as they have been, the species that remain will be welcome to the place." In a column a few weeks later Cargill suggests, "The national motto should read 'Out of many only one sort of people' " ("Returning to the Battle", *Daily Gleaner,* 15 January 1998, A4). Christine Nunes, in her piece "Looking at the Caribbean from Outside" (*Daily Gleaner,* 9 December 1997, A16), says, "[I]ncreasingly I am feeling like an outsider in my own country. Anthony Winkler, in 'Coming [*sic*] Home to Teach' conveys this feeling very well. . . . Increasingly, because my skin is white, I am

rejected by my countrymen, yet I have no other passport, nor do I have permission to live and work elsewhere." Diana McCaulay expressed this feeling of marginalization most poignantly in her piece, "The Mango, the Ackee and the Breadfruit" (which won the 1991 *Lifestyle* magazine and Heinemann Publishers short story competition): "the urge to write is on me again – to tell of this land which is still mine, white though I am. Can it be true that . . . I can lay no claim to this land because of my European ancestors?" (*Lifestyle*, March–April 1992, 40–44). And in her *Sunday Gleaner* column of 20 August 1995, entitled "Real Jamaicans" (9A, 10A), she said, "I have a friend who insists that I am not a Jamaican . . . because I am white. Growing up, I soon realized that I would never enjoy what Anthony Winkler described as that 'most fundamental of freedoms in my own country, anonymity in a public place.' . . . I often feel Jamaica has never accepted me . . . they conclude that if you criticize the cruelty, incompetence and corruption that are undeniable features of our national life – you should emigrate. What is meant but not usually said is: you don't belong here anyway." (It should be noted that this column appeared shortly after the writer was hauled over the coals for an unfortunate reference in a previous column ["When a Man Cleans House", *Sunday Gleaner,* 30 July 1995, 4A] to running out of clean underwear because she was without a domestic helper.) More recent expressions of marginalization are to be found in Ashley Gambrill's "Between Your World and Mine" and Carolyn Gomes's "Jamaica's Promise and Pain", both appearing in the column "It's My Write" in the Arts section of the *Sunday Observer,* on 16 January 2000 and 18 June 2000 respectively. Gambrill's piece opens with a reference to "the sense of cultural exclusion I have struggled with as a white Jamaican" (p. 19). Says Gomes: "I feel the weight of my white skin, and my upper-class Jamaica descend on my stomach and twist me away from my being into my masquerade. It is a mask I don't [choose] to wear but am forced to bear when the eyes [of a poor black person] remind me of my otherness" (p. 3).

5. Edward (Kamau) Brathwaite, *Contradictory Omens: Cultural Diversity and Integration in the Caribbean* (1974; reprint, Kingston: Savacou Publications, 1985), 38.

6. See *Wasafiri* 22 (1994–95): 69–78.

7. Evelyn O'Callaghan, " 'Jumping Into the Big Ups' Quarrels': The Hulme/Brathwaite Exchange" (paper presented at the Fifteenth Annual Conference on West Indian Literature, University of the West Indies, St Augustine, Trinidad, 1996).

8. Michelle Cliff, "Clare Savage as a Crossroads Character", in *Caribbean Women Writers,* ed. Selwyn R. Cudjoe (Wellesley, Mass.: Calaloux, 1990), 265. Cliff expounds on the meaning she has attached to the name: "Her first name means . . . light-skinned . . . and light-skinnedness in the world in which Clare originates . . . stands for privilege, civilization, erasure, forgetting. . . . Her surname

... is meant to evoke the wildness that has been bleached from her skin. . . . A knowledge of history, the past, has been bleached from her mind. . . . She is fragmented, damaged, incomplete" (p. 265).

9. Cliff, *Free Enterprise* (1993; reprint, London: Penguin, 1995).

10. Cliff, interview by author, St George's, Grenada, 21 May 1998.

11. Cliff, *The Store of a Million Items: Stories* (Boston: Houghton Mifflin, 1998), 59. Subsequent references appear parenthetically in the text.

12. All the individual poems by Ford-Smith quoted in this chapter are to be found in *My Mother's Last Dance.*

13. Honor Ford-Smith, "Grandma's Estate", in *Lionheart Gal: Life Stories of Jamaican Women,* by Sistren with Honor Ford-Smith (London: The Women's Press, 1986), 181. Subsequent references appear parenthetically in the text.

14. Cliff, "Clare Savage", 265.

15. Melville, "Beyond the Pale", 742.

16. Benítez-Rojo, "Three Words Toward Creolization", 61; also see chapter 1.

17. Melville, *Shape-shifter* (1990; reprint, London: Picador, 1991), 157.

18. Melville, *The Ventriloquist's Tale* (1997; reprint, London: Bloomsbury, 1998), 7. Subsequent references are to this edition and appear parenthetically in the text.

19. Melville, "Beyond the Pale", 740.

20. Melville, *The Migration of Ghosts* (London: Bloomsbury, 1998).

21. Melville, "Beyond the Pale", 743.

22. Robert Antoni, interview by author, Kingston, Jamaica, 29 April 1998.

23. Jane Bryce, "From Carnivalesque to Carnival or Who Foolin' Who? Robert Antoni's *Divina Trace*" (paper presented at the Twelfth Annual Conference on West Indian Literature, University of the West Indies, Mona, Jamaica, 1993), 12.

24. Benítez-Rojo, "Three Words Toward Creolization", 61.

25. Brathwaite, *Contradictory Omens,* 36.

26. Robert Antoni, interview.

27. Edward (Kamau) Brathwaite, *The Development of Creole Society in Jamaica, 1770–1820* (London: Oxford University Press, 1971), 311.

Chapter 5

1. Anthony C. Winkler, interview by Annie Paul, *Caribbean Review of Books* 7 (February 1993): 20.

2. Wayne Brown, "The Lunatic", first of a three-part review of *The Lunatic,* in his column "In Our Time", *Trinidad Express,* 25 April 1989, 9.

3. Barbara Lalla, *Defining Jamaican Fiction: Marronage and the Discourse of Survival* (Tuscaloosa: University of Alabama Press, 1996), 133.

4. Winkler, interview by author, Atlanta, Georgia, 14 July 1996.

5. Winkler, "Anthony Winkler: 'The Lunatic' . . . and Other Madnesses", interview by Donal James Black, *Lifestyle,* November–December 1990, 20.

6. Winkler, interview, 14 July 1996.

7. Winkler, "Anthony Winkler", 20.

8. Glynis Salmon, conversation with author, Kingston, Jamaica, June 1998.

9. Lalla, *Defining Jamaican Fiction,* 117.

10. Mervyn Morris, *Is English We Speaking* (Kingston: Ian Randle, 1999), 14.

11. Ibid., 9–10.

12. Winkler, letter to author, 4 March 1994.

13. Frederic G. Cassidy, *Jamaica Talk: Three Hundred Years of the English Language in Jamaica* (Kingston: Institute of Jamaica; London: Macmillan, 1961), 2–3.

14. Winkler, letter to author, 4 March 1994.

15. Jean Rhys, "Let Them Call It Jazz", in *Tigers Are Better-Looking,* 44–63.

16. John Hearne, "At the Stelling", in *Best West Indian Stories,* ed. Kenneth Ramchand (Walton-on-Thames: Nelson Caribbean, 1982), 67–80.

17. Examples of such slippage are easy to sense, but sometimes harder to pinpoint. In de Lisser's *Jane's Career,* occasionally the dialogue in dialect reads as though the author composed it in standard English and then attempted to translate it: for example, "God! It is there that people dress an' enjoy themself! Every evenin' when I was dere I used to go for a long car drive, right roun' de belt-line" (p. 4). In Rhys's "Let Them Call It Jazz", the register abruptly changes from time to time: "She tell me the house very old, hundred and fifty year old, and she and her husband live there since long time. . . . Then she tells me . . ." (p. 46). In Hearne's "At the Stelling", one wonders if an over-zealous editor may have tampered with the text: "The two of we talk so. . . . The grass stay high, and the ground hard with sun. It is three mile to where the Catacuma run black" (p. 67); or "Because de rifle is Government . . . so it is him have a right to de rifle" (p. 68). Cargill, in *Jamaica Farewell,* sometimes combines a high and low register in a curious mix: "That is the art of it," [the hangman expounds.] "You gets so you can tell the drop needed at a glance. I used to have them weighed, but long time now I don't bother" (p. 213).

18. Cargill, interview.

19. Morris Cargill, "The Lunatic", *Sunday Gleaner,* 7 June 1987, 10A.

20. Wayne Brown, "A Naipaullian Fable", second of a three-part review of *The Lunatic, Trinidad Express,* 26 April 1989, 9.

21. Bob Shacochis, "An Island in the Sun: Two Novels of Jamaica", review of *The Lunatic* and *No Telephone to Heaven* by Michelle Cliff, *Washington Post, Book World,* 2 August 1987, 14.

22. Winkler, letter to author, 7 January 1983.

23. Michael Thelwell, "Fishermen in Troubled Waters", review of *The Painted Canoe, Washington Post, Book World,* 16 November 1986, 10.

24. M.H. Abrams, *A Glossary of Literary Terms,* 6th ed. (Fort Worth: Harcourt Brace, 1993), 175.

25. Anthony C. Winkler, e-mail to author, 15 July 1998.

26. Wayne Brown, "The Child of Nature", third of a three-part review of *The Lunatic, Trinidad Express,* 27 April 1989, 9.

27. Lalla, *Defining Jamaican Fiction,* 135.

28. Shacochis, "Island in the Sun", 14.

29. Lalla, *Defining Jamaican Fiction,* 139.

30. Brown, "The Child of Nature".

31. Brown, "The Lunatic".

32. Lalla, *Defining Jamaican Fiction,* 138.

33. Thelwell, "Fishermen in Troubled Waters", 10.

34. Brown, "The Lunatic".

35. Cargill, "The Lunatic".

36. Shacochis, "Island in the Sun", 1.

37. Brown, "The Lunatic".

38. Ibid.

39. Shacochis, "Island in the Sun", 14.

40. See Lalla, *Defining Jamaican Fiction,* 147.

41. Ibid., 134.

42. Ibid., 146.

43. Brown, "The Child of Nature".

44. Melville, *Shape-shifter,* 98.

45. Shacochis, "Island in the Sun", 14.

46. Brown, "The Child of Nature".

Chapter 6

1. Shacochis, "Island in the Sun", 14.

2. Winkler, interview, 14 July 1996.

3. Simon Dentith, *Bakhtinian Thought: An Introductory Reader* (London and New York: Routledge, 1995), 66.

4. Mikhail Bakhtin, *Rabelais and His World,* trans. Helene Iswolsky (Bloomington: Indiana University Press, 1984), 88, 439.

5. Extending from Cassidy's definition – "to stoop down; to squat on the heels" – *butu* in contemporary Jamaican usage means "low, low-class, low-bred, uncultured, uncouth".

6. St Augustine embraced the Neoplatonist philosophy of the superiority of the spirit world over the material world, which had been adopted into Christian teachings through the influence of Plotinus (see *Growth of Ideas: Knowledge, Thought, Imagination* [1965; reprint, New York: Doubleday, 1966], 10:128–29). St Augustine was also heavily influenced by Manichaeanism, which claimed that good has a separate source from evil: God is good, while all of matter is evil (see p. 53).

7. Martin Schade met Winkler through their mutual friend, the late Vicky Kenmay, to whom *The Duppy* is dedicated. Kenmay, an American who resided in Jamaica, died in February 1996, the year before *The Duppy*'s publication.

8. Martin Schade, interview by author, Kingston, Jamaica, 24 February 2000.

9. Martin Schade, "Riddim of Creation: A New Theology Offered", *Daily Gleaner,* 22 January 2000, B12. And in Schade's letter to the Father General of the Society of Jesus (dated 1 September 1999) in which he explains his decision to leave the Society, he commends the Society for "its spirituality of finding God in all things".

10. Schade, interview.

11. Schade, "Riddim of Creation".

12. Schade, interview.

13. Ibid.

14. Ibid.; Winkler, telephone conversation with author, 1 March 2000.

15. I am very grateful to Father Gerard McLaughlin, SJ, and his fellow Jesuits Father Oliver Nickerson and Father John Surrette, for taking the time to read *The Duppy* and to discuss with me its theology, Roman Catholic and otherwise, as well as current conservative versus radical debates within the church. (The interview took place in Kingston, Jamaica, on 25 November 2000.) Interestingly, all three priests expressed great enthusiasm about *The Duppy* and its theology, as did Martin Schade when interviewed (as well as the Catholic deacon Ronnie Thwaites in his radio interview of Winkler [Power 106 FM, May 2000]), although none of them saw the book's theology as being especially Catholic.

16. See, as just one of innumerable possible examples of this view, an editorial review of the book *Papal Sin: Structures of Deceit* in the Catholic journal *Cross Currents: The Wisdom of the Heart and the Life of the Mind* (50, no. 3 [Fall 2000]: 291–93). The review, entitled "Structures of Sin", suggests approvingly that the book's author, Garry Wills, is "a Catholic layman who is as mad as hell and just won't take it any more. Not only is his book a rousing polemic against all that is dreadful in the Roman Catholic Church, it applies with equal force to other institutions" (p. 291). The description could easily apply to Winkler and *The Duppy.*

17. In his article, "Capital Punishment and the Intrinsic Goodness of Man" (*Daily Gleaner,* 10 January 2001, A4), Roman Catholic deacon Peter Espeut suggests

that a recent pastoral letter by the twenty-two Roman Catholic bishops of the Antilles supports the view that, contrary to the beliefs of "the disciples of Calvin" and others, man is fundamentally good and therefore "capital punishment is morally wrong for Christians". Espeut's article produced a number of energetic responses in the press, including that of Martin Henry (letter to the editor, *Daily Gleaner*, 16 January 2001, A5). Henry states that "[t]his view is more the product of Humanist thought, particularly manifested in modern 'sinless' sociology and psychology and New Ageism, than it is of Christian theology", and that "Mr Espeut writes as a deacon of the Roman Catholic Church who should take the trouble to get his theology right. . . . It is the Roman Catholic Church . . . which historically has had the darkest view of human nature. . . . Deacon Espeut's enlightened view is a remarkable departure which could well be considered heretical by his Archbishop".

18. This observation was made by Father McLaughlin (interview, 25 November 2000).

19. Bakhtin, *Rabelais and His World*, 29.

20. Dentith, *Bakhtinian Thought*, 66.

21. Carolyn Cooper, *Noises in the Blood: Orality, Gender and the "Vulgar" Body of Jamaican Popular Culture*, Warwick University Caribbean Studies (London: Macmillan Caribbean, 1993), 7.

22. Ibid., 5, 2, 11.

23. Lalla, *Defining Jamaican Fiction*, 133, 139.

24. Ibid., 139.

25. Shacochis, "Island in the Sun", 14.

26. Lalla, *Defining Jamaican Fiction*, 134.

27. *West Coast Review of Books*, May 1987.

28. Lady Saw, "Wuk With You", from *Passion*, VP Records, catalog no. 1493.

29. Louise Bennett, *Selected Poems* (Kingston: Sangster's Book Stores, 1982), 21–22.

30. Cooper, *Noises in the Blood*, 50.

31. Seminar discussion with Robert Antoni, Sixteenth Annual Conference on West Indian Literature, University of Miami, 1997.

32. Joe Pereira, "Babylon to Vatican: Religion in the Dancehall" (paper presented at the Sixteenth Annual Conference on West Indian Literature, University of Miami, 1997).

33. Cooper, *Noises in the Blood*, 22.

34. Bakhtin, *Rabelais and His World*, 317, 339.

35. Brown, "A Naipaullian Fable", 9.

36. Bakhtin, *Rabelais and His World*, 19.

37. "Gyal Man" by Johnny P, quoted in Cooper, *Noises in the Blood*, 155.

38. Bakhtin, *Rabelais and His World*, 34.

39. Dentith, *Bakhtinian Thought,* 79.
40. Bakhtin, *Rabelais and His World,* 122–23.
41. Ibid., 340, 336.

Chapter 7

1. *Contemporary Authors* 123 (Detroit: Gale Research Co., 1988), 477.
2. Winkler, e-mail to author, 11 November 1998.
3. Sandra Pouchet Paquet, "West Indian Autobiography", *Black American Literature Forum* 24, no. 2 (Summer 1990): 357–78.
4. V.S. Naipaul, "Prologue to an Autobiography", in *Finding the Centre* (1984; reprint, London: Penguin, 1985), 40. Subsequent references appear parenthetically in the text.
5. Winkler, interview, 14 July 1996.
6. Winkler, interview by author, Kingston, Jamaica, 12 April 1996.
7. Winkler, "Anthony Winkler", 19.
8. Ibid., 15.
9. Winkler, interview, 14 July 1996.
10. Ibid.
11. Winkler, "Anthony Winkler", 19.
12. Pouchet Paquet, "West Indian Autobiography", 358.
13. Robert Sayre, "Autobiography and the Making of America", in *Autobiography: Essays Theoretical and Critical,* ed. James Olney (Princeton: Princeton University Press, 1980), 149–50.
14. Ibid., 160.
15. Ibid., 167.
16. Pouchet Paquet, "West Indian Autobiography", 359, 358.
17. Ibid., 359.
18. Ibid., 373.
19. Ibid., 365.
20. Rachel Manley, *Drumblair: Memories of a Jamaican Childhood* (Kingston: Ian Randle, 1996). Subsequent references appear parenthetically in the text.
21. Pouchet Paquet, "West Indian Autobiography", 360.
22. Earl Lovelace, *Salt* (1996; reprint, New York: Persea Books, 1997), 5.
23. Quote from Winkler appearing on a promotional item produced by Kingston Publishers, *c.*1987–88.
24. Winkler, "The Looks That Blind Us", in the column "International Atlanta", *Atlanta Constitution,* 17 October 1994, A9.
25. Ramchand, *West Indian Novel,* 226.

26. Winkler, interview, 12 April 1996.
27. Winkler, e-mail to author, 24 November 1998.
28. Winkler, interview, 12 April 1996.
29. Winkler, e-mail to author, 6 November 1998.
30. Winkler, interview by Annie Paul, *Caribbean Review of Books,* 20.
31. Winkler, letter to author, 1 January 1983.
32. Winkler, interview, 12 April 1996.
33. Ibid.
34. Ibid.
35. Ibid.
36. Ibid.
37. Ibid.
38. The terms "Syrian" and "Lebanese" are often used interchangeably in Jamaica.
39. Winkler, "Anthony Winkler", 17.
40. Winkler, radio interview, KLAS FM, February 1995.
41. Winkler, letter to author, 23 September 1982.
42. *Contemporary Authors,* 477.
43. Several stories have recently been published in the *Sunday Observer*'s supplement, *The Arts.* All but one, "The Annihilation of Fish", are set in Jamaica; "Fish", set in America, features a Jamaican protagonist. The collection *The Annihilation of Fish and Other Stories,* containing a number of the *Observer* stories plus many others, has since been published by Macmillan (Oxford: 2004).
44. Winkler, interview, 14 July 1996.
45. Winkler, letter to author, 15 September 1993.
46. "The Annihilation of Fish", written in 1975, appears in the anthology *Bearing Witness: The Best of the Observer Arts Magazine 2000,* ed. Wayne Brown (Kingston: Jamaica Observer, 2000), and subsequently as the title story of the collection *The Annihilation of Fish and Other Stories.*
47. Winkler, "Anthony Winkler", 20.
48. Winkler, interview by Annie Paul, *Caribbean Review of Books,* 20–21.
49. Winkler, "Tony Winkler's Atlanta", *Skywritings,* July–August 1996, 64. Subsequent references appear parenthetically in the text.
50. Winkler, interview, 14 July 1996.
51. Ibid.
52. See the bibliography for details of these interviews.
53. Winkler, interview, 14 July 1996.
54. All quotes from Winkler, interview, 14 July 1996.
55. Ibid.

Selected Bibliography

Anthony C. Winkler

Books

Winkler, Anthony C. *The Annihilation of Fish and Other Stories.* Oxford: Macmillan, 2004.

———. *The Crocodile.* Unpublished manuscript, first draft completed 1999.

———. *Dog War.* Unpublished manuscript, first draft completed 1991.

———. *The Duppy.* Kingston: Kingston Publishers, 1997.

———. *Going Home to Teach.* Kingston: Kingston Publishers, 1995.

———. *The Great Yacht Race.* Kingston: Kingston Publishers, 1992.

———. *The Lunatic.* Kingston: Kingston Publishers; Secaucus: Lyle Stuart, 1987.

———. *The Mary Anne Papers.* Unpublished manuscript, *c.*1973.

———. *The Painted Canoe.* Kingston: Kingston Publishers, 1983.

Short Stories

Winkler, Anthony C. "The Annihilation of Fish". In *Bearing Witness: The Best of the Observer Arts Magazine 2000,* edited by Wayne Brown, 11–21. Kingston: Jamaica Observer, 2000.

———. "The Man Who Knew the Price of All Fish". In *Significance: The Struggle We Share,* edited by John H. Brennecke and Robert G. Amick, 103–9. Beverly Hills: Glencoe Press, 1971.

Articles

———. "The Looks That Blind Us". In the column "International Atlanta", *Atlanta Constitution,* 17 October 1994: A9.

———. "Tony Winkler's Atlanta". *Skywritings,* July–August 1996, 64–66.

Published Interviews

Winkler, Anthony C. "Anthony Winkler: 'The Lunatic' . . . and Other Madnesses". Interview by Donal James Black. *Lifestyle,* November–December 1990, 15–20.

———. Interview by Annie Paul. *Caribbean Review of Books* 7 (February 1993): 17+.

Personal Interviews and Correspondence

There has been extensive communication between Winkler and the author (letters, e-mail, telephone conversations and personal contact) since they first met in 1981. Below are listed only the exchanges drawn upon most heavily in this book.

Winkler, Anthony C. E-mail to the author, 6, 11, 15, 17, 24, 25 November 1998.

———. Letters to the author, 23 September 1982, 7 January 1983, 26 January 1984, 15 September 1993, 4 March 1994.

———. Interview by author. Kingston, Jamaica, 12 April 1996.

———. Interview by author. Atlanta, Georgia, 14 July 1996.

———. Telephone interview by author, 1 March 2000.

Other Sources

Published Works

Allfrey, Phyllis Shand. *The Orchid House.* 1953. Reprint, Oxford: Clio Press, 1992.

Antoni, Brian. *Paradise Overdose.* New York: Simon and Schuster, 1994.

Antoni, Robert. *Blessed Is the Fruit.* New York: Henry Holt, 1997.

———. *Divina Trace.* New York: The Overlook Press, 1992.

Arbell, Mordechai. *The Portuguese Jews of Jamaica.* Kingston: Canoe Press, 2000.

Bakhtin, Mikhail. *Rabelais and His World.* Translated by Helene Iswolsky. Bloomington: Indiana University Press, 1984.

Balutansky, Kathleen M., and Marie-Agnes Sourieau, eds. *Caribbean Creolization: Reflections on the Cultural Dynamics of Language, Literature, and Identity.* Gainesville: University Press of Florida; Kingston: The Press, University of the West Indies, 1998.

Benítez-Rojo, Antonio. "Three Words Toward Creolization". In Balutansky and Sourieau, *Caribbean Creolization,* 53–61.

Bennett, Louise. *Selected Poems.* Kingston: Sangster's Book Stores, 1982.

Brathwaite, Edward (Kamau). *Contradictory Omens: Cultural Diversity and Integration in the Caribbean.* 1974. Reprint, Kingston: Savacou Publications, 1985.

———. *The Development of Creole Society in Jamaica, 1770–1820*. London: Oxford University Press, 1971.

———. "A Post-Cautionary Tale of the Helen of Our Wars". *Wasafiri* 22 (Autumn 1995): 69–78.

Brereton, Bridget. "The White Elite of Trinidad, 1838–1950". In Johnson and Watson, *The White Minority in the Caribbean*, 32–70.

Bryce, Jane. "From Carnivalesque to Carnival or Who Foolin' Who? Robert Antoni's *Divina Trace*". Paper presented at the Twelfth Annual Conference on West Indian Literature, University of the West Indies, Mona, Jamaica, 1993.

Bryan, Patrick. Unpublished paper on Alice Spinner, *c.*1995.

Busby, Margaret, ed. *Daughters of Africa: An International Anthology of Words and Writings by Women of African Descent from the Ancient Egyptian to the Present*. New York: Pantheon Books, 1992.

Cargill, Morris. *Jamaica Farewell*. 1978. Reprint, New York: Barricade Books, 1995.

Carmichael, Mrs. *Domestic Manners and Social Condition of the White, Coloured, and Negro Population of the West Indies*. 2 vols. 1833. Reprint, New York: Negro Universities Press, 1969.

Cassidy, Frederic G. *Jamaica Talk: Three Hundred Years of the English Language in Jamaica*. Kingston: Institute of Jamaica; London: Macmillan, 1961.

Chapman, Esther. *Study in Bronze: A Novel of Jamaica*. 1928. Reprint, London: Chantry Publications, 1952.

Cliff, Michelle. *Abeng*. 1984. Reprint, London: Penguin, 1991.

———. *Claiming an Identity They Taught Me to Despise*. Watertown, Mass.: Persephone, 1980.

———. "Clare Savage as a Crossroads Character". In *Caribbean Women Writers,* edited by Selwyn R. Cudjoe, 263–68. Wellesley, Mass.: Calaloux Publications, 1990.

———. *Free Enterprise*. 1993. Reprint, London: Penguin, 1995.

———. *The Land of Look Behind*. Ithaca: Firebrand Books, 1985.

———. *No Telephone to Heaven*. 1987. Reprint, New York: Random House, 1989.

———. *The Store of a Million Items: Stories*. Boston: Houghton Mifflin, 1998.

Cobham, Rhonda. "Herbert George de Lisser (1878–1944)". In *Fifty Caribbean Writers: A Bio-Bibliographical Sourcebook,* edited by Daryl Cumber Dance, 166–77. Westport, Conn.: Greenwood, 1986.

———. Introduction to *Black Fauns,* by Alfred Mendes, i–xvi. London: New Beacon Books, 1984.

Contemporary Authors 123. Detroit: Gale Research, 1988.

Cooper, Carolyn. *Noises in the Blood: Orality, Gender and the "Vulgar" Body of Jamaican*

Popular Culture. Warwick University Caribbean Studies. London: Macmillan Caribbean, 1993.

Curtin, Philip D. *Two Jamaicas: The Role of Ideas in a Tropical Colony, 1830–1865.* Cambridge, Mass.: Harvard University Press, 1955.

De Lisser, H.G. *Jane's Career.* 1913. Reprint, New York: Africana Publishing, 1971.

———. *Morgan's Daughter.* 1930–31. Reprint, London: Macmillan Caribbean, 1980.

———. *Myrtle and Money.* Published in *Planter's Punch* 4, no. 4 (1941–42).

———. *Psyche.* 1942–43. Reprint, London: Macmillan Caribbean, 1980.

———. *Susan Proudleigh.* London: Methuen, 1915.

———. *Under the Sun: A Jamaica Comedy.* London: Ernest Benn, 1937.

———. *The White Witch of Rosehall.* 1929. Reprint, London: Macmillan Caribbean, 1982.

Dentith, Simon. *Bakhtinian Thought: An Introductory Reader.* London and New York: Routledge, 1995.

Douglass, Lisa. *The Power of Sentiment: Love, Hierarchy, and the Jamaican Family Elite.* Boulder: Westview, 1992.

Drayton, Geoffrey. *Christopher.* 1959. Reprint, London: Heinemann Educational Books, 1972.

Durie, Alice. *One Jamaica Gal.* Kingston: The Jamaica Times, 1939.

Edwards, Bryan. *History, Civil and Commercial, of the British West Indies: With a Continuation to the Present Time.* 3 vols. 1793. Reprint, New York: AMS Press, 1966.

Emtage, J.B. *Brown Sugar.* London: Collins, 1966.

Fanon, Frantz. *The Wretched of the Earth.* Translated by Constance Farrington. 1961. Reprint, New York: Grove, 1968.

Ferguson, James. "The Worlds of Lawrence Scott". *Caribbean Beat,* May–June 2000, 48–52.

Figueroa, John, ed. *Caribbean Voices.* Washington and New York: Robert B. Luce, 1971.

Ford-Smith, Honor. "Grandma's Estate". In *Lionheart Gal: Life Stories of Jamaican Women,* by Sistren with Honor Ford-Smith, 175–97. London: The Women's Press, 1986.

———. *My Mother's Last Dance.* Toronto: Sister Vision, 1997.

Froude, J.A. *The English in the West Indies, or The Bow of Ulysses.* London: Longman, Green and Co., 1888.

Gregg, Veronica Marie. *Jean Rhys's Historical Imagination: Reading and Writing the Creole.* Chapel Hill: University of North Carolina Press, 1995.

Griffith, Glyne. *Deconstruction, Imperialism and the West Indian Novel.* Kingston: The Press, University of the West Indies, 1996.

Growth of Ideas: Knowledge, Thought, Imagination. Vol. 10. 1965. Reprint, New York: Doubleday, 1966.

Hall, Douglas. *In Miserable Slavery: Thomas Thistlewood in Jamaica, 1750–86.* Warwick University Caribbean Studies. London: Macmillan Caribbean, 1989.

Harris, Wilson. *The Palace of the Peacock.* 1960. Reprint, with a note by the author and an essay by Kenneth Ramchand, London: Faber and Faber, 1998.

Hearne, John. "At the Stelling". In *Best West Indian Stories,* edited by Kenneth Ramchand, 67–80. Walton-on-Thames: Nelson Caribbean, 1982.

———. *The Faces of Love.* London: Faber and Faber, 1957.

———. "Roger Mais: Part of a Life". Incomplete manuscript, n.d., accessed courtesy of the Hearne family.

———. "Roger Mais: A Personal Memoir". *Bim* 6, no. 23 (1955): 147–48.

———. *Voices Under the Window.* London: Faber and Faber, 1955.

Hearne, John, and Rex Nettleford. *Our Heritage.* Kingston: University of the West Indies, Department of Extra-Mural Studies, 1963.

Henderson, John. *Jamaica.* London: A. and C. Black, 1906.

Hoetink, H. " 'Race' and Color in the Caribbean". In Mintz and Price, *Caribbean Contours,* 55–84.

Holzberg, Carol S. *Minorities and Power in a Black Society: The Jewish Community of Jamaica.* Lanham, Md.: North-South Publishing, 1987.

Hulme, Peter. "The Place of Wide Sargasso Sea". *Wasafiri* 20 (Autumn 1994): 5–11.

———. "A Response to Kamau Brathwaite". *Wasafiri* 23 (Spring 1996): 40–50.

Issa, Suzanne. *Mr. Jamaica Abe Issa: A Pictorial Biography,* edited by Jackie Ranston. Kingston: Suzanne Issa, 1994.

Johnson, Howard, and Karl Watson, eds. *The White Minority in the Caribbean.* Kingston: Ian Randle; London: James Currey, 1998.

Jones, Evan. "The Lament of the Banana Man". In Figueroa, *Caribbean Voices,* 86.

———. "The Song of the Banana Man". In Figueroa, *Caribbean Voices,* 4.

———. *Stone Haven.* Kingston: Institute of Jamaica Publications, 1993.

Lalla, Barbara. *Defining Jamaican Fiction: Marronage and the Discourse of Survival.* Tuscaloosa: University of Alabama Press, 1996.

Levy, Michèle. Introduction to *Pablo's Fandango,* by Alfred Mendes, v–xi. Harlow: Longman, 1997.

Lewis, Gordon K. *Main Currents in Caribbean Thought: The Historical Evolution of Caribbean Society in Its Ideological Aspects, 1492–1900.* Kingston: Heinemann Educational Books (Caribbean), 1983.

Lewis, M.G. *Journal of a West India Proprietor, 1815–17.* 1834. Reprint, London: George Routledge and Sons, 1929.

Lipsitz, George. *The Possessive Investment in Whiteness: How White People Profit from Identity Politics.* Philadelphia: Temple University Press, 1998.

Livingstone, W.P. *Black Jamaica: A Study in Evolution.* 1899. Reprint, London: Sampson Low, Marston, and Co., 1900.

Long, Edward. *The History of Jamaica, or General Survey of the Antient and Modern state of that Island: With Reflections on its Situations, Settlements, Inhabitants, Climate, Products, Commerce, Laws and Government.* 3 vols. 1774. Reprint, London: Frank Cass, 1970.

Lovelace, Earl. *Salt.* 1996. Reprint, New York: Persea Books, 1997.

Macmillan, Mona. *The Land of Look Behind: A Study of Jamaica.* London: Faber and Faber, 1957.

Maingot, Anthony P. "Haiti and the Terrified Consciousness of the Caribbean". In Oostindie, *Ethinicity in the Caribbean,* 53–80.

Mais, Roger. *Black Lightning.* London: Cape, 1955.

———. *Brother Man.* London: Cape, 1954.

———. *The Hills Were Joyful Together.* London: Cape, 1953.

Manley, Rachel. *Drumblair: Memories of a Jamaican Childhood.* Kingston: Ian Randle, 1996.

McCaulay, Diana. "The Mango, the Ackee and the Breadfruit". *Lifestyle,* March–April 1992, 40–44.

McDonald, Ian. *The Hummingbird Tree.* 1969. Reprint, Oxford: Heinemann, 1992.

———. "No Other Home". In *Enterprise of the West Indies,* edited by George Lamming, with an afterword by Lloyd Best, 29–32. Port of Spain: Trinidad and Tobago Institute of the West Indies, 1999.

Melville, Pauline. "Beyond the Pale". In *Daughters of Africa: An International Anthology of Words and Writings by Women of African Descent from the Ancient Egyptian to the Present,* edited by Margaret Busby, 739–43. London: Cape; New York: Pantheon Books, 1992.

———. *The Migration of Ghosts.* London: Bloomsbury, 1998.

———. *Shape-shifter.* 1990. Reprint, London: Picador, 1991.

———. *The Ventriloquist's Tale.* 1997. Reprint, London: Bloomsbury, 1998.

Mendes, Alfred. *Black Fauns.* 1935. Reprint, London and Port of Spain: New Beacon Books, 1984.

———. *Pablo's Fandango.* Edited by Michèle Levy. Harlow: Longman, 1997.

———. *Pitch Lake.* 1934. Reprint, London and Port of Spain: New Beacon Books, 1980.

Mills, Charles. "Race and Class: Conflicting or Reconcilable Paradigms?" *Social and Economic Studies* 36, no. 2 (1987): 69–108.

Mintz, Sidney W. "Ethnic Difference, Plantation Sameness". In Oostindie, *Ethinicity in the Caribbean,* 39–52.

Mintz, Sidney W., and Sally Price, eds. *Caribbean Contours.* Baltimore and London: Johns Hopkins University Press, 1985.

Morris, Mervyn. *Is English We Speaking.* Kingston: Ian Randle, 1999.

Naipaul, V.S. "Prologue to an Autobiography". In *Finding the Centre,* 13–72. 1984. Reprint, London: Penguin, 1985.

Nettleford, Rex M. *Mirror Mirror: Identity, Race and Protest in Jamaica.* 1970. Reprint, Kingston: Kingston Publishers, 1998.

Nugent, Maria Skinner, Lady. *Lady Nugent's Journal of Her Residence in Jamaica from 1801 to 1805.* 1907. Reprint, edited by P. Wright. Kingston: Institute of Jamaica, 1966.

O'Callaghan, Evelyn. " 'Jumping Into the Big Ups' Quarrels': The Hulme/Brathwaite Exchange". Paper presented at the Fifteenth Annual Conference on West Indian Literature, University of the West Indies, St Augustine, Trinidad. 1996.

Omi, Michael, and Howard Winant. *Racial Formation in the United States: From the 1960s to the 1990s.* London and New York: Routledge, 1994.

Oostindie, Gert, ed. *Ethnicity in the Caribbean.* Warwick University Caribbean Studies. London: Macmillan Caribbean, 1996.

Pereira, Joe. "Babylon to Vatican – Religion in the Dancehall". Paper presented at the Sixteenth Annual Conference on West Indian Literature, University of Miami, 1997.

Pieterse, Jan Nederveen. *White on Black: Images of Africa and Blacks in Western Popular Culture.* New Haven and London: Yale University Press, 1992.

Pouchet Paquet, Sandra. "West Indian Autobiography". *Black American Literature Forum* 24, no. 2 (Summer 1990): 357–78.

Pratt, Mary Louise. *Imperial Eyes: Travel Writing and Transculturation.* London and New York: Routledge, 1992.

Raiskin, Judith L. *Snow on the Cane Fields: Women's Writing and Creole Subjectivity.* Minneapolis and London: University of Minnesota Press, 1996.

Ramchand, Kenneth. Introduction to *Jane's Career,* by H.G. de Lisser, v–xvi. New York: Africana Publishing, 1971.

———. Introduction to *Pitch Lake,* by Alfred Mendes, i–xii. London: New Beacon Books, 1980.

———. *The West Indian Novel and Its Background.* London: Faber and Faber, 1970.

Redcam, Tom [Thomas Macdermot]. *Becka's Buckra Baby.* Kingston: Times Printery, 1907.

———. *One Brown Girl and –.* Kingston: Jamaica Times Printery, 1909.

Rhys, Jean. *Jean Rhys: Letters 1931–1966.* Selected and edited by Francis Wyndham and
Diana Melly. 1984. Reprint, London: Penguin, 1985.

———. *Smile Please.* 1979. Reprint, London: Penguin, 1981.

———. *Tigers Are Better-Looking: With a Selection from* The Left Bank. 1968. Reprint,
London: Penguin, 1972.

———. *Voyage in the Dark.* 1934. Reprint, London: Penguin, 1969.

———. *Wide Sargasso Sea.* 1966. Reprint, edited by Angela Smith, London: Penguin,
1997.

Roberts, W. Adolphe. *Six Great Jamaicans: Biographical Sketches.* Kingston: Pioneer
Press, 1952.

Robotham, Don. *Vision and Voluntarism: Reviving Voluntarism in Jamaica.* Grace,
Kennedy Foundation Lecture 1998. Kingston: Grace, Kennedy Foundation, 1998.

Roediger, David R. *The Wages of Whiteness: Race and the Making of the American
Working Class.* London: Verso, 1991.

Sayre, Robert. "Autobiography and the Making of America". In *Autobiography: Essays
Theoretical and Critical,* edited by James Olney, 146–68. Princeton: Princeton
University Press, 1980.

Schade, Martin. "On Being Catholic". *Catholic Opinion,* January–February 2000, 33.

Scott, Lawrence. *Witchbroom.* 1992. Reprint, Oxford: Heinemann Educational Books,
1993.

Scott, Michael. *Tom Cringle's Log.* 1838. Reprint, London: J.M. Dent and Sons, 1915.

Sistren Collective, with Honor Ford-Smith. *Lionheart Gal: Life Stories of Jamaican
Women.* London: The Women's Press, 1986.

Smith, M.G. *The Plural Society in the British West Indies.* 1965. Reprint, Kingston:
Sangster's Book Stores; Berkeley and Los Angeles: University of California Press,
1974.

Smith, R.T. "Race and Class in the Post-Emancipation Caribbean". In *Racism and
Colonialism: Essays on Ideology and Social Structure,* edited by Robert Ross, 93–119.
The Hague: Martinus Nijhoff, Publications of the Leiden Centre for the History of
European Expansion, 1982.

Spinner, Alice [Augusta Zelia Fraser]. *Lucilla: An Experiment.* London: Kegan Paul,
Trench, Trubner and Co., 1896.

———. *A Study in Colour.* London: T. Fisher Unwin, 1894.

Steel, M.J. "A Philosophy of Fear: The World View of the Jamaican Plantocracy in a
Comparative Perspective". *Journal of West Indian History* 27, no. 1 (1993): 1–20.

Stephenson, Clarine. *Undine: An Experience.* New York: Broadway Publishing, 1911.

Tanna, Laura. "Evan Jones: A Man of Two Worlds". *Jamaica Journal* 18, no. 4
(November 1985–January 1986): 38–45.

Trollope, Anthony. *The West Indies and the Spanish Main.* 1859. Reprint, London: Dawsons of Pall Mall, 1968.

Personal Interviews

Antoni, Robert. Interview by author. Kingston, Jamaica, 29 April 1998.
———. Seminar discussion. Sixteenth Annual Conference on West Indian Literature, University of Miami, 1 April 1997.
Cargill, Morris. Interview by author. Kingston, Jamaica, 5 March 1995.
Cliff, Michelle. Interview by author. St George's, Grenada, 21 May 1998.
McLaughlin, Gerard, Oliver Nickerson and John Surrette. Interview by author. Kingston, Jamaica, 25 November 2000.
Melville, Pauline. Interview by author. St George's, Grenada, 20 May 1998.
Schade, Martin. Interview by author. Kingston, Jamaica, 24 February 2000.

Periodicals

Daily Gleaner, October 1996, December 1997–January 1998, January 2000, January 2001
Sunday Gleaner, January 1959, June 1987, July–August 1995, December 1997–May 1998
Sunday Observer, January–June 2000
Trinidad Express, 25–27 April 1989
Washington Post, "Book World", November 1986, August 1987

Index

Abeng (Cliff), 68; guilt theme in, 43; whiteness in, 38

Allfrey, Phyllis Shand: critique of writings of, 21; guilt theme in, 42

Aloysius (*Lunatic*), 3, 40, 62, 79; characterization of, 31, 32, 79, 88–89, 90–101; 107–8; and God, 90, 92, 97; and language, 88; and madness, 94–98

Amélie (*Sargasso*): coloured seductress stereotype, 34

America. *See* United States

American autobiographies, 134–35

American heaven: depiction of, 114–15

Americans: depiction of, 116

Amerindian theme: in Melville, 74

"Amputation for Two Voices" (Ford-Smith): identity in, 71

Amy (*Under the Sun*): characterization of, 58, 62

Angwin (*Great Yacht Race*): whitening of, 56–57

Annie Palmer (*White Witch*): and obeah, 26–27

Annihilation of Fish and Other Stories, The (Winkler), 5, 165; publication, 5

Another Life (Walcott): as autobiography, 136

anti-white sentiments: Manley regime and, 149

Antoinette (*Sargasso*), 24; and England, 41; faithful nurse stereotype, 29

Antoni, Brian, 16; and faithful nurse stereotype, 29; and guilt, 43; and margin-

alization, 40, 66; and rejection of blackness, 39

Antoni, Robert, 16, 166; and the creole experience, 76–79, 80–81; and faithful nurse stereotype, 29

Ascom, Rachel (*Faces of Love*): and whiteness, 37

Atlanta: Winkler and, 165–66

autobiography: Cargill, 47–55; Rhys, 27; West Indian, 131; Winkler and, 4, 48–53, 54–55, 131–33, 136–38; writing the, 133–34

Baba, 154

bad Negro stereotype: in white West Indian literature, 28

Bakhtin, Mikhail: philosophy, 105, 112, 121, 126, 128, 129

Baps (*Duppy*): characterization, 31–32, 112, 113, 114–15

batty imagery, 127–29

Becka's Buckra Baby (Redcam), 29, 30

Benítez-Rojo, Antonio, 167; on creolization, 11, 19

Bennett, Louise: and power of women, 125

black consciousness: socialism and, 65–70

black female servants. *See* faithful nurse stereotype

Black Lightning (Mais), 31

black male protagonists: in white West Indian literature, 30, 31, 62; Winkler's, 3, 31–32, 40, 62, 63–64, 79, 80, 85–110, 112, 113, 114–15, 145 black nanny stereotype. *See* faithful nurse stereotype

black protagonists: Winkler's, 3, 29, 31–32, 40, 62, 63–64, 79, 80, 79, 85–110, 112, 113, 114–15, 145

black self-hatred: in *The Duppy,* 113–14; in *Going Home to Teach,* 144; in white West Indian literature, 49–51, 59–60

blackness: in Robert Antoni, 78–79; Cliff and, 38; in *The Great Yacht Race,* 62, 63; in Jamaica, 10–11; rejection of, 39; and slavery, 144–45; in *Stone Haven,* 61; in white West Indian literature, 21–22, 23–45; Winkler and, 39–40; in Winkler, 79

Blessed Is the Fruit (Antoni): creolization in, 76, 77, 81; faithful nurse stereotype in, 29

Body parts: Winkler's treatment of, 112, 127–29

Bowen (*Great Yacht Race*): murder of, 27

Brathwaite, Edward Kamau: and creolization, 81; and white creoles, 66

Brother Man (Mais): black protagonist in, 31

Brown, Christopher (*Under the Sun*): whitening of, 57

Brown, Wayne: critique of *The Lunatic,* 89, 109–10, 126

brown-skinned characters. *See* coloured characters

Brown Sugar (Emtage), 21, 22, 23

bush: personification of (*Lunatic*), 88, 102, 105

Busha (*Lunatic*): characterization of, 88–89, 96, 97–98, 106, 107, 108; and socialism, 96–98

Cargill, Morris: background, 19, 42, 47–54, 55, 66; and Jamaica, 22–23; critique of *The Lunatic,* 89; madness in writings of, 44, 48; migration of, 48–53; negativity of, 47–48.

Caribbean identity: ambiguity in, 76; and whiteness, 11, 19, 38–39

Carmichael, Mrs: stereotypes of the good and bad Negro, 28

carnivalesque, the: Winkler and, 112; in *The Duppy,* 126–29

Cayuna novels: Hearne's, 38

Chapman, Esther, 35

Charlene (*Yacht Race*): characterization of, 58–59

Christopher (Drayton), 21, 24; obeah in, 26

Christophine (*Sargasso Sea*): faithful nurse stereotype, 28, 29; and obeah, 26

Claiming an Identity They Taught Me to Despise (Cliff): whiteness in, 38, 71

class: and colour in Jamaica, 49–52, 55, 65; and race, 145

Cliff, Michelle, 166; background, 17, 18; guilt theme in writings of, 43; search for identity, 67–69, 71, 72, 81; and whiteness, 11, 38

Cobham, Rhonda: on de Lisser's writing, 23, 37, 53–54

colonialism: and black self-hatred, 36, 114; and madness in Jamaican society, 96–99; and race, 9–12; and religion, 117; and societal distortion, 44, 49–50, 55; Winkler and, 5, 28, 140–41

colour: in the Caribbean, 167; and class in Jamaica, 49–50, 55, 65; dynamics of, 9–16; and identity, 67–69, 71, 72, 75, 81, 152; and privilege in Jamaica, 10–11, 14–16

coloured characters: in white West Indian literature, 32–38; Winkler's, 32, 56–58

coloured middle class: de Lisser and the, 61; in *Stone Haven,* 59–60; Winkler and the, 59, 62

coloured seductress stereotype: in white West Indian literature, 34

Cooper, Carolyn: on Bennett, 125; and subversion in Jamaican popular culture, 121

Cornélie (*Orchid House*), 33, 34

Cosway, Daniel (*Sargasso Sea*), 33

creole: defining, 17–18

creole identity: in *Witchbroom,* 67, 75

creoles: status of, 41. *See also* hybridity
créolité: defining, 18–19; 39, 76
Creolization: in *Divina Trace,* 76, 79; and identity, 76
Crocodile, The (Winkler), 5, 164
culture: Winkler's definition of, 140
Curtin, Philip: and social structure in Jamaica, 12
Cynthia (*Stone Haven*): characterization of, 60, 61–62

dancehall, 125–29
Daughters of Africa, 39
de Lisser, H.G.: background, 17, 53–54; and the middle class, 57, 60; negativity in, 43–44; racist attitude, 25; satirization of the English, 41; treatment of coloured characters, 29–30, 34, 37: and the upper class, 60–61, 62–63; use of Jamaican language, 88
decay imagery: in white West Indian writing, 24
Development of Creole Society (Brathwaite): and pluralism in West Indian society, 81
dialectical incarnationalism: defining, 118
Divina Trace (Antoni), 76, 77; ambiguity and identity in, 76; faithful nurse stereotype in, 29
Doctor (*Painted Canoe*): nihilism of, 103
Dog War (Winkler), 5, 164
doomed mulatto: in white West Indian literature, 34. *See also* coloured characters; hybridity
Douglass, Lisa: on elite families in Jamaica, 13–14, 16; and the "myth of origin", 55–57
Drayton, Geoffrey: analysis of writings of, 21
Drumblair (Manley), 136; as biography, 137, 138; comparison with *Going Home to Teach,* 138
Du Bois, W.E.B., 12
Duppy, The (Winkler): analysis of, 111–29; plot, 4, 6; blackness in, 40, 59–60; hopefulness in, 44

educational system: critique of Jamaica's, 141–43
Edwards, Bryan: racism of, 25
Egbert (*Duppy*): as Baps's conscience, 114
elite families: Jamaica's, 55–56
Emtage, J.B.: critique of writings of, 21–22; racist attitude of, 24–25
England: white West Indians and, 40–41
evil: in *The Painted Canoe,* 101

Faces of Love, The (Hearne): and whiteness, 37
faithful nurse stereotype: in *Blessed Is the Fruit,* 29, 78–79; in white West Indian literature, 28–29; Winkler's subversion of, 29
Father Huck (*Great Yacht Race*): vision of heaven, 120
fatty power, 123–24
fear: in white West Indian writing, 26–28. *See also* terrified consciousness
Foggy Cumberbatch (*Brown Sugar*), 21
Ford-Smith, Honor: and blackness, 38; search for Identity, 69–72, 72, 81
Free Enterprise (Cliff): blackness in, 68
free will: in *The Duppy,* 119
Froude, J.A.: coloured stereotypes in writings of, 34; on creoles, 41; negativity in, 44; Ramchand's critique of, 22

Gip (*Christopher*): faithful nurse stereotype, 28, 29
God: depiction of, 4, 90–92, 97,111, 114; and goodness, 114, 128–29; and pumpum, 125–26, 128
Going Home to Teach (Winkler): as autobiography, 4, 48–53, 54–55, 106,131–33, 136–38; blackness in, 40; challenge to established religion in, 118; comparison with *Drumblair,* 136–37; as Jamaican history, 136; madness in, 48, 159, 160; and marginalization of white Jamaicans, 65–70; migration in, 47, 53; publication, 4, 6, 130; racism in, 48; whiteness in, 9–12; writing, 134

good Negro stereotype: in white West Indian literature, 28
goodness: in *The Duppy,* 114, 127–29
Grace (*Stone Haven*): Jones's treatment of, 58, 61
Great Yacht Race, The (Winkler): 2, 31, 32; characterization of Missus Grandison in, 32; coloured middle class in, 62; fear in, 27–28, 31; publication of, 4; whitening theme in, 56–57
Griffith, Glyne: on race, 11
grotesque: Winkler's use of the, 112, 127–29
guilt: in white West Indian literature, 42–43, 67
Guyana: Portuguese in, 14

Harris, Wilson: and hybridity, 39
hatred of whites. *See* anti-white sentiments; reverse discrimination
Hearne, John: background, 17; and whiteness, 37–38
heaven: Winkler's depiction of, 4, 111–12, 113, 115, 120
Henderson, John: on creoles, 41
Hills Were Joyful Together, The (Mais), 31
hood imagery: in *The Duppy,* 112, 113; in *The Lunatic,* 103–4
hopefulness: in Winkler's writing, 44
hopelessness: in white West Indian literature, 44
human body: Winkler's exaggeration of the, 123
Hummingbird Tree, The (McDonald): white West Indian identity crisis in, 42; guilt in, 43
hybridity: Melville and, 73–76; in white West Indian literature, 38–39, 167

identity: and language, 87–88; Melville and, 73–76; and pumpum, 103, 104, 106, 123; and race, 13; and whiteness, 67–72, 108; Winkler and, 88, 89, 93, 100, 101
independence: Jamaicans and, 147, 149

Inga (*Lunatic*): characterization of, 3, 40, 88, 89, 93, 100–101, 102; and pumpum, 103, 104, 106; and whiteness, 108
insanity. *See* madness
interracial unity: in *Blessed Is the Fruit,* 77–79, 80–81

Jamaica: colour and class in, 49–50, 55, 96; elite families in, 55–56; reverse discrimination in, 67–70, 96, 149; slave revolts in, 25; socialism in, 96, 97; whiteness in, 9–12, 14, 16; Winkler and, 85–86, 152–69
Jamaica Farewell (Cargill), 22; migration in, 47–53; racism in, 48–52
Jamaica white: defining, 16–17
Jamaican heaven: in *The Duppy,* 113, 115, 119
Jamaican identity: Winkler and, 139–41
Jamaican society: *The Lunatic* and satirical treatment of the, 88–89; madness in the, 96
Jamesons (*Going Home to Teach*): and exclusivity of whites, 150
Jane's Career (de Lisser), 29, 30, 34, 58; Jamaican language in, 88
Jews: in Jamaica, 14, 55
Jones, Evan: background, 17, 54; treatment of coloured characters, 36
Josephine (*Witchbroom*): faithful nurse stereotype, 29

Lady Nugent's Journal, 41
Lady Saw: and pumpum power, 124, 125
Lalla, Barbara: analysis of *The Lunatic,* 121–22
Lally (*Orchid House*): faithful nurse stereotype, 28, 29
"Lament of the Banana Man" (Jones), 62, 63
Land of Look Behind, The (Cliff): guilt theme in, 43; and whiteness, 67
landscape: Aloysius and the Jamaican, 100–101; in *Wide Sargasso Sea,* 24

language: in *The Lunatic,* 86–87; and West
Indian writing, 87
Lattimer, Mark (*Voices*): and whiteness, 37
Lebanese: in Jamaica, 14, 54
Lewis, Gordon K.: on the tainted blood
theme in West Indian literature, 35, 36
Lewis, M.G. "Monk", 25, 26
Lilla (*Blessed Is the Fruit*): and the creole
experience, 77
Lipsitz, George: on whiteness, 12, 14–15
Livingstone, W.P.: racism of, 22
Long, Edward: racism of, 22, 25
"Looks That Blind Us, The" (Winkler),
151
Lucea (*Study in Bronze*): and coloured
alienation, 35
Lunatic, The (Winkler): analysis, 85–100;
blackness in, 40, 79; hopefulness in, 44;
Jamaican language in, 86–87; madness in,
44, 159; plot, 3, 6; popular response to,
1; publication of, 85, 130; pumpum in,
102–6, 112; satire in, 88–89; sex in, 88,
97; subversion of status quo in, 121–22

Macdermot, Thomas. *See* Tom Redcam
Macmillan, Mona: on white West Indians'
love for England, 41
madness theme: in *Blessed Is the Fruit,* 77;
in *The Lunatic,* 88, 90–98, 109–10; in
The Painted Canoe, 96; in *Stone Haven,*
60; in white West Indian writing, 28, 44,
48, 60; in *Wide Sargasso Sea,* 24; in
Winkler's works, 158–61
Magdalena (*Divina Trace*): identity and
ambiguity in, 76
Mais, Roger: and blackness, 31
Majolie (*Orchid House*): and obeah, 26
"Man Who Knew the Price of All Fish,
The" (Winkler), 134
Manley, Edna, 136, 137; and nationalism
of the 1930s, 31
Manley, Michael, 136, 137, 143; and
migration of Jamaican professionals, 148;
and racism, 146, 147; and socialism, 52,
146, 149

Manley, Norman, 136, 137
Manley, Rachel: biographical writing of,
136–38
marginalization: of white West Indians, 27,
40, 65–80, 150–52
Marly: white alienation in, 35, 37
Mason, Bertha (*Jane Eyre*): and creole experience, 71
Mason, Mrs (*Jane's Career*): de Lisser's treatment of, 60
Mavis (*Stone Haven*): Jones's treatment of,
59–60
McCaulay, Diana, 66
McDonald, Ian: and guilt theme, 43; and
identity theme, 42
"McGregor's Journey" (Melville): burden of
whiteness in, 109–10
Melville, Pauline: and the creole experience, 73–76, 81; and hybridity, 38; and
whiteness, 11
Mendes, Alfred: treatment of black charac-
ters, 30
migration: in *Going Home to Teach,* 47–49;
in *Jamaica Farewell,* 47–53; of Jamaican
professionals, 148, 160–64, 165–66;
Winkler and, 132–33, 161–64
Migration of Ghosts, The (Melville): creole
identity in, 75
Mildred (*Yacht Race*): caricature of faithful
nurse, 29
Mintz, Sidney: on whiteness, 10
Miriam (*Stone Haven*): Jones's treatment of,
60, 63
Miss B (*Duppy*): and fatty power, 123
Missus Grandison: faithful nurse stereotype, 29, 32; strength of, 62; and
pumpum power, 125
Morgan's Daughter (de Lisser): coloured
seductress stereotype in, 34
mulatto stereotypes. *See* coloured stereotypes
My Mother's Last Dance (Ford-Smith), 38,
69, 72
Myrtle and Money (de Lisser): doomed
mulatto theme in, 34

Naipaul, V.S.: on writing, 132, 134
nationalism: and blackness in West Indian literature, 31
nature: Aloysius and the hostility of, 100–101
Nettleford, Rex: definition of Jamaica white, 16–17
Newton, Stanley (*Stone Haven*): whitening of, 56
No Telephone to Heaven (Cliff): blackness in, 68; whiteness in, 38
Nugent, Lady: on creoles, 41; racism of, 25
Nunes, Christine, 66

obeah: and fear among white planters, 26
Old Rose (*Christopher*): and obeah, 26,
ole negar: defining, 144–45
Olivier, Sir Sydney, 30
One Brown Girl and – (Redcam), 29
One Jamaica Gal (Durie), 30
Orchid House, The (Allfrey), 21, 24; guilt in, 42; obeah in, 26
original sin: defining, 118–19
out-of-order theme: in *The Duppy,* 117; in *The Lunatic,* 85, 88, 94, 97, 99, 102; in Winkler's work, 1–2, 20

Painted Canoe, The (Winkler): blackness in, 79; murder in, 96; plot, 3, 90–91; publication, 1, 2; Zachariah in, 90–92; villagers in, 94; whiteness in, 101
Paradise Overdose (B. Antoni): faithful nurse stereotype in, 29; guilt theme in, 43: rejection of blackness in, 39; white marginalization in, 40, 66
"Parrot and Descartes, The" (Melville), 76
Pitch Lake (Mendes), 30, 31
popular culture: Cooper on subversion in Jamaican, 121
Portuguese: in Guyana, 14
Pouchet Paquet, Sandra: on autobiographical writing, 131, 134, 135, 136, 138
poverty: and class in Jamaica, 146
Power of Sentiment, The (Douglass): and the "myth of origin", 13–14, 55–56

pumpum: and the carnivalesque, 112; God and, 116, 117, 120–21, 124–26; power of, 103–6, 123–24; role of, 99, 128

race: and class, 12, 65, 145–46; and colonialism, 9–12
racial categorization, 10–11, 13, 145–46
racial purity: and white West Indians, 39
racism: in Jamaican society, 49–50, 96; in American society, 145; in white West Indian literature, 48
Raiskin, Judith: definition of creole, 17–18
Ramchand, Kenneth: on white West Indian writers, 13, 21–24, 26, 28, 37, 61, 66, 152
Redcam, Tom: treatment of black characters, 29
religion: and colonialism, 117–19; and sex, 125; and women, 116, 120, 125
reverse discrimination: Manley regime and, 67–70, 96, 149
Rhys, Jean: autobiography, 27; and blackness, 39–40, 42; critique of writings of, 21; and fear, 27; and guilt theme, 42; and marginalization, 40–42; negativity in, 44
Roediger, David: on working-class racism, 12
Roman Catholicism: Winkler's subversion of, 4, 117–25

Saarem, Mr (*Lunatic*): Winkler's characterization of, 106–8
Sandi (*Sargasso Sea*), 33
Sarah (*Lunatic*), 106
Sayre, Robert: on autobiographical writing, 134–35
Schade, Martin: definition of dialectical incarnationalism, 118
Scott, Lawrence: and the creole identity, 75; guilt in writings of, 43
Scott, Michael: and fear among white planters, 26; on white West Indians' love for England, 41
Seawell, Gracie (*Under the Sun*): de Lisser's treatment of, 60
self-hatred: white, 80–81, 151; white West

Indian literature and black, 49, 51; Winkler and black, 96–97, 113–14, 149
self-identity: and autobiography, 135, 136, 138; Winkler's search for, 138–39
Service (*Lunatic*): 88–89, 99, 103, 104; nihilism of, 103
sex: in *The Lunatic*, 102–6; and religion, 116, 120, 124–25; and tourism, 99–101; Winkler's treatment of, 112, 113, 116. *See also* pumpum
sexuality. *See* pumpum
Shape-shifter (Melville): and hybridity, 74
Shubert (*Lunatic*): characterization of, 94
Sistren Theatre Collective: Ford-Smith and, 71
slackness: in *The Lunatic*, 89, 112, 122–23; in *The Duppy*, 123
slavery: punishment under, 28; Winkler on impact of, 140–41, 144
Smile Please (Rhys): terrified consciousness, 27; blackness in, 39, 40; societal distortion in, 44
Smith, M.G.: and pluralist social structure, 12
socialism: in 1970s Jamaica, 97–98; Winkler and, 46, 51, 52, 146–49
societal madness: in *The Lunatic*, 94–98; in Winkler's work, 158–59
"Song of the Banana Man" (Jones), 60, 62, 63
Stone Haven (Jones): as autobiography, 54; blackness in, 59; coloured characters in, 36, 59–60; madness in, 60; whitening in, 56
Store of a Million Items, The (Cliff): and the search for identity, 69
Study in Bronze (Chapman): coloured dilemma in, 35
Susan Proudleigh (de Lisser), 30
Swiffles (*Under the Sun*): and whiteness, 61

tainted blood theme: in white West Indian literature, 34–36
terrified consciousness theme: in *The Great Yacht Race*, 27–28; in white West Indians,

13; in white West Indian writing, 21, 23, 24–28
theology: in *The Duppy*, 118–21
Tom Cringle's Log (M. Scott): on fear among white planters, 26; on white West Indians' love for England, 41
tourism: Winkler's satirization of, 99–100
"Transactions": marginalization theme in, 69
Trollope, Anthony: on white West Indians' love for England, 41

Under the Sun (de Lisser): coloured middle class in, 57, 60, 62; near-white upper middle class in, 60–61; satirization of the Englishman, 41; whitening theme in, 57
United States: Cargill and, 52; colour in, 10–11; racism in, 145; whiteness in, 14–15; Winkler and, 42, 114–16, 127, 133, 138–40, 152, 160–61, 164–66

Vel (*Blessed Is the Fruit*): and the black experience, 77–78; faithful nurse stereotype, 29
Ventriloquist's Tale, The (Melville): identity in, 74–75
Voices Under the Window (Hearne): whiteness in, 37, 38
Voyage in the Dark (Rhys): blackness in, 39; England in, 41

Walcott, Derek: autobiographical writing of, 136
West Indian autobiographers, 134–36
West Indian identity: and autobiography, 134–36, 138
West Indian literature: and use of language, 87–88; white marginalization in, 40–41, 66–67; white writers in, 21–45
West Indian Novel and Its Background, The (Ramchand). *See* Ramchand
West Indian society: race in, 13; pluralism in, 12, 81; whiteness in, 14–15
white Jamaicans: marginalization of, 15–16, 65–73, 79–81

white people: depiction of, 48–49, 57–59, 69, 109; Winkler's depiction of, 106–8, 116, 150

white self-hatred: Winkler and, 80–81, 151

white West Indian literature, 21–45; bad Negro in, 28; black male protagonists in, 30, 31; blackness in, 21–45; coloured characters in, 32–38; creole consciousness in, 73–77, 79, 80–81; faithful nurse stereotype in, 28–29; good Negro in, 28; guilt in, 67; tainted blood theme in, 34; terrified consciousness in, 23–28; white marginalization in, 40–41, 66–67; and whiteness, 9–20

white West Indian writers, 21–45, 65–81; Winkler's relationship with, 2, 5–6, 166–68

white West Indians, marginalization of, 15–16, 65–81. *See also* creoles

White Witch of Rosehall, The (de Lisser): coloured seductress stereotype in, 34; negativity in, 44; obeah in, 26

whiteness: defining, 5, 10–20; and exploitation, 107–8; and identity, 9–20, 65–81; in Jamaica, 9–12, 13–18, 19–20; and privilege, 13–15, 68, 69–71; in Winkler's works, 80, 106–8, 149–51, 152

whitening: in de Lisser, Jones and Winkler, 56–58; of Jamaica's elite families, 55; process of, 36

Wide Sargasso Sea (Rhys), 21, 24: England in, 41; madness in, 44; obeah in, 26

Widow Dawkins (*Lunatic*): and pumpum, 103–4, 105; treatment of, 89, 94

Winkler, Anthony: autobiography, 48, 52–53, 131–34, 136, 138–40; background, 1–5, 46–48, 52–53, 54–55, 131–34, 138–40, 152–58, 160, 161–66;

black male protagonists, 3,4, 31, 32, 40, 62, 63–64, 79, 80, 85–110, 112–15, 127, 145; internalized black identity, 40, 51, 53, 80, 152, 158, 167; and Jamaican identity, 42; and marginalization, 32, 40, 80, 151–52; and middle class, 58–59, 62, 137; migration of, 46–48, 52–53, 138–40, 164–66; use of the Jamaican language, 86–88; and white people, 106–8, 149–51; and whiteness, 9–16, 40, 45, 50, 53, 80, 149–51, 152, 166; on writing, 87, 132–34, 165, 166, 167

Winkler, Cathy, 131, 132, 145, 161–64

Winkler, grandfather (paternal), 132, 152–53, 157, 161, 163–64

Winkler, grandfather (maternal), 48–49, 156, 157

Winkler, grandmother (paternal), 132, 161, 163, 164

Winkler, Louis Jr., 3, 154–56

Winkler, Myrtle, 3, 138, 153

Witchbroom (L. Scott): faithful nurse stereotype in, 29; guilt theme in, 43; madness in, 44; rejection of blackness in, 39

women: and power, 104–6, 120, 123–25; white West Indian writers' treatment of black, 28–30; coloured, 33–35

working-class racism: in the United States, 12

writers: white West Indian, 16–18, 21–45, 166–68

Wynter, Sylvia: on Mais, 31

Zachariah (*Painted Canoe*), 79; characterization of, 3, 31, 32, 40, 62, 79, 90–92, 96